Saving the Reservation

JOE GARRY

AND THE BATTLE

TO BE INDIAN

Saving the Reservation

JOE GARRY

AND THE BATTLE

TO BE INDIAN

John Fahey

UNIVERSITY OF WASHINGTON PRESS

Seattle and London

Saving the Reservation: Joe Garry and the Battle to Be Indian
is published in part with support from
the Joel E. Ferris Foundation.

Library of Congress Cataloging-in-Publication Data

Fahey, John.
 Saving the reservation : Joe Garry and the battle to be Indian / John Fahey.
   p.   cm.
 Includes bibliographical references and index.
 ISBN 978-0-295-99537-3
 1. Garry, Joe, 1910–1975.   2. Skitswich Indians—Biography.   3. Indian
activists—United States—Biography.   4. Indian civic leaders—United
States—Biography.   5. Indians of North America—Politics and government.
6. Indians of North America—Government relations—1934-   7. National
Congress of American Indians—History.   8. Self-determination, National—
United States.   I. Title.
E99.S3 G373   2000   305.897'0092—dc21   [B]   2001035249

Frontispiece: Joe Garry, 1957, by Boise photographer Virgil Parker.

This portrait was exhibited in the annual show of the Photographic Society
of America and was adapted for a National Congress of American Indians letterhead. (Arlene Owen family collection)

For the emerging generation:
Elizabeth, James, Megan, and Ryan

Contents

Preface

This book is not a history of the National Congress of American Indians. Neither is it an inclusive account of government-Indian relations during the 1950s. It is the story of a remarkable American, Joseph R. Garry, who changed the course of events, who expunged the past as determinant of the future.

The termination era of Garry's time was but one swerve in the twisting trail of government-Indian concerns. In the middle of the twentieth century, approximately 350,000 Indians lived on reservations scattered across the United States. The Indian communities and the individuals who lived in them varied widely in education, income, and degree of assimilation into the white majority. These demographics, the long distances between native constituents, and differences in political sophistication faced anyone who sought to unite the tribes as a political force.

If you are not acquainted with the conduct of Indian administration, the plethora of legislation and regulation directed at American Indians may seem bewildering. How do you keep in mind the turns of political intent, the legal precedents, and the 2,200 laws and rules that affect only Indian persons and tribes? I have tried to simplify the discussion of such matters, but obviously the story of men and women at war in the political arena requires some attention to the "bullets."

For at least eighty years before Garry's day, the notion of assimilating natives into the general population dominated legislative and societal posture toward American Indians. As evidence mounted confirming failure of the allotment program, an ameliorating stance emerged: Reconstitute native cultures, through economic strengthening of impoverished and lethargic tribes, to become self-supporting in a pluralistic society.

After World War I, John Collier, an idealistic social reformer, popularized Indians' rights and the values of native culture. As commissioner of Indian affairs under President Franklin D. Roosevelt, he championed a radical policy of transferring extensive powers to tribal governments and reestablishing tribal land bases. His program passed Congress in 1934 as the Indian

Reorganization Act, but the old paternalism of federal oversight continued by way of the secretary of the interior's power of final decision.

Throughout federal management of Indians, economic assistance, education, and public services to most tribes have been inadequate. Joseph Garry came on the scene when Congress, recognizing the shortcomings of Indian policy and administration, embraced a rising sentiment to "free" the Indians, to terminate federal supervision and aid. Garry not only fought termination but he set in motion forces that underlie Indian relations with the U.S. government today.

I suggest that in reading this book you fix two measures firmly in your mind: House Concurrent Resolution 108, declaring that Congress will terminate federal jurisdiction over Indians as quickly as possible; and Senate Concurrent Resolution 280, conferring on the individual states jurisdiction over Indians. Remind yourself often that the view of the Bureau of Indian Affairs conveyed here is that of the Indians. For most reservation Indians, the local bureau office had been the primary point of contact with the federal government for a century. Garry, in breaking that pattern, strove to deal with government at its highest administrative level.

Garry confronted the double challenge of shaping Indian policy for the nation and trying to make it work on his home reservation. He encountered predictable cleavages in the Indian population: factions opposing tribal leaders, progressives against traditionalists, urban versus reservation Indians. He turned the conduct of tribal business from its ancient habit—consensus of elders—to parliamentary procedure, committees, and compromise.

Garry occupied many offices at once, and I have separated them in the narrative for easier understanding. Consequently, the story occasionally returns to something you have already read. You may wish for more precision—dates, a timeline, etc.—to guide you through the narrative. But in Garry's time, events tumbled over events, and I try to evoke the fever of those years by giving attention more to *what* than *when*.

There is no way, in a text of modest length, to credit all of the actors who played significant roles in the complex events that occupied Garry. I regret that many are mentioned only in passing, or are left out altogether.

When I began to think of a book about Joe Garry, I asked informed individuals in many parts of the United States for their impressions of his work. Garry brought the Indians into the twentieth century, said one; he showed Indians the importance of organizing and lobbying, said another. He elevated Indians to a political and social force in American life. He stalled wholesale termination of federal responsibility for Indians. He convinced America that Indians were ready and able to do business as equals. Their comments persuaded me that a book about Garry was not merely warranted but necessary.

Three who knew Garry in different ways contributed substantially to this story: his niece, Jeanne Givens; Rev. Thomas E. Connolly, S.J., pastor at Sacred Heart Mission, DeSmet; and Robert D. Dellwo, longtime legal counsel to the Coeur d'Alene tribe. They not only talked to me at length about Joe Garry but read a rough-draft manuscript and made insightful suggestions that have been incorporated into the narrative.

Father Connolly always spoke of this period as "the last Indian war," on the premise that the field of termination and consent of the governed had been a battleground—the last great stand of American Indians for their homelands and for justice. There is certainly truth in that interpretation, and I hope that the war really has now ended.

From manuscript to publication, this story and author benefited from the graceful professionalism of Julidta Tarver, former managing editor of the University of Washington Press, and from perceptive editing by Rick Harmon, former editor of the *Oregon Historical Quarterly*.

The special burden of keeping the author going, listening patiently to complaints about the agony of composition, recording identifications of pictures, and maintaining a serene household falls to my wife, Peggy. I would never finish a book project without her support.

Thank you all.

Saving the Reservation

JOE GARRY

AND THE BATTLE

TO BE INDIAN

1 Emergency!

*D*ecember 9, 1953: They left Phoenix with disaster looming, a tempest gathering, those delegates to the tenth convention of the National Congress of American Indians. They left Phoenix's fabricated greenery and its tufa-rock capitol, with sculpted Truth and Justice atop, to go back to their reservations, dismayed and angry at the U.S. Congress's callous repudiation of century-old promises and its threat to end Indian life as they knew it.

In the summer of 1953, less than four months before the Phoenix convention, Congress had adopted, in House Concurrent Resolution 108, a policy of cutting off all federal supervision and protection of Indian tribes at the earliest possible date, and had directed the secretary of the interior to draft bills before the end of the year that would bounce selected tribes. They called it "termination."

It was the phrase "at the earliest possible date" that shocked Indians. That the Feds wanted to be done with them came as no surprise. But the prospect of indiscriminate, speedy termination was appalling. In the convention at Phoenix, the delegates buzzed of little else.

The prospect of disaster fell heavily on the new president of the NCAI, Joseph R. Garry, the forty-three-year-old chairman of a small tribe in northern Idaho, the Coeur d'Alenes. He knew he had to do something to stall termination—but what? Leaving Phoenix, he puzzled over possibilities as he drove to Tucson to speak at a conference of the American Anthropological Association. There, a New York socialite generous in her support of Indian causes, Corinna Lindon Smith, snared him for a round of introductions. He was, for the moment, a social catch—the new man in office, handsome in business suit and crisp white shirt, with a friendly grin and a quiet modesty. (Smith slipped him $200 for trip expenses.)

He drove next to Santa Fe to call on Oliver La Farge, anthropologist and Indian apologist and president of the prestigious Association on American Indian Affairs. They talked into the night.

Then, to Denver for a first long colloquy with Helen Peterson, executive secretary of the NCAI, and with D'Arcy McNickle, one of the nation's noted Indians and a founder of the NCAI. "What I learned there," Garry said, "convinced me that I should go to Washington personally to . . . determine how we could best meet the serious situation brought on by legislation affecting our American Indian people." Peterson, her mother, and her son volunteered to ride with Garry in the round-nosed old Buick sedan he waggishly called "the Coeur d'Alene beer wagon." Helen thereafter remembered the old car "as a symbol of when we had so very little."[1]

Garry and Peterson talked strategy as the Buick lumbered toward the national capital. They resolved to renew the NCAI, because, Helen felt, "it had been heavily influenced by or reflective of Oklahoma tribes" in its first ten years; and now it faced the quickened pace of Congress toward ending trusteeship.

The new president brought a new perspective to the Indian congress, as well as a broader—and, he and Helen resolved, a more aggressive—agenda. Through ten- and twelve-hour wintry days on the road, with Helen's son chattering to Joe to keep him alert, Joe Garry and Helen Peterson hashed out what they would do.[2]

But Garry was surprised by how little they had to work with. The NCAI was broke. Those first hours in Washington stuck in Garry's memory "as cold, gloomy days for NCAI. . . . Anyone without a proven devotion to the Indian cause was really taking the test now." Since walking was cheap, he and Peterson set out on foot to introduce themselves to members of Congress.[3]

To Peterson and Garry, and to those working with them, a demonstration of the NCAI's new vigor seemed imperative: They determined to call tribal representatives to Washington for a massive show of united Indian opposition to the new direction of Congress. Garry was not inexperienced in confrontation. Three years earlier he had led delegates from seven Pacific Northwest tribes to Washington to demand repeal of a federal leasing program for Indian lands.

The call to meet went out over Garry's signature: "The National Congress of American Indians is calling an 'Emergency Conference of American Indians on Legislation' in Washington, D.C. . . . The crisis . . . now faces us in urgent and clear cut terms." Referring to House Concurrent Resolution 108 as "the forewarning" (McNickle called 108 the bell that caused the cow to kick over the bucket), Garry continued: "Most of the pending legislation, if passed, would result in the end of our last holdings

on this continent and destroy our dignity and distinction as the first inhabitants of this rich land. The supreme test for our strength and our will to
survive, as Indians, is now before us."+ With this announcement, the NCAI
sent each tribe a summary of legislative proposals before Congress and a
questionnaire asking the tribe's position on termination and other bills.

Garry's summons hit home. The Indian community was already in an
uproar over strictures on their choice of legal counsel, over Bureau of Indian
Affairs intrusions into tribal elections, over curbs on tribal control of funds
and lands, and over centralization of the bureau under Dillon S. Myer,
who had taken office as commissioner in May 1950. In his work as a tribal
chairman, Garry well knew the bruising rigidity of Myer's regime.

Myer's ignorance both of Indian sensibilities and the 2,200 regulations
governing Indians, as well as his brusque personality, presented an ideal
target to critics: He epitomized the enemy figure who fuels a crusade. One
of the most ravaging attacks on him was carried out by Felix S. Cohen,
former counsel to the secretary of the interior and author of the standard
Handbook of Indian Law, in an article entitled "The Erosion of Indian
Rights, 1950–1953," published in the *Yale Law Journal* in February 1953.
Cohen, citing restrictions on individual freedom and Indian control of property, criticized changes in the power structure of the bureau. He also cen-
sured bureau campaign literature seeking to influence a Blackfeet tribal
election, its proposed regulations to control the selection and services of
tribal attorneys, its oblique attacks on tribal self-government, its sales of
Indian land to non-Indian buyers, its obtrusions into tribal credit systems,
and its misuse of tribal funds. Cohen concluded that Indian rights had
eroded substantially in Myer's three years in office, and he warned that
critics of the bureau often were answered by attacks on their integrity.[5]

Cohen viewed government critically, pointing to a "tendency of any government bureau to expand its power . . . when the people subject to the
bureau's activities are without many of the normal avenues of protest, publicity, and legal redress." His article reached an influential, if limited, read-
ership, one that might be moved to phone or write friends in Congress.

A strong Indian voice at the time was that of Clarence Wesley, described
by Senator Barry Goldwater as "one of Arizona's outstanding citizens, a
San Carlos Apache." Wesley was general manager of Apache Tribal
Enterprises, a respected businessman in his home state. Goldwater inserted
some of Wesley's blunt views in the *Congressional Record:*

"American citizens, including public officials, generally don't know what the Indian issues really are. . . . The real issues are continuing ownership of land; development of human and natural resources; protection of rights solemnly promised by treaty and law; honor in Government dealing with conquered peoples; our day in court on our claims; real opportunity for education of the same quality as is available to non-Indian citizens; adequate Federal assistance in reservation development . . . an end to bureaucratic dictatorship . . . an end to wasteful and constantly changing, insensitive administration of our affairs.

There is something radically wrong with the kind of Federal supervision of Indian affairs we have had when, after 135 years of Indian administration, Indians face more problems than ever.[6]

Garry resolved to lead a crusade against the abuses highlighted by Cohen and Wesley, and to mount an evangelical uprising to confront the real issues of the Indian condition. Myer's resignation did not lessen Garry's determination. Myer was succeeded in July 1953 by a Gallup, New Mexico, banker, Glenn L. Emmons, who stoked the tumult with his first pronouncement: His policy as commissioner would be to "liquidate the trusteeship of Indians as quickly as possible."[7]

February 25, 1954: When the Indian emergency conference opened, delegates represented forty-three tribes from twenty-one states and Alaska. Three dozen responded with written positions on pending legislation. As Helen Peterson counted registrants, she realized that this was "the biggest demonstration by American Indians ever," comprised of men and women representing a third of the nation's Indian population. For some tribes, this was a first encounter with other Indians. Differences in symbol and dress intrigued them. The Seminole group, for one, came barefoot into Washington's February chill. Many who attended had never been to the nation's capital before, had never seen a listing of pending legislation, had never spoken to a member of Congress.[8]

Nineteen non-Indian organizations sent observers, with such diverse groups as the Japanese American Citizens League, the American Legion, and the Montana Farmers Union seated side by side with the Indian advocacy groups such as the Association on the American Indian Affairs, the Indian Rights Association, and the Institute of Ethnic Affairs—this last the agency of John Collier, the former commissioner of Indian affairs who had fashioned the Indian Reorganization Act, allowing tribes to form as corporations.

With the Subcommittee on Indian Affairs conducting hearings on the termination of certain tribes, Garry and Peterson had set the dates for their emergency conference to fit into a brief recess in the hearings schedule. But when Congress juggled its dates, Garry urged delegates to spend a few hours listening to Flathead termination sessions. Many who acted on his suggestion heard D'Arcy McNickle assail the two options presented by the Flathead bill: a referendum on forming a Montana corporation to manage tribal assets; or a trustee to liquidate Flathead property. About half the Flatheads no longer lived on the reservation, McNickle declared, and they "will want to divide everything before the subject is fully considered."

Senator Arthur V. Watkins, the subcommittee chairman, butted into the testimony to remind Indian speakers that Congress intended to end their status as wards, snapping, at one point, that the "Supreme Court had held that Congress could repudiate any treaty at any time." He conveyed an air of rectitude that was almost terrifying, one onlooker thought. Delegates to the emergency conference left the hearing with new fears after witnessing the impatient and curt chairman.[9]

On another day, delegates invaded the Senate and House office buildings to meet briefly with their congressional representatives. Otherwise, the emergency conference ran as might have been expected: sessions to explain bills before Congress, speeches by bureau spokesmen (one ventured his opinion that off-reservation Indians had a "vested right" to participate in tribal decisions on termination), and expressions of support from advocacy groups.

In a roll call of tribes, delegates spoke the views of their own people:

Comanche-Kiowas: "Our people have little schooling and cannot write or speak English."

Osages: "Indians must stand together to protect what we have."

Kaibab band of Paiutes: "This [competency] bill would benefit only the predatory interests seeking our resources."

Yakimas: "If termination bills are passed for a few tribes, they will be extended to all. The suddenness of this action is serious."

Caddos: "Let us join together in our common fight."

Gila River Pima-Maricopas: "If we don't defeat these bills, we will be swept away."

Eastern Cherokees: "Watch out for new bills. Some will be camouflaged, but they will keep coming."

Omahas: "Glad we have this Indian organization by which we . . . can unite in strength and fight for our rights."

Seminoles: "Florida Seminoles have poor quality land, little education, and low income. . . . They don't know how to do business."

Colvilles: "Promises made in the past should still hold today."

And so on. Some speakers mentioned local problems, some offered draft resolutions, and nearly all opposed termination and commended the NCAI.[10]

Before adjournment, the delegates approved a Declaration of Indian Rights, which read in part:

In exchange for Federal protection and the promise of certain benefits, our ancestors gave forever to the people of the United States title to the very soil of our beloved country. . . . Today the Federal Government is threatening to withdraw this protection and these benefits. We believe that the American people will not permit the Government to act in this way if they know these proposals do not have Indian consent; that these proposals, if adopted, will tend to destroy our tribal government; that they may well leave our older people destitute; and that the effect of many of these proposals will be to force our people into a way of life that some of them are not willing or are not ready to adopt.[11]

At Garry's request, Congressman E. Y. Berry of South Dakota inserted the declaration into the *Congressional Record*. While the emergency conference probably raised Indian expectations beyond the NCAI's capacity to perform at the time, it generated a demand for Joe Garry as a speaker on Indian conditions.

Clarence Wesley delivered the concluding address:

We have come great distances and at great expense. . . . We came because we believe that the future of the American Indian people is at stake. . . . Either the United States government will recognize its treaty and statute obligations to the Indians . . . or we continue down the bitter road toward complete destruction.

For more than 130 years the government has been paving this road for us. And—speaking from my experience on the San Carlos Reservation—I would say it's one of the few good paving jobs it's done for the Indians. . . . The man who came here a week ago from a poor 10-acre allotment isn't going to find a fertile half-section when he gets back home. That's why I feel it is so important for us to keep the unity we have found here when we return to our homes . . . All we ask now is time, an effective voice in our nation's councils, and the help we need to help ourselves.[12]

2 "The Chance of Our Indian Lifetimes"

*W*hen the National Congress of American Indians held its organizing convention in 1944, Sgt. Joe Garry was with the army in Europe. He was one of the new generation targeted by the founders of the NCAI in their call for delegates, one of those "away at war" who would come home "dissatisfied with the way things were before they went into the armed services. They are going to want more to say about the management of their local affairs."[1]

"Indians in the armed forces who write home . . . indicate a determination to be more articulate in their affairs hereafter," observed one of the NCAI planners, D'Arcy McNickle. "Even before the war certain regional Indian organizations had formed and there is every indication that these will continue and be strengthened after the war. . . . Indians are going to organize whether anybody likes it or not. They can organize badly and fall victims to houligan [*sic*] leaders who will destroy the opportunity . . . or they can organize with foresight and become in time a force to be reckoned with."[2]

The NCAI expected veterans toughened against discrimination, but it aimed mainly at Indians "who think beyond their reservation borders," in the phrase of another of the planners, Archie Phinney. To his mind, this was the moment to launch a movement for all Indians, and he did not want to waste it. He had been talking of Indian organization for years and had no desire to hold back now. "We need to go the whole way in some manner," Phinney told McNickle. "Here is the chance of our Indian lifetimes."[3]

Yet they were not sure how to begin. The pathway to Indian political unity is strewn with the headstones of aborted starts. One of the strongest had been that of the Society of American Indians, founded in 1911, devoted to "the honor of the race and the good of the country." It enlisted perhaps 1,500 members, some of the outstanding Indian spokesmen of its time. The president of the United States, senators, noted scientists, and ranking officials of the Indian Service (Bureau of Indian Affairs) spoke at its conventions. It made America "Indian-conscious." But it lasted only a few years and foundered on one man's political ambition.[4]

There had been more recent tries. W. F. Semple, a Tulsa, Oklahoma, attorney, drew together Indians at the 1936 Tulsa Indian Exposition to talk about a national movement, and in October 1938 he convened a cadre who adopted a constitution and elected officers—Semple as president—calling themselves the Inter-Tribal Indian Council. They proposed a central council of one member from each tribe of a hundred or more members.[5]

Ben Dwight, administrative assistant to Oklahoma governor Robert Kerr, worked with Semple. He invited Phinney, a Nez Perce Indian then working as a Bureau of Indian Affairs field agent, to attend the first meeting. But Phinney stayed away, for he regarded Semple's plan as "based on the questionable principle of trying to create a movement with leadership as a starting point . . . mainly from non-reservation sources," he wrote to Dwight. Phinney went on: "My hope for an inter-tribal organization of deep and lasting significance comes from the feeling that a sound basis for inter-tribal relations and organizations is only beginning to develop now throughout the country as a result of the new consciousness and interest in self-government the Indians are expressing in their present social and economic programs. At present this is a purely reservation phenomenon but only in its growth will the prerequisites for sound inter-tribal activity be established. At that time, leaders will rise from the masses of the Indian population, and the policies and purposes of any organization they may have will come from and represent the everyday problems and hopes of tribespeople."[6]

Phinney was not alone in believing Indian organization must spring from the reservations. He, McNickle, Ruth Muskrat Bronson, and other Indian notables had, in September 1939, participated in a seminar ("The North American Indian Today") in Toronto, cosponsored by Yale and Toronto universities. They were among the U.S. and Canadian delegates who walked out of the conference on its final day, convinced that most of those attending had become so acculturated that they no longer represented reservation Indians. The walkouts framed a resolution "hoping that the need for an all-Indian conference . . . will be felt by Indian tribes [with] delegates limited to bona fide Indian leaders, [a] conference . . . free of political, anthropological, missionary, administrative, or other domination." They had lit a spark for action. After Toronto, letters of McNickle, Phinney, and others fairly bristled with an eagerness to get started.[7]

Like Phinney, McNickle and Bronson then both worked for the Bureau of Indian Affairs, housed during wartime in the massive Merchandise Mart in Chicago. As the dream of a national Indian movement rising from the reservations gripped them, they kept in touch through a bureau field agent in Chicago, Charles E. J. Heacock, and each began to assume a role: Heacock as conduit and convenor, Phinney as goad and visionary, McNickle as well-placed diplomat, and Bronson as the one who would not let their resolve waver.

It fell to McNickle, as administrative assistant to the commissioner, John Collier, to sound out the boss. "The Commissioner has finally come around in his thinking to agreeing that an organization of Indians such as you have been proposing for several years would be worthwhile, and valuable, if it truly represented Indian leadership," he reported to Phinney.[8]

Both McNickle and Phinney traveled often for the bureau. As they visited tribes, they probed Indian interest in a national organization. It was mixed. Many tribes struggled to find a middle ground between young and elders, and between reservation and off-reservation factions. They were so mired in local affairs they could not think nationally. Yet Phinney's assessment was encouraging: He found "a group of Indians in Arizona (about 90 in number) who are organized and who take interest in affairs of Indians at large. You will find all over the Indian country, Indians who think beyond their reservation borders. . . . We have fine leadership on the reservations even though many of these leaders do not always get on with their councils."[9]

McNickle canvassed southwestern reservations—Hopi, Navajo, Apache, and Papago. He, too, was encouraged. And Phinney noted regional meetings of tribal delegates at such diverse sites as Minneapolis, Billings (Montana), Carson City (Nevada), and Phoenix, where there "arose spontaneously . . . the idea of national Indian conventions."[10]

While Phinney and McNickle were on the road, Charlie Heacock invited bureau Indians to lunch in his office to discuss Indian solidarity. Some showed interest, others not much. The brown-bag group shuffled participants, but gradually consensus emerged. They seized on an unusual meeting of thirty or forty Indian staffers, called by Collier for another purpose, to bring up the idea of organizing Indians. After a lively session, twenty-four of the group petitioned Collier to continue meetings "for discussion of the many problems with which Indians and the Indian Service are daily confronted." Charlie's lunches had born fruit.[11]

Indians in the Chicago office were still debating the form of organization—whether it should have regional units, whether it should ally with racial minorities, who should be in charge, and other questions—when Heacock summoned twenty-two prominent Indians to convene as a "working committee on national Indian organization" in May 1944 at the Chicago YMCA on LaSalle Street. They were: Arthur O. Allen, Sioux; Ruth Bronson, Cherokee; Mark L. Burns, Chippewa; Cleo D. Caudell, Choctaw; Ben Dwight, Choctaw; David Dozier, Pueblo; Amanda H. Finley, Cherokee; Kent FitzGerald, Chippewa; Roy E. Gourd, Cherokee; Lois E. Harlin, Cherokee; Charles Heacock, Sioux; Erma O. Hicks, Cherokee; George LaMotte, Chippewa; Leona Locust, Cherokee; Carroll Martell, Chippewa; Randolph N. McCurtain, Choctaw; D'Arcy McNickle, Cree; Charlotte Orozco, Chippewa; Peter Powlas, Oneida; Ed Rogers, Chippewa; Harry L. Stevens, Apache; and Archie Phinney. All but Dwight and Dozier worked for the Indian Service.[12]

Here the National Congress of American Indians was born. In three days the committee worked out a statement of purpose—"the organization would hope to speak for the American Indian, but . . . its authority and powers could consist only of what were granted it by its membership"—and drafted a constitution. They agreed that active membership would be limited to Indians, but they left defining "Indian" to the tribes. They talked over the financing of an organizing convention, the question of who should be invited, and the "immediate specific project of rendering assistance to Indian men and women returning from military service." They adjourned to reconvene minutes later as a constitutional convention, and then approved a draft constitution by Dwight, Phinney, Allen, Heacock, and McCurtain.

That done, the working committee adjourned and reconvened again to organize under their new constitution as the National Council of American Indians. They chose Mark Burns (a Bureau of Indian Affairs field representative in Minnesota) as president, named an executive committee, and determined to call a national convention in Denver. Ruth Bronson, consultant at large in the bureau, and Chester Faris, secretary of the Indian Rights Association (who attended as an observer), encouraged the committee in summarizing remarks, and the group adjourned, satisfied that they had done what they came to do.

The little band of bureau Indians who set out for Denver from Chicago—Gourd, Hicks, Heacock, Locust, Harlin, LaMotte, and Peru Farver—had mixed hopes. McNickle came from Washington and Phinney from Idaho. The two men expected to take roles in leading the new union of Indians, and yet they did not want the organization to appear to be a front for bureau policies, as some Indians suspected. They had ruled out a partnership with the bureau's National Indian Institute precisely for that reason. They realized that they were, as Phinney remarked, "estranged from Indian life" by living in cities and working for the government. And Heacock added wryly, "Articulate Indians capable of Indian leadership and independent thought . . . are not too popular" with the rank and file on reservations.[13]

McNickle hoped the new organization might provide social services as well as promote Indian views, and Phinney believed it could be a forum for "developing a scientific sociology of United States Indians."

The convention call had gone out over Ben Dwight's signature, setting a starting date of November 15. Burns followed with letters to tribal councils urging reservation Indians to lead the new organization. Dwight asked each tribe to contribute $100 as a start-up fund. No one gave anything. McNickle had canvassed prospective donors for money to pay delegates' expenses, but November closed on them so fast that the founders had to ask each participant to pay his or her own costs.

Eighty delegates came from fifty tribes in twenty-seven states, mostly Plains and Midwestern Indians. Only four represented Arizona, three New Mexico, three California, and three Montana. Phinney, newly assigned to the Northern Idaho agency, represented Idaho. Nobody attended from tribes in either Washington or Oregon. By and large, these were progressive, younger Indians who held positions of leadership in their tribes; they were literate, accustomed to dealing with bureaucracy, and sure of themselves. Looking them over, an aged Oklahoma Comanche rose to caution them to "remember the ignorant older Indians."

Basil Two Bears offered an invocation in Sioux, ending with a war whoop that so startled a convention in another room that delegates dashed into the lobby, thinking someone had been stabbed. The boldness of their gambit stirred the delegates, and the first hours passed in brisk declarations of what this new organization ought to be. They approved the Chicago draft of a

A section from a group picture of delegates at the organizing convention of the National Congress of American Indians in 1944. Left to right: William Short, second president of the NCAI; George La Motte; Roy Gourd; Justice N. B. Johnson, first president of the NCAI; and Ben Dwight. (Helen Peterson collection)

preamble: "to secure to ourselves and our descendants the rights and benefits to which we are entitled, to enlighten the public toward a better understanding of the Indian race, to preserve Indian cultural values, to seek an equitable adjustment of tribal affairs . . . under treaties with the United States, and otherwise to promote the common welfare of the American Indians." [14]

The choosing of officers set off a spirited debate. Despite Dwight's assurance in his keynote address that the bureau delegation "had only the good of Indian people at heart," many opposed electing Indian Service employees to office. William W. Short, Oklahoma Chickasaw stockman who looked like a movie cowboy, snapped, "We have been as suspicious of the Indian Bureau as we are of the Jap, and frankly we don't have any use for John Collier." Will Rogers, Jr., son of the famed cowboy humorist, objected to Short's remark. Then another Oklahoman, District Judge Napoleon B. Johnson, graying and erect, stepped in as mediator, calming the rumpus, and a proposed rule barring government employees from office was abandoned. [15]

The delegates passed resolutions to put a "legislative agent" in Washington, D.C., to lobby for Indian causes; to start a newsletter; to support improved training for Indians hired by the government; to seek funds for graduate education; to survey Indian opinion; and to set up a legal-aid bureau to help tribes without attorneys. They changed the name of their new organization to National Congress of American Indians.[16]

They adopted a draft constitution and elected Johnson president and Dan Madrano—a Caddo Indian and an Oklahoma state representative—secretary. A Denver newspaper hailed "the all-tribal constitution, the first of its kind in the United States," judging the story worthy of page 10. The aplomb of the Oklahoma delegates and their familiarity with parliamentary procedure allowed them to call the tune, as the Chicago group played second fiddle. Nevertheless, Archie Phinney and D'Arcy McNickle were named to an eight-member executive committee.

On November 18, the convention's final day, sixty-nine delegates posed for a group picture beside the terra-cotta face of the Cosmopolitan Hotel, with some good-natured joshing when the photographer stood them in front of the hotel bar. The seven women in the picture wore stylish street clothing, the men wore business suits, and except for classic Indian profiles here and there, a few ten-gallon hats, and one head of braided hair, the image could have passed as a photo of realtors from Toledo.

To Judge Johnson fell the task of defining the NCAI. An adroit tactician, he saw the congress as a political body. The congress, variously headquartered in Tulsa, then Claremore (Oklahoma), used Ruth Bronson's home as its Washington office for its first years, although it rented an office in an old building on Dupont Circle as a mailing address. It had no paid staff and no money to hire anyone. (Bronson had volunteered as executive secretary.) Two months passed before Johnson assembled the executive committee for a day in Chicago.

The first step, as Johnson perceived his role, was to show that the NCAI could do something. He seized on the issue of claims for ceded tribal lands. After years of talking about the monumental obstacles that tribes faced in petitioning to sue in the Court of Claims, Congress was moving toward vesting jurisdiction in a special court. President Roosevelt had vetoed such a bill in 1934, but a revised one was making its way through Congress with backing from Republican Karl Mundt, Democrat Henry Jackson, and Secretary of the Interior Harold Ickes (who fancied that when Indian claims were settled, Indians would give up dreams of huge federal payoffs, perhaps give up their reservations, and take their place in the mainstream of American life).

Johnson devoted most of his first presidential year—when he was not working as judge—to lobbying for an Indian Claims Commission, in the name of the National Congress of American Indians. The congress even drafted its own version of a bill, but Senator Jackson introduced the measure that eventually passed.

Johnson's other great effort went into an *amicus curiae* brief filed with the Supreme Court in the Shoshones' unsuccessful suit for compensation for ceded lands. The NCAI was showing it could do something. "During the past year, NCAI has devoted practically its entire effort to bringing about enactment of the Indian Claims Commission bill," Johnson wrote to his executive committee. He had gone to Washington twice to lobby for the bill; Ben Dwight had also gone twice, and had persuaded Oklahoma governor Robert Kerr to recommend it in person to President Truman. "I have one of the pens" that Truman used to sign the measure on August 13, 1946, Johnson crowed. "Its passage will lend great prestige to our organization."[17]

The act created a singular legal channel for Indians: a commission of three to adjudicate tribal claims for lands ceded. It gave tribes five years to submit their cases and was itself to expire after ten. It heard pleas that could not be advanced in other courts, empowered the commission to revise treaties, and encouraged poor tribes to pay lawyers contingency fees. While Ickes had urged the commission to conduct its own inquiries, its failure to do so inevitably threw claims cases into an adversarial format, tribe against government.

So few living witnesses to old times remained that anthropologists, historians, and appraisers testified on the basis of their studies of Indian life and territory, and from their work came a good many accounts of aboriginal peoples. The act expanded a legal specialty, Indian law. But for all its promise of quieting ancient discontents, the commission got tacky regard from Congress. In order to clear their crowded calendar, commissioners were forced to use staff attorneys to hear testimony, and the staff sat at desks in hallways. Clerks' files cluttered the reception area. The commission was not able to print findings but issued them in mimeograph. Yet, for Indians, it was the beginning of the future—a future with money for tribal operations and self-improvement.

The claims bill had not yet passed Congress when the National Congress of American Indians held its second annual convention, this time in Browning, Montana, hosted by the Blackfeet, who paid the executive committee's travel expenses. The relatively remote location attracted fewer progressive leaders and more "blanket Indians," reservation conservatives. These delegates passed a resolution barring Indian Service employees from policymaking positions and enlarged the executive committee by adding Lorene Burgess, a Blackfeet, and feisty Robert Yellowtail, the outspoken former superintendent of the Crow reservation.

This second convention drew delegates from only twenty-two tribes, and its business was hobbled by bickering between traditionalists and progressives. The nation's press gave it only passing notice. Browning had been chosen as a demonstration of Indian unity in the heart of Indian country. From this standpoint, and as public relations, the convention fizzled. From that time on, the NCAI would meet in larger cities (the next year, in Oklahoma City).

As the global war in Europe and the Pacific wound down, the NCAI looked forward to the return of its young veterans to infuse new energy into the struggle for Indian unity. Congress, meanwhile, turned again to domestic affairs. While Indians were not their most urgent business, members of Congress from states with substantial Indian populations set themselves to resolve old problems of Indian separateness.

In their view, settlements ordered by the Indian Claims Commission would advance assimilation. But the 1934 Indian Reorganization Act, which empowered tribes to write their own constitutions, was another matter. The chairman of the Senate Committee on Indian Affairs, Elmer Thomas of Oklahoma, and Sen. Burton K. Wheeler of Montana, whose name was linked to the Indian Reorganization Act (the Wheeler-Howard act), now considered it a mistake and called for its repeal, arguing that the legislation helped Indians develop economic programs and tribal governments, making them more separate than ever.

While the act stayed on the books, the continuing debate over its effectiveness convinced conservatives in both houses of Congress and both parties to call for a searching investigation of Indian conditions. Senator Mundt expressed hope that the inquiry would result in abolishing the Bureau of Indian Affairs. Off-reservation Indians applauded him.

As architect of the reorganization act, Commissioner of Indian Affairs

Collier now fell constantly under fire. He resorted, recklessly, to attacking the senior staff professional of the Senate committee, Albert A. Grorud, whom he had once refused to hire after D'Arcy McNickle whispered that Grorud speculated in California Indian lands. Sensing a payback, Collier asserted that in writing Senate Partial Report 310, highly critical of the Indian Reorganization Act and the Indian Service, Grorud distorted the consensus of the committee. Collier was wrong. The senators backed the report.[18]

Collier's presentation of his budget request turned out to be his swan song. It had been apparent, observed Assistant Commissioner William Zimmerman, Jr., "that the forward momentum of the Collier regime was running down." Indeed, a number of tribes, including the Navajos, wanted Collier out. Collier resigned in 1945, succeeded by his own choice for the post, William A. Brophy, who had been counsel to the Pueblos. But Brophy was not the NCAI's preference: The congress had petitioned the Truman Administration for a commissioner of Indian blood. Brophy's health forced him to take leave for much of his time in office, and Zimmerman ran the bureau in his stead.

Rather than risk rallying to Collier, Judge Johnson steered the NCAI effort to lobbying for Alaskan tribes who were then demanding reservations and legislation to preserve their traditional hunting and fishing sites. Secretary of the Interior Ickes had reserved more than 1.5 million acres for Indians and Eskimos and intended to set aside more. Of course, white commercial fishermen denounced him.[19]

Johnson also opened a legal-service bureau to furnish tribes with copies of bills and reports from Congress, headed by the indefatigable Ruth Bronson. Despite her full-time employment with the Bureau of Indian Affairs, Bronson opened a full-time NCAI office, staffed by volunteers, "thus achieving one of our basic aims," she wrote Archie Phinney. Before this, she added, Indian delegations visiting the capital city at great expense often did not understand how to arrange meetings with federal officers or members of Congress. As many as forty delegations came each year.[20]

The National Congress of American Indians appeared to be making headway. Although the Navajos, the nation's largest tribe, would not join, its returning veterans did. And in 1947, for the first time, four tribes paid dues to the NCAI, a total of $407.[21]

This is when Joe Garry discovered the NCAI. Attending a dinner hosted by Bronson to solicit tribal memberships, the handsome, well-spoken veteran, who was then rising in the political affairs of Pacific Northwest tribes, was pampered by the hostess. When he visited Washington, Garry joined the informal breakfast circle that Bronson gathered around her.

They talked of many things. Bronson wrote to Garry that she found his ideas "intensely interesting." The breakfast muster covered raising money for the NCAI, the plight of Navajos, denial of voting rights to Indians of Arizona and New Mexico, farm loans for Indians, the unfulfilled promise to train Indians for posts in the Indian Service, and so on. But the foremost topic of conversation was Acting Commissioner Zimmerman's testimony under subpoena before the Senate Committee on Civil Service.[22]

The committee intended to reduce the number of government employees. Zimmerman had gone before it, innocently enough, to talk about releasing some who worked for the bureau, mentioning tribes he felt could handle their business without federal oversight. The notion of terminating supervision, and thereby cutting the federal payroll, animated some committee members, and they directed Zimmerman to come back the next day with a list of tribes ready to take over their own affairs. He named the Klamaths of Oregon and the Menominees of Wisconsin, among others, and he offered draft bills to convert their tribal governments into corporations with lives of fifty years.

Arthur Watkins, a slight, earnest senator from Utah, howled in his reedy voice that Zimmerman had sounded a wake-up call to Congress. According to Watkins's understanding of the acting commissioner's testimony, about 40,000 Indians were "ready for immediate freedom from further federal control." Senator Wayne Morse, Republican from Oregon, introduced a bill to terminate the Klamaths, and Hugh Butler, Republican from Nebraska, offered a bill to terminate the Menominees, Flatheads, Osages, Potawatomies, and Indians of California and North Dakota.[23]

Zimmerman may not have sparked termination—he surely had not meant to—but no matter how often he protested that his testimony was wantonly "misquoted and misinterpreted," his words roused Congress to action. In termination, Senator Watkins had found a bully pulpit.

The National Congress of American Indians did not grasp immediately the effect of Zimmerman's testimony. Indeed, the NCAI endorsed, as Johnson phrased its view, "a planned program . . . for the progressive liquidation of the Indian Service." For the moment, the Indian congress busily publicized the distress of the Navajos: Ranges were overgrazed, herds reduced, children diseased, schooling neglected. The NCAI forecast wide-spread starvation among the Navajos, it supported court suits to require Arizona and New Mexico to allow Indians to vote and to serve on juries, and, with the Association on American Indian Affairs, it pursued lawsuits to lift restrictions on social services provided to Indians in those same two states.[24]

Garry went to the 1948 NCAI convention in Denver, representing the Affilated Tribes of Northwest Indians as well as the Coeur d'Alene and Kalispel tribes. The Denver delegates reelected Johnson as president, even though he was now a justice of the Oklahoma Supreme Court, with less time for Indian affairs. While the convention was well attended, only seven tribes paid dues—a total of $1,232. The congress relied on small founda-tion grants to maintain its Washington office and pay for mailings.[25]

The 1948 convention yielded an unexpected dividend: Helen Peterson, an Oglala Sioux and director of the Denver Commission on Community Relations, was enchanted by a two-page *Denver Post* photo spread of NCAI speakers. "I nearly burst with pride at discovering these magnificent Indians," she enthused later. Rather stocky and short, with dark hair and black-rimmed glasses, Peterson was already known as an energetic and capa-ble administrator, bright and articulate. She could be gracious, and she could be steely. She joined the NCAI, and in the next decade she and Joe Garry would be prime movers of the Indian congress.[26]

The 1949 convention in Rapid City, South Dakota, drew a record 212 delegates, many of them young activists. As president of the Affiliated Tribes of Northwest Indians, Garry took part in a panel discussion of a bill before Congress to give jurisdiction over Indians to the states. He steered a mid-dle course, generally favoring federal oversight, warning that a sudden change in Indian administration "might be dangerous," and urging tribes to cooperate with each other to improve federal relations. Garry predicted that the states, given control, would immediately impose taxes on Indians.

While his prosaic talk was not at all inspiring, as a person Garry impressed the younger Indians, the veterans who wanted action from the NCAI. He was named to the NCAI executive committee and to the res-olutions committee for the 1950 convention. Again the delegates elected Johnson as president, and the executive committee hired Louis Bruce, a Sioux Mohawk, as paid executive director, succeeding the overworked vol-unteer, Bronson. Bruce, former youth director of a New York dairymen's

association, was an outspoken easterner much impressed with his new eminence. He irked western reservation Indians, who were already murmur-
ing that Oklahomans and former bureau people bossed their congress.

Among their twenty-nine resolutions, the delegates protested realignment of the Bureau of Indian Affairs, which had closed forty district offices
and created eleven "area" offices—another level of bureaucracy between
the bureau and the tribes. This change had been in the works for some
time, as part of a reorganization of the executive branch recommended by
the Hoover Commission. When it took place, an NCAI attorney said that
"members of Congress were by no means fully conscious of what was being
done . . . but are now faced with an accomplished fact, one that they do
not like." Seven Northwest tribes sent a futile joint telegram to the
Washington, Oregon, and Idaho congressional delegations, asking them
to amend the appropriations bill to ban funding for area offices.

The convention also heard reports of the NCAI's efforts to assist
Navajos during the preceding winter. The NCAI had been hampered in
fund raising because it was not tax-exempt (it was, after all, a lobbying
agency). After the convention, Bronson, McNickle, and Johnson incorporated a separate entity, the NCAI Fund, Inc., to solicit and manage contributions for NCAI purposes. However, the NCAI Fund did not pass
muster with the Internal Revenue Service, and six months later its name
was changed to Arrow, Inc., a tax-exempt corporation attached to the NCAI
only by the requirement that Arrow's trustees would be appointed by the
business committee of the NCAI.[27]

Arrow, an acronym for American Restitution and Righting of Old
Wrongs (according to Peterson), would be an unruly offspring, and soon
it would go its own way. It never raised much money for the NCAI, and
funding continued to be a problem for the congress. Dues from tribes
totaled only $1,040 in 1949. Many simply did not have funds to contribute.
Tribal delegates, including Joe Garry, begged or borrowed to attend the
annual meeting. Joe often cadged contributions from neighboring farmers who leased Indian lands.

At this 1949 convention Garry met Leona Tremble, a Bureau of Indian
Affairs employee with a young daughter, who came from a politically active
and educated Pine Ridge reservation family. In the words of one who
watched their relationship flower, "Leona got her hooks into Joe and did
not let go." She and Joe married in Las Vegas on December 29, 1953.

After the convention, Garry and Frank George of the Colville reservation (second vice-president of the NCAI) headed to Washington to protest the establishment of area offices, which they called "no-man's-land" between Washington and the reservations. They charged that area directors were too far from reservations to know what was going on, and that the new level of bureaucracy produced only "waste and delay." At Garry's request, Idaho congressman Compton I. White offered an amendment to the general appropriations bill to abolish area offices, asking that the funds for these offices be spent instead on "the improvement of services to Indians in their home communities." Protests proved futile; White's amendment failed.[28]

If the bureau realignment truly caught Congress off guard, it also underscored a lack of direction in Indian affairs. The Truman Administration seemed indecisive about Indians. The bureau provided scant guidance, offered no long-range program, and expressed its mission simply as termination. And Congress groped for a cheaper Indian policy that might, at last, solve the "Indian problem."

Before the NCAI opened its convention in 1950, the new commissioner of the Bureau of Indian Affairs had taken office. Dillon Myer, at age sixty-one, was a twenty-four-year federal employee with a reputation for tackling unpopular assignments. He had directed the War Relocation Authority that herded Japanese Americans into internment camps during World War II, and then managed the Federal Housing Administration. Appointed commissioner of a rudderless Bureau of Indian Affairs on May 5, 1950, Myer cleaned house. He brought in his own management team and accepted the resignations of five of the bureau's top-rank officials, including William Zimmerman. He publicly humiliated some who stayed on, among them Ruth Bronson. Myer believed that any agency, regardless of its mission, could be drummed into shape through rigorous managing. His people did not need to know Indians; they needed to know management.

Myer's appointment dismayed the National Congress of American Indians. They had hoped that their keynoter of 1948, Will Rogers, Jr., would become commissioner; but when sounded out, Rogers had deferred to Myer. The new commissioner contracted with a study group from Princeton University to analyze the bureau's field organization and policies. The researchers saw the bureau's primary missions as providing Indians with services that other citizens received from state and local governments, and assisting Indians toward assimilation. They found—no surprise—the bureau's field staff and budgeting inept, and they scored tribal councils as impractical for equating religion with business. These findings, and congressional intent, as Myer perceived it, formed his program.[29] Under a darkening bureaucratic sky, the National Congress of American Indians strained to blunt Myer's edicts, but its esprit ebbed. Bruce and Bronson had been appointed to a blue-ribbon Indian Advisory Committee for the Interior Department, but the committee rarely met and its deliberations were not publicized. Embarrassed by Myer's public comments, Bronson resigned from the Indian Service.[30]

Bruce did not stay long as executive director, and was succeeded, temporarily, by John Rainer, a Taos Pueblo. Rainer's tenure was calculated to appease southwestern tribes growing impatient with domination of the congress by Oklahomans.

While dissent brewed in its ranks, the NCAI did not lack external challenges. Alaskan tribes continued to resist inroads on their lands, and they opposed a rider on an Alaskan statehood bill that would wipe out Indian reserves. Blackfeet protested arbitrary land leases. Colorado River Indians turned to the NCAI in their appeal for payment on their lands used for Japanese internment camps. Fort Berthold, Standing Rock, and Cheyenne River tribes contested hydroelectric projects that would flood their lands. Paiutes at Pyramid Lake decried Senator Pat McCarran's persistent efforts to force sales of their land to squatters. On many reservations, superintendents meddled in tribal business. The NCAI busily carried these protests to Congress.

With the NCAI's day-to-day coaching, said NCAI attorney James E. Curry, "the quality of Indian delegations to Washington has continued to improve. In the old days, Indians used to come to Washington thoroughly confused about their purposes. . . . Now that the delegations have help from the NCAI, they usually stick to their purposes and get a fair hearing.[31] But with the punishing demands, the NCAI's tiny staff and volunteers struggled to maintain a stopgap pace. And any missed opportunity soured a tribal council somewhere.

Joe Garry collected the shards of tribal discontent like colored pebbles in a stream, forming them into a mosaic of coercion and thralldom. He now saw political terrain beyond the Northwest, and he contemplated the obstacles of cultural and geographic distance that separated tribes. He also arrived at his own uncomplicated convictions: Indians must control their tribal affairs, regain their lands, build an economic base, and educate their young.

But he was snatched away from the cause shortly after the 1950 annual convention. As an enlisted army reservist, he was called to duty with the combat engineers in Korea. He reported on September 12, 1950, leaving behind an Indian community in near revolt against the Bureau of Indian Affairs and a commissioner bent on whipping them into line.

Strife between Myer and the National Congress of American Indians came to a head in the fall of 1950 when President Truman, heeding Indian petitions, canceled an order to transfer the superintendent of the Pyramid Lake reservation, who opposed Senator McCarran's raid on Paiute lands. (The Paiutes were clients of NCAI attorney James Curry.) In November, Myer issued new rules requiring his approval of attorneys who contracted with Indian tribes. Speaking for the NCAI, John Rainer accused Myer of "attempting to dictate to the Indian people what attorneys they may hire . . . or whether they shall be permitted to have any attorneys at all."[32]

Curry, who represented more than forty tribes as counsel or in claims suits, asserted that the stringent attorney code was, in fact, an attack on him. He and Rainer were not alone in their protests; other voices decried Myer's code. The American Bar Association judged that the commissioner lacked authority to approve contracts between attorneys and "organized" tribes (those with constitutions and bylaws). Former commissioner John Collier chimed in that Myer's policy amounted to "imprisonment of Indian litigation and legal representation," and the *New York Times* editorially called the code "a retrogressive step in the treatment of the American Indian and one that ought to be stopped."[33]

Eventually, the secretary of the interior, after hearing forty-four witnesses and representatives of the American Bar Association, all speaking against Myer's policy, rejected the regulations. Myer and his successors nonetheless continued, by various means, to obstruct tribal contracts for legal services.

When Myer addressed the 1951 NCAI convention the following June in St. Paul, he did not dwell on lawyer contracts, choosing instead to assure the delegates that no master plan was in the making to end government wardship wholesale. A master plan of that sort, he said, would "be one of the worst mistakes we could make in Washington for the solution of all

Indian problems. I believe that we must develop our programs locally in consultation every step of the way with the Indians who will be affected." However, Myer did not win over his suspicious listeners. When the delegates passed a resolution to do away with area offices, Myer said he would not consider it.[34]

Alarmed by tribal defections and meager contributions, the convention planners hoped this meeting would rekindle the fervor of the NCAI's first years, and to that end they brought back one of the originals, D'Arcy McNickle, to sound new challenges. A slight, erudite man, curly-haired, peering through round glasses, McNickle recalled the early years: "One reason we succeeded, I believe, is that we did not attempt too much. We avoided talking big." He reminded the delegates of the NCAI's success in lobbying for the Indian Claims Commission.

McNickle's was a reasoned speech, a call for united action. "In my opinion," he said, "the situation is dangerous. . . . Congress has been giving warnings for the past several years that appropriations for the benefit of Indians must come to an end . . . that the Bureau of Indian Affairs must be abolished and the Indians turned loose. . . . The Indians themselves and this organization can bring about a larger concept of the Indian problem by taking action. . . . The Indian tribes have resources which, if used to the utmost, could make a . . . fundamental attack on the poverty and lack of opportunity which now confront our Indian people. . . . I ask, what alternative have we?"

McNickle proposed a new program for the NCAI, "as a challenge to your thinking and to your desire to be leaders among your people." The delegates, he urged, should inventory the resources of their reservations, ask Congress for funds to develop them, buy back their reservation lands, and demand a federally financed training program comparable to the GI bill for veterans.[35]

Whatever fire McNickle's challenge lit, membership applications and dues payments to the NCAI continued to fall off. Some of the inner circle saw the NCAI as "dead for all practical purposes," its organizational confidence lost and $5,000 in debt.[36]

Shouldering this dismal burden fell to Frank George, named executive director in 1951. Burly, round-faced, dark-skinned, astute, and independent, George, a Nez Perce, had been tribal-relations officer for the Colville reservation. He had attended the organizational meeting of the Governors'

At the Missoula National Congress of American Indians convention, left to right: Frank George, Joe Garry, and Alex Saluskin (Yakama). (Dellwo collection)

Interstate Council for Indian Affairs, was elected its vice-president, and offered the governors one of his usual blunt observations: The council should not adopt policies without referring first to the tribes affected. Privately, he believed the council's agenda was to end federal guardianship and put Indian land on state tax rolls. One of the council's stated objectives was to transfer the Indian Health Service to the U.S. Public Health Service, an action the NCAI opposed.

George was a hard worker, a founder of the Affiliated Tribes of Northwest Indians, highly regarded not only for his good sense but for his skill at reporting. (He had learned shorthand at the Haskell Institute.)[37]

He went about reviving the NCAI mightily, trying to be everywhere at once. As a result, he was absent from the Washington office for days at a time, and out of touch. The workaday business of the NCAI—lobbying, guiding visiting delegations, issuing news bulletins—went undone. And he was not bringing in dues or foundation grants. Bill Short scolded George. Bronson, McNickle, and Robert Bennett urged him to quit.

As the months passed, the NCAI became unable to pay George for his services. Undoubtedly George wrote to Garry in Korea about his problems. He had taken to addressing Joe, in the pidgin of Korea, as "Cho Kolley." Shortly after September 1, 1951, Garry returned to the United States with a medical discharge for arthritis. Soon he was back with the Coeur d'Alene business council, the Affiliated Tribes, and the NCAI executive council. He called a meeting of the officers of the Affiliated Tribes to discuss what they might do to unscramble the NCAI and to get George his back pay.

Garry found that the Northwest tribes believed they were being manipulated by "professional" Indians. George Adams, a Skokomish, and vice-president of the Affiliated Tribes, warned that western Indians "should be very wary of the 'professional' Indians whose ideologies were not synchronized with true Indian thinking." [38]

As the 1952 NCAI convention approached, suspicions among the northwest Indians divided the NCAI hierarchy. George resisted domination by those he regarded as "white" Indians, "big city professional Indians," meaning Short, Bronson, McNickle, and Elizabeth Roe Cloud. All of them had been with the NCAI from the first. At the convention, the NCAI dissolved its business council, handing over to Arrow, Inc., the responsibility for its finances. However, that did not sit well with delegates who questioned Arrow's performance. And when Bill Short succeeded Johnson as president, George believed the grass-roots reservation Indians had been betrayed.

The Indian convention met soon after the national elections, gathering at the Cosmopolitan Hotel in Denver, site of its organizing conclave. Both national political parties had nailed Indian planks into their platforms: The Democrats pledged "prompt final settlement of claims," and the Republicans offered "equal opportunities."

With Dwight Eisenhower's victory, Myer seemed sure to be replaced as commissioner. The NCAI executive council endorsed Alva A. Simpson, Jr., New Mexico welfare director and chairman of the Governors' Interstate Indian Council, for the post. Robert Yellowtail scoffed that Simpson's supporters were "the old Collier-Zimmerman crowd, backed by Felix Cohen." Then Bill Short announced that he would be a candidate, publicly repudiating George's endorsement of Simpson, and telegraphed senators that George was "no longer executive director" of the NCAI.

The new commissioner would be neither Simpson nor Short, but Glenn L. Emmons, a New Mexico banker. George bitterly inferred that

Short had sold out Simpson. To a friend, George wrote, "I called Bill Short what he is, and he didn't like it."[39]

Garry was dismayed by this public show of discord, and by Short's treatment of Frank George. Dissent within the executive committee and open conflict between Short and George undermined George's credibility as a spokesman for the NCAI. Although he had not resigned, he could not realistically act for the congress. Bronson and McNickle, fearing collapse of the organization, induced Helen Peterson to take over as executive director, and Short hired her. She agreed to work six months to plan a 1953 convention and, in her words, "help the organization to regroup." But the executive committee's choice of Phoenix for the meeting set off another uproar, with reservation Indians crying that the convention was "rigged" by "professional" Indians who chose a site too expensive for grass-roots delegates.[40]

The 1953 convention loomed as crucial, not only because factions tattered the NCAI but because Congress had begun in earnest to press drastic changes in Indian administration. A California congressman introduced a bill to transfer criminal jurisdiction over California Indians from the federal government to the state, and members of congress in Minnesota, Nebraska, Oregon, and Wisconsin wrote in support of the legislation. The bill passed as Public Law 280, and the NCAI—crippled by internal conflict—lobbied as best it could for amendments to the act to require the consent of Indians.

While Public Law 280 aroused opposition from many, House Concurrent Resolution 108, introduced by Wyoming representative William Harrison and sponsored in the Senate by Henry Jackson of Washington, evoked little argument in Congress. It passed as routine business on August 1, 1953, declaring as the "policy of Congress" an end to federal trusteeship as rapidly as possible. This resolution, which would obliterate a 150-year-old system of relations between Indians and the federal government, sounded patriarchal—the great father freeing his children—but, in fact, it aimed at quick riddance.

Joe Garry, in the political maelstrom that shook the NCAI and propelled Congress, set out to change the leadership of the National Congress of American Indians. Using a tax raid on Coeur d'Alenes as his pretext, he traveled the West to raise a defense fund, and as he visited western tribes he heard their views and propounded his own.

As the convention date neared, Garry called a meeting of the Affiliated

Tribes for the ostensible purpose of forming a united front. Thus he built a constituency, and when delegates gathered for the 1953 annual convention, Garry presented himself as a candidate for president, a devoted reservation Indian ready to throw out the city-bred Oklahomans. "At that meeting," recalled Helen Peterson, "Garry ran a very dignified and sophisticated campaign to become president." One of the most respected western leaders, Clarence Wesley, nominated him.[41]

"Joe Garry was a very, very impressive man," in Peterson's opinion, "with great leadership quality, and it was not surprising that he won rather easily. . . . Joe had a commanding voice, a very deliberate manner of speaking, and he was a man of great dignity. There was a quality about Joe Garry of royalty."[42]

3 The Crucial Year

*I*n the days after the emergency session of 1954, the year took shape ominously. Congress uncaged plans that hovered like rapacious vultures over the Indian community. These "legislative proposals," warned the National Congress of American Indians, "constituted the gravest threat to Indian properties and rights since the General Allotment Act of 1887."

Congress deliberated bills to terminate federal management of Flatheads, Klamaths, Menominees, Makahs, Sacs and Foxes, Potawatomies, Kickapoos, Turtle Mountain Chippewas, Seminoles, and bands in New York, Utah, Texas, Oregon, and Nevada. The hearings were under way when the NCAI emergency conference began.

New laws repealed the federal prohibition on liquor sales to Indians, leaving regulation to the states; conferred civil and criminal jurisdiction over Indians on half a dozen states, "making possible a similar extension to the remainder"; and lifted the archaic ban on sales of firearms to Indians.[1]

Congressional committees called for studies to evaluate tribal governments organized under the Indian Reorganization Act and of law enforcement on reservations; they also wanted surveys of Indian lands that might be taxed under state jurisdiction. These proposals and demands were cloaked in the rhetoric of freedom, citizenship, and equal opportunity for Indians. In the words of the House Interior and Insular Affairs Committee, "The objectives, in bringing about the ending of the Indian segregation . . . are (1) the end of wardship or trust status as not acceptable to our American way of life, and (2) the assumption by individual Indians of all the duties, obligations, and privileges of free citizens."

And to critics of its headlong rush to jettison the Indians, Congress warned of self-styled spokesmen who opposed termination for personal gain. "The real Indians," it asserted, "have been drowned out by the high-powered propaganda machine of the 'professional Indians' and their manipulators."[2]

Across the capital city, one of the so-called professional Indians, Helen Peterson, wrote to Bill Short, former president of the NCAI: "It is just mighty hard for either of us [Peterson or Bronson] to get any letters written with the terrific pressure and demands and workload. It is an absurdity to think of trying to run this office in any kind of creditable manner with less than five or six fulltime people. Even then each person has to work long, hard hours and be able to do three or four different jobs.

"I assume that what you . . . want is a vigorous and responsible organization and NCAI is fast becoming that, but it is surely going to mean that we have to have more adequate financing."[3]

The NCAI office, housed in an older building on DuPont Circle, was sparsely equipped: a hand-turned mimeograph; some secondhand furniture; a red carpet donated by the Wilkinson law firm when it redecorated; and an air-conditioner (given by Dr. Paschal Sherman) that ruffled curtains purchased from Sears, Roebuck. Two volunteers (retirees from the Bureau of Indian Affairs), one of whom liked to watch birds from the office window, comprised the staff.[4]

One is tempted to see a David-versus-Goliath confrontation in the Indian resistance to ending federal controls—a whole government marshaled against a few native Americans—but, in fact, very few members of Congress grasped, or were even interested in, Indian affairs. A handful found in the issue of Indian relations a useful pulpit; some considered it a recurring chore. "The field of Indian affairs has been, through the years, one of the most neglected, least understood, and lightly treated of all the areas requiring Congressional consideration," Peterson wrote to a supporter, suggesting he use her words to lobby for Indians: "Casual inquiry reveals that a large proportion of United States Congressmen have no experience or interest or contact with the Indian people and they, therefore, leave the entire responsibility for Indian legislation in the hands of the Indian Subcommittee. . . . While it may be thought that Indian legislation, after all, affects only a very small racial minority in this country (something like 400,000 people) there is much more at stake. . . . The issue with Indians is *not* integration as is so universally thought even by citizens and congressmen of good will. The Indians are the only aborigines in this country. Our treatment of them reflects the moral character of our Nation."[5]

Congress had other matters on its collective mind: While Senator Joseph McCarthy alleged the presence of Communists in high positions of the U.S. government, Arthur Watkins chaired a committee to censure him;

Puerto Ricans opened fire on a sitting House of Representatives from the visitors' gallery; President Eisenhower circumvented Congress by executive agreements with foreign nations; and the French retreated from Vietnam, baring Asia to a perceived threat of Communist expansion. And individual members of Congress were preoccupied with their regional projects: for example, Frank Church of Idaho pursued a laboratory for his state to produce electricity from atomic energy.

But, while the NCAI strove to raise money and to maintain an Indian presence before Senate and House committees, Congress pushed ahead with Indian bills. Joe Garry pitched membership and donations for the NCAI wherever he traveled. At home, in Idaho, he sponged contributions from his neighbors. His father, Ignace, gave five dollars. Others staged bingo games, blanket dances, bazaars, greeting-card sales, and so on to raise a few dollars to mail to Washington. Sometimes the NCAI paid overdue office rent with two- and three-dollar checks from the day's post. When he was in the NCAI office in Washington, D.C., Garry walked to a nearby Catholic church to give prayerful thanks for contributions.

Arrow, the fund-raising subsidiary, contributed almost nothing. Shortly after the emergency conference, Peterson and Garry visited Arrow's New York office. They were appalled. A white benefactor, Susan B. Hyde, had recently been photographed wearing a war bonnet and riding in an automobile with "National Congress of American Indians" on its side.

"That kind of publicity turned the stomachs of a lot of Indians," snorted Peterson. Arrow shared an office with the Committee for an Effective Congress, branded as a Communist front. "If that had been publicized, it would have destroyed NCAI," in Peterson's opinion. The walls featured photographs of emaciated Indian children. Garry "was revolted at the idea of using children, showing them in their worst state, to beg for money that was spent so foolishly as this stationwagon parading in New York," Peterson recalled. Garry and Peterson concluded that the Arrow office must close.[6]

In a letter to McNickle, then working in a health-education center in Crown Point, New Mexico, Garry urged that Arrow's funds be transferred to a special trustee "until all the details of relationship" between Arrow and the NCAI could be worked out, and that "the New York office of Arrow be closed" until the boards of Arrow and the NCAI "consider there is sufficient agreement, staff, resources, and planning to re-open a New York

office." Doubtless Garry sensed that Arrow and the NCAI would separate, and he did not want the NCAI burned in the process.[7]

Slowly tribes signed up as members of the NCAI. Garry and other solic-
itors increased membership from twelve (with dues of $806) in 1953 to nine-
teen (with dues of $3,206) in 1954. (Dues were assessed according to size
of the tribe.) Raising a few dollars was indeed difficult. The Kalispel council, for one, voted 15–0 to join the NCAI but did not have the $30.10 fee.
Chairman Raymond Pierre wrote Garry that they would apply for a grant
to pay.

"Our financial support has been greatly increased," observed Peterson,
"but nowhere in proportion to the demands on the office for service.
Consequently, the office goes on month after month, hanging on by the
skin of its teeth." A number of tribes relied on the NCAI for information
and support before congressional committees without formally joining.
And fortunately an angel appeared: the Robert Marshall Civil Liberties
Trust, which granted funds to match what the NCAI raised. In 1954 the
trust gave $13,800, and the NCAI finished the year with $913.59 in its bank
account.[8]

The National Congress of American Indians would need all the aid it
could muster. Branding the five-score Indian bills introduced in the
Eighty-third Congress as "the most frightening and threatening to Indian
property and rights in this century," the NCAI maintained that one of these
bills would class an Indian property owner "competent" to manage his
own affairs and release him and his heirs from federal jurisdiction; one,
authored by Senator McCarran, would wipe out constitutional guaran-
tees for Indians; another would transfer responsibility for Indian health
to the Public Health Service; and five would terminate tribes. The NCAI
resisted them all, and toiled to persuade Congress to amend House
Concurrent Resolution 108 and Public Law 280.[9]

On the other hand, the National Congress of American Indians took
no position on the termination of tribes that had voted for it. These included
the Menominees and Klamaths, whose members seemed beguiled by expectations of large per-capita payouts. Neither did the NCAI oppose or comment on the termination of small bands in Texas, Utah, and western Oregon
that had not asked for help. However, while the NCAI took no position,
its president did. Joe Garry argued against termination at every opportunity. One story has it that Garry, addressing the Klamath council, had con-

vinced a majority to reconsider their vote for termination until a faction walked out to defeat a quorum.[10]

Congress could not hope to treat tribes equally. Maybe the Menominees and Klamaths had resources, but the Seminoles of Florida contended that they "did not have members advanced enough to take care of the administration of tribal property," that their tribal cattle business made no profit, and that their members still lived in native "chickees," open on all sides with cabbage-palm or palmetto-leaf roofs.[11]

Many bills duplicated those already before Congress, or proposed small changes, and a number would fail, such as one sponsored by Sen. Barry Goldwater to define as Indians only those of half-blood or more. Determining who qualified legally as "Indian" was a dilemma of long-standing. Even the NCAI left that to individual tribes.

While a special committee, pursuant to House Resolution 89, conducted a "full and complete investigation and study of the activities and operations of the Bureau of Indian Affairs," Congress relied on data obtained from an elaborate self-study of the bureau in 1952 under Dillon Myer. Congress acknowledged that the self-study—a complex review squeezed into an inflexible format—was unreliable, but tribal delegates still had to overcome misinformation from the report in dealing with members of Congress.[12]

As the special committee examined the bureau, the committee's frustrations seeped into capitol cloakrooms. Well before the findings were published in September, they had become matters of common talk among members of Congress concerned with Indians: The special committee grumbled that they could not find out what Indians thought because there was no recognized channel for opinion, and they complained that the technical and geographic details of Indian legislation were almost beyond understanding. They suspected that tribes manipulated membership rolls; they discovered again what everyone knew—that Indian administration was often venal and corrupt; they wondered whether Indian advocates—including the National Congress of American Indians—really spoke for Indians. All in all, the committee concluded that Indian affairs were a hodgepodge, a muddle of Congress's own making.

Still, Congress pressed on. Hearings on termination of the Flatheads, or more properly, the Confederated Salish and Kootenai Tribes of the Flathead Reservation, moved into the field. The governor of Montana warned, "Because this measure would set a precedent for similar legislation affecting other tribes, [I] think it imperative [that] extreme care and caution be exercised in drafting the provisions." [13]

The Flatheads numbered 4,213 persons, with 644,015 acres of trust lands that embraced a pine forest, a hydroelectric dam and two potential damsites, two tribal businesses (a mineral bath and a lakeshore resort), and a 14,300-acre irrigation project. About half of the Flatheads lived off the reservation and, like most off-reservation Indians, saw termination as a chance for a generous distribution of assets. The Confederated Tribes had formed a government by council under the Indian Reorganization Act. Their constitution allowed voting on tribal business only by those who lived on the reservation.

Senator Watkins, in precise, rigid fashion, conducted field hearings in person; all across the country he made promises to persuade tribes to endorse termination. At a mass meeting in Polson, Montana, Joe Garry and Dennis Dellwo, secretary of the irrigation project, spoke forcefully against termination, and as a result, the reservation Flatheads voted almost unanimously against it. When Watkins interrupted Garry, Joe turned his back on the senator and said to the Indians gathered, "I am speaking to you, brothers," and went on with his remarks.

One witness before Watkins's traveling committee spoke passionately: "Let me assure this committee that there is no mystery or question as to how the Indian people feel about the proposed bill. . . . They are opposed to it, and more: they are disillusioned, and they are bitter. They cannot understand how the great American Government could strike such a final and irrevocable blow against them." [14]

The Intertribal Policy Board of Montana, representing all seven reservations and Montana's landless Indians, also advised against Flathead termination. McNickle, a Cree who grew up on the Flathead reservation, called the termination bill "hasty and ill-advised," and he urged the committee to let the Indians choose either to keep their reservations intact, to manage it as corporate property, or to break it up. If not that, McNickle cautioned, the tribe should at least be given time to learn to manage its affairs, without "every possible string attached" by the Department of the Interior. Watkins retorted, "We don't intend to deprive them of their God-given right to make a few of their own mistakes." [15]

Other witnesses made the necessary comments about the sanctity of treaties and the honor and integrity of the nation. As the hearing went on, it became clear that, in their minds, the Flatheads were defending not only their assets and their lands but their very existence as a people. The hearing, as a preview of termination proceedings, offered no comfort to other tribes, for the questioning was acerbic at times, and a majority of the committee had obviously made up their minds beforehand.

Asked if Congress meant to extend termination beyond the tribes already under consideration, Watkins averred that Congress meant to "do something about ending the status of Indians as wards as rapidly as possible." He concluded: "We have a duty to perform in accordance with the resolution adopted by the Congress." Except for a short written statement from the NCAI, that remark closed the sessions.

In the weeks after the Flathead hearings, Helen Peterson monitored the termination bill, and William Zimmerman, now employed by the Association on American Indian Affairs, lobbied against it with tribal attorney George Tunison. Peterson wrote to Walter McDonald, Flathead council chairman, urging him to leave nothing to chance: Make sure members of Congress "understand clearly that the majority of your Tribe is very much opposed to this bill." Call on the National Catholic Welfare Conference for support, and write letters to the *Washington Post*, she advised.[16]

The strategy paid off. By adjournment of the Eighty-third Congress's second session, the Flathead bill lay stalled in committee. In this session Congress had passed no act to cut loose a tribe that resisted termination.

Congress was by no means done with termination, but it moved on to other business. Montana congressman Wesley D'Ewart introduced a "competency" bill, one of many then under consideration. Congressman D'Ewart cannily excluded Indians of Oklahoma, New Mexico, and Arizona, who had been part of earlier proposals, "removing some of the strongest pressure against the bill," the NCAI pointed out. Attorney Felix Cohen put the bill's purpose in plain language: "to make it easier for Indians who don't want to be Indians to get rid of their special status." D'Ewart called it an "emancipation" bill, and Cohen, in testimony before the House Committee on Interior and Insular Affairs, described it as "one of the most far-reaching bills to come before this committee in the past 25 years."[17]

In simple terms the bill provided that an Indian could apply to the secretary of the interior for a "decree of competency." If the individual were deemed competent, the Interior Department would turn over all of the Indian's trust property to him; neither the applicant nor his family would any longer be subject to laws governing Indians. The Affiliated Tribes of Northwest Indians protested that release of trust property might "force liquidation of an entire tribe's assets."

At its Phoenix convention, the National Congress of American Indians had pointed out the danger: "An Indian obtaining a decree of competency would still retain an interest and voice in tribal affairs and the tribe would be required to share with him any future division of assets. In the course of time as the automatic feature of the law took effect, a majority in any tribe would hold certificates of competency and could force the liquidation of even such a reservation as the Navajo." For the NCAI, Helen Peterson sent out dozens of letters to tribes urging them to call on their congressional representatives to oppose competency. In his letters, Garry called the bill "one of the most wicked ever introduced."[18]

D'Ewart's draft slipped through the subcommittee with no hearing and seemed almost certain to sail through the full committee with a recommendation for passage. To his Indian clients, Cohen reported:

> I have found in discussing the bill with various Congressmen, there is a widespread impression that this 'emancipation' bill is something Indians want in order to be free of special Bureau restrictions. It is very hard to make Congressmen realize that this bill will not actually eliminate authority over a single Indian, but that the bill will cut down on Federal Indian hospital services, schooling, and other essential public services, not only for Indians who want to remove themselves from Federal jurisdiction, but also for the children of such Indians. . . . If these points are made clear to interested Congressmen by a majority of the Indian groups affected, I think there is still a fighting chance of defeating this pending legislation.[19]

When no Indian appeared to testify against the bill at the committee hearing, the NCAI and its president mounted a furious campaign to deluge Congress with protests from Indian tribes. Peterson spent $425 of the NCAI's precious funds on telephone calls and telegrams exhorting tribes to protest to Congress. Letters and telegrams flowed into Washington. For example, Martin Vigil, chairman of the All-Pueblo council, wrote: "The competency bill, aside from its grossly unfair provisions, is absurdly impractical. Proponents . . . either have no understanding of New Mexico economy or are completely callous and indifferent." [20]

Garry adopted a telling strategy: He went directly to Idaho representatives Hamer Budge and Gracie Pfost, asking them to exclude Idaho from the bill and to persuade other members of Congress to seek exemption for their states. "Your work on Pfost and Budge really paid off," Peterson exulted: "They started the ball rolling that got the bill recommitted and Pfost obviously was acting on your instructions and Budge stated plainly that he had . . . heard from all the tribes in his state. They were largely responsible for the action to recommit. After they started it, then [George] Shuford of North Carolina, [James] Haley of Florida, and finally and reluctantly [E. Y.] Berry had to ask for exclusion of South Dakota. That wrecked Mr. D'Ewart's playhouse." [21]

Competency was dead in the Eighty-third Congress.

The tribes responded less emphatically to House Resolution 303, intended to transfer the Indian Health Service to the Public Health Service on the flimsy premise that combining two underfunded agencies might produce one with enough money to run it. Transfer was part of Glenn Emmons's three-point program to turn Indian health over to the Public Health Service, to improve Indian education, and to relocate Indians from reservations to cities.

"Basically the problem with both [health] services is inadequate appropriations," Peterson observed, "and many of us feel that shifting the responsibility will not solve this problem. We think, in the end, Indians will simply be stripped of those special services." Nonetheless, care for Indians varied from reservation to reservation, and neglected tribes had little to lose by the transfer. The Indian Health Service maintained only fifty-six hospitals—clinics, really—and few employed more than one physician. They were generally obsolete, poorly equipped, and only ten were accredited. Emmons pointed out that seventy-seven doctors made up the entire medical staff of the Indian Health Service, and contract physicians living near reservations cared for tribes as they had time available from their regular practices.

Garry's own Coeur d'Alene tribe had been covered by a contract physician who died in 1951 and was not replaced. After that, any Coeur d'Alene who required diagnosis or treatment had to apply by mail on a bureau form to the Northern Idaho agency, ninety miles distant in Lapwai. As Garry put it, "Only those Indians with advanced cases would take the time and the chance to apply. . . . Even then one is not sure whether he would qualify since eligibility for assistance is based on a certain degree of indigency and availability of [agency] funds." Mailed applications went first to Spokane and then to Lewiston, Idaho, en route to Lapwai. Responses took at least a week, even for the "simple advice of a physician."[22]

Navajos, San Carlos Apaches, and the Montana Intertribal Advisory Board favored transfer to the Public Health Service. Other tribes, when they gave an opinion, opposed transfer. Peterson observed that "it took the Indians a long time to get in gear but the opposition has been mounting." As the bill passed conference committee and both houses, ready for the president's signature, the National Congress of American Indians was caught in an equivocal position.

Frank George, while executive director, had testified that the NCAI supported the transfer. Peterson was limited to saying that the NCAI merely passed along the views of various tribes. Meanwhile, she fretted, "One of the [tribal] Governors from Oklahoma . . . who said he had requested a very substantial tribal contribution to NCAI told me he'd withdraw his request for the contribution if we had endorsed 303 — he may have been kidding me but he didn't smile."[23]

Legislation transferring responsibility for Indian health to the Public Health Service was signed by the president and scheduled to take effect on July 1, 1955. The service, still underfunded, then began renovating hospitals and recruiting additional staff, housing people and equipment in 250 surplus army barracks dismantled for reassembly on Indian reservations. It hurried to build facilities for the Navajo that would test for tuberculosis. But contract physicians continued to be the lot of many tribes.[24]

Congress also considered wrapping Indian agricultural extension into the Department of Agriculture's services offering advice and demonstrations through county agents. More than 5,000 Indian boys and girls nationwide already took part in 4-H clubs. Backers of the transfer argued that, through a merged extension service, Indian adults would learn to work with their white neighbors (overlooking the reality that Indians were rarely welcome in granges or farmer associations). Senator Watkins added his caustic opinion that the transfer would advance Indians "under the spur of necessity." The National Congress of American Indians opposed the idea, for much the same reason it resisted the health transfer: Combining two underfunded programs was unlikely to produce one better program. The bill to combine, weakened by the requests of New Mexico and Arizona to be excluded (the same strategy that defeated competency), failed to pass the Senate.[25]

For months, Indian advocates had lobbied for an amendment to Public Law 280 that would require Indian consent before passing jurisdiction to states. "Consent," as contrasted to "consultation," had become one of those buzzwords that, by repetition, made members of Congress testy. Passed in 1953, Public Law 280 granted jurisdiction over criminal offenses committed by or against Indians in Indian "country" to the states of California, Minnesota (excepting the Red Lake reservation), Oregon (except the Warm Springs reservation), Nebraska, and Wisconsin. It also granted the states jurisdiction over civil causes of action to which Indians were a party, and it allowed jurisdiction to pass to a state whether the Indians in question favored it or not. Delegates to the 1953 NCAI convention had unanimously adopted a resolution offered by fifty-two tribes asking that Public Law 280 be amended to require consultation with, and consent of, the Indians affected.

The House Committee on Interior and Insular Affairs, impatient with piecemeal changes in Indian administration and eager to get on with pushing Indians toward assimilation, prodded Congress to extend Public Law 280 to all the states, and the California bill was amended to do so. There had been little tribal resistance to Public Law 280, even though President Eisenhower, when he signed it, had urged amending it to give Indians a voice.

Subcommittees in both houses intimated that they would approve an amendment for "consultation" with Indians before states could assume jurisdiction. But that was not enough. The National Congress of American Indians, in a legislative bulletin, called the notion of "full consultation" with Indians "a mockery—Congress and the Administration have clearly demonstrated that they don't mean the same thing the Indians mean by 'consultation.'" The NCAI held out for "consent."[26]

Meanwhile, members of Congress from several states began having second thoughts about Public Law 280 when the California legislature published a 493-page study of how enforcement of the law would operate in that state. Was California to consider Indians as wards? What would be the law's effect on school districts, welfare benefits, and medical services?

What would be the impact on roads, irrigation projects, property tax exemptions, surveys and maps of Indian lands?[27]

Joe Garry was in Idaho campaigning for a seat in the state house when an amendment for consultation came up for hearing in Congress. If the government was going to hand over jurisdiction to the states, what better place for an Indian than in the state legislature? Helen Peterson had been talking with members of Congress, she reported to Garry. "I said we insisted on 'consent'—not consultation in the bills to amend P.L. 280," she wrote, "and I understand that Watkins said that meant we wouldn't get any bill."[28]

But at the emergency conference the previous February, Frank George had framed a resolution calling only for consultation. "Again we're caught by our own carelessness," Helen went on. "That is not the same as our [1953] convention resolution which asks for 'consent.' It is clear to me that 'consultation' does not mean the same to Congress or the Bureau as it means to the Indians therefore, we should not agree to consultation when consent is what we want."

Garry was in Idaho. Peterson, headed for Nashville, hired attorney Glen Wilkinson to go to the hearing on behalf of the NCAI. "One of the reasons I hired Glen to represent us in that one hearing only is to go another step toward getting the entire firm to take a more active part on the *general* bills affecting Indians," she explained. The firm of Wilkinson, Boyden, Cragun and Barker was perhaps the most prestigious law office in the capital with a substantial Indian clientele. It had won the largest fee in claims history in the Ute case, and it represented Garry in a suit (the Nicodemus case) against taxes on income from trust land. The Wilkinson firm could be a strong ally for the NCAI.[29]

John Cragun of the Wilkinson firm had represented the NCAI earlier against Senator McCarran's futile bill to revise the Constitution to omit Indians from Congress's power to regulate commerce. And Cragun was often in the NCAI office, courting Hilda Henderson, a new staff member.

Wilkinson told the committee that the NCAI wanted a bill to require "consent of the Indian citizens affected . . . prior to surrender of civil and criminal jurisdiction to the various states," and he proferred a copy of the NCAI convention resolution for consent, "adopted unanimously by representatives of fifty-two tribes."[30]

Wilkinson stuck to legal considerations in his testimony, pointing out that the phrase "'fully consulted' has no defined meaning in law. . . . The meaning of 'fully consulted' seems incapable of definition when applied to an Indian tribe." After the hearing, the Senate amended Public Law 280 to remove all states other than the original five (California, Minnesota, Nebraska, Oregon, and Wisconsin). "This victory for the Indians," Peterson said in a bulletin to tribal chairmen, "came because your organization and you individually . . . informed your Senators of your position." The job now was to persuade the House to do the same.[31]

Senator Watkins floated a minority statement: "The issue is consent versus consultation. Although the immediate issue is restricted to civil and criminal jurisdiction, there will be an inevitable tendency to expand the principle to all other fields of Indian administration." In other words, the senator worried that if the NCAI could get "consent" into this legislation, it could expand "consent" to all Indian bills.[32]

As summer's humidity softened into fall and leaves turned orange in the capital, the House Special Subcommittee on Indian Affairs released its study of the activities and operations of the Bureau of Indian Affairs. In its brown paper cover, House Report 2680 held no surprises: Its content had leaked all summer long. While the report consisted of only thirteen pages, an appendix of more than 500 pages, compiled from the bureau's study of itself ordered by Dillon Myer, was attached.

Fully in concert with Congress's resolve to dump Indians as quickly as possible, the subcommittee recommended that the major functions of the Bureau of Indian Affairs be discontinued or handed over to other agencies, federal or state. Some of the recommendations—transfer of health to the Public Health Service, for instance—had already been decreed. Bureau operations in six states—California, Michigan, Nebraska, South Carolina, Texas, and Wyoming—could be discontinued immediately, the subcommittee said. Indians in those states could handle their own affairs.

Dealing with Indians as tribes was "impractical," in the subcommittee's view, and the "proposition that it is possible to release Indians from Indian Bureau supervision, jurisdiction by jurisdiction, under a fixed series of selected criteria, is open to question." In other words, unplug the Indians in one doing. Dissolve tribal governments formed under the Indian Reorganization Act, get the bureau out of the land business and let Indians handle lands themselves, and "free" the Indians of special restrictions, the subcommittee urged. In sum, the report concluded, Congress should stay on the track mapped by House Concurrent Resolution 108.[33]

The National Congress of American Indians countered that "the same type of reasoning prevailed in the [Eighty-third] Congress as in the period leading up to the General Allotment Act of 1887." In its call for the annual convention, the NCAI revisited 1887: "Lawmakers proposed then to 'civilize' the Indians by passing laws that would force them to abandon their ways and adopt those of the 'white man'; today they would 'liberate'—or 'assimilate'—or 'integrate' the Indians by legislation that would lead quickly to dispossessing them of their lands, their tribal existence, and special rights granted to them by treaties.[34]

If nothing else, House Report 2680 set an Indian agenda for the Eighty-fourth Congress and for the coming 1954 NCAI convention in Omaha. All in all, the National Congress of American Indians concluded, the crucial year of 1954 had not been a bad one.

Surely the NCAI was stronger than before. Garry had traveled all across the West to enlist members, Peterson had held together the business in Washington, and tribal delegations had done their work with Congress.

For his part, Sen. Arthur Watkins told a newspaper reporter that "because of Congress' interest, more progress had been made by Indians in the past few years than in the previous twenty-five." What he meant by that, he did not explain.[35]

4 Turning Points

*I*n that crucial year of 1954, the National Congress of American Indians surged in visibility and prestige as the instrument of Indian peoples. Joe Garry, Helen Peterson, and others lifted it from near calamity by the skinniest of bootstraps, using Congress and the Bureau of Indian Affairs as targets for the NCAI's arrows. The Indians hit an issue—consent of the governed—that reached to the core of the American conscience and needed no apology. Thereafter they cried "consent" to thwart Congress's convoluted schemes to shed them.

"The NCAI is making the country Indian-conscious through its public relations work," Paschal Sherman would observe to delegates at the 1954 convention in Omaha. "It is making Indians realize they can do something for themselves through cooperative effort and that they have in NCAI an organization which can help along and direct that effort."[1]

Delegates had looked forward to the meeting in a spirit of muted triumph. Helen Peterson circulated her mimeographed reprise of major Indian bills, headed "Indians Come Out Better Than Expected in 83rd Congress." She wrote: "Although the sum total of the Indian bills introduced in the 83rd Congress was probably the most frightening and threatening to Indian property and rights in this century, the Indians showed . . . that by concerted action through their organization, the National Congress of American Indians, and their tribal organizations, that they *could* get attention, consideration for their point of view, and effective support for their position from reasonable and friendly Congressmen. Several Senators and Representatives brilliantly defended Indian rights."[2]

"Senators and representatives defending Indian rights": This was a key Garry-Peterson strategy, for Garry realized that the NCAI must preempt the assault on Indian rights by not merely opposing Congress but by putting forth the Indians' own solutions to the problems driving Congress. Garry hoped for a day when Congress would deliberate on bills drafted by Indians. The year 1954 marked the beginning of the effort to define an Indian program and publicize it, to identify friends in Congress, and to advance alter-

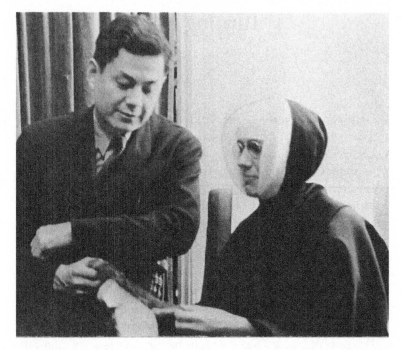

A youthful Joe Garry with Sister Providencia, apparently during Joe's assignment in Washington to show Indian crafts. (Arlene Owen family collection)

natives to termination. This agenda would preoccupy the NCAI at its 1954 convention in Omaha, its 1955 gathering in Spokane, and its 1956 meeting in Salt Lake City.

Sen. James E. Murray, a Montana Democrat, was one of the Indians' well-placed friends in Congress. Surveying the possibility of a Republican sweep in the fall of 1954, Murray's volunteers called on the Indians for support. "Murray is probably the number one man in the Senate in his importance to Indians," one said. "He is now ranking minority member of the committee on Insular and Indian [*sic*] Affairs and is in line for the chairmanship if a Democratic Senate is elected."[3]

Sister Providencia, an activist sociology professor at the College of Great Falls, acted as one of Senator Murray's pipelines to Indian constituents. A native of Anaconda, Montana, the nun had taught at several Indian schools—she had known Joe Garry at Sacred Heart Mission—before coming to the college. Daughter of Cong. John Tolan of California, she was drawn to grass-roots political action by the plight of impoverished, abandoned Indians. Sister Providencia, once fixed on a goal, did not give up. She called on Indians to vote for Murray, and Indian spokesmen, at her urging, made statements and wrote letters to Montana news media. Murray was reelected, and would become chairman of the pivotal Senate Committee on Interior and Insular Affairs, aware that Indians had demonstrated some power, on his behalf, in voting booths.[4]

Dates for the NCAI convention had been shifted to avoid a conflict with national elections. By the time Garry and his wife, Leona, set off for the 1954 convention in Omaha, he knew he had lost his first bid for the Idaho house of representatives. But he would run again.

Helen Peterson had written Garry that, as president, he was entitled to a suite in Omaha; but in a second letter the same day she reported that the NCAI did not have enough money for his expenses. She warned: "The convention this year may very well be the most critical for Indians in this century. . . . There can be no doubt that the accumulated bills in the last session were the gravest threat to Indian property and rights since the Allotment Act of 1887. . . . To consolidate the gains of this year and to plan for the future may never be more important than now."[5]

The convention opened with a buffalo-steak buffet, and President Garry brought the delegates to order with a tomahawk-shaped gavel given him by Oglala Sioux at Pine Ridge. An Omaha newspaper called Garry "a man who had helped spear-head resistance to a whole raft of so-called 'termination' bills" in Congress. The *New York Times* wrote of Garry: "He . . . led in opposing the removal of the Government in Indian affairs." In his address, Garry declared that Indians "must move on to a program of our own." He was reelected president.[6]

As chairman of the resolutions committee, D'Arcy McNickle crafted nearly twenty statements, to which delegates added ten from individual tribes. One called for extending the life of the Indian Claims Commission "until all claims filed shall have been finally adjudicated"; another was the standard call for amending Public Law 280 "to require consent by referendum vote of the Indians affected"; and another asked for "repudiation and withdrawal" of House Concurrent Resolution 108.

McNickle strove to state the Indian position on pending bills in clear language, and to draw public attention to the biased misinformation on which Congress relied. Delegates approved his nine-page commentary on House Report 2680, the subcommittee study of Indian administration. "We find it hard to believe that these men [the subcommittee] could have read the report," McNickle said, "because the report reveals profound ignorance of Indian issues." House Report 2680, he observed, revealed that the subcommittee members "believe that complex problems of human adjustment" could be solved by passing a law to "be used as a club, if necessary, to make Indians conform to the wishes of Congress."[7]

To the subcommittee's recommendation that jurisdiction over Indian lands be taken from the bureau, McNickle declared, "The day when trusteeship is removed altogether will be the beginning of the end for a people who once were masters in their own house. . . . Where tribes were persuaded to allot their lands . . . sales at foolish prices have been taking place at the rate of hundreds of acres a day."

McNickle asserted that members of Congress, due to the complexity of Indian affairs and lack of time, relied too much on staff. As a matter of fact, NCAI officers believed that the subcommittee staff professional, Albert A. Grorud, had written the vitriolic House Report 2680 and that subcommittee members merely rubber-stamped it. Grorud—a man in a key position who was committed to termination—was anathema to the NCAI. (John Collier had earlier expressed a similar conclusion about Grorud, and thirty years after her tenure at the NCAI, Helen Peterson still reviled Grorud as "a rotten character, spilling out venom in congressional reports.")[8]

An important plank in every Indian platform was preservation of Indian landholdings. Land, essential to his program for Indians, was one of Garry's special concerns. He believed that Indians must hold onto and expand their lands as an economic base for business development and to maintain tribal identity. He told returning war veterans that they must preserve their property: "If you get drunk and go to jail, and you have 160 acres, you are still a gentleman. But if you lose that 160 acres and go to jail, you are a bum."[9]

Peterson had reminded him, before the convention, to "be thinking of the points that ought to be covered in the draft of a bill on fractionated or heirship lands." McNickle wrote a resolution urging Congress to grant tribes first-purchase rights on heirship allotments, and to provide a revolving fund to assist tribes in such purchases. A legacy of the General Allotment Act of 1887, "heirship" was the term used for the process by which heirs of an Indian allottee inherited equal portions of an allotment, their heirs in the next generation inherited shares, and as each generation passed, shareholders multiplied. By one estimate, in the mid-1950s about 6 million acres of Indian land, in individual tracts, belonged jointly to six or more heirs of original owners.[10]

Shortly after the convention, Garry handed the task of drafting an heirship bill to the Wilkinson law firm. Paschal Sherman (for the NCAI) and five attorneys reviewed a draft by John Cragun, who acted as team leader. One attorney's version would have had Congress, as a matter of policy, assist tribes in holding onto their land, "in opposition to the view, occasionally espoused by Senator Watkins, that Indians might as well get off the land and move to the cities."[11]

Drafting a bill to suit the tribes proved complex, and Cragun warned his team that "we may have trouble selling a particular plan to the Department of the Interior unless it contains a lot of provisions which we do not want. . . . It strikes me maybe at some other time the tribes would drive a better bargain than they can right now." Important as heirship was to tribes, it was, after all, only a bargaining chip in Congress. Timing and political friends would be pivotal, as lands, termination, consent, and economic development of the reservations would dominate Indian affairs in Congress for the rest of the fifties.

Cragun learned that the Department of the Interior held fast to two principles: It would not agree to Indian tribes having a voice in the disposition of private reservation lands (which allotments were), and it would resist federal loans. Peterson passed Cragun's memo on to Garry with her penned marginal comment: The refusal to finance land buys, she wrote, "will leave poor tribes utterly unable to solve their problems."[12]

In his remarks in Omaha, Sherman had mentioned that a "Yakima law" for heirship lands, and a proposal to restore lost tribal lands to Colvilles as an incentive to terminate, might be models that would appeal to Congress for general bills applying to all tribes. The prospect of the Colville bill becoming a model for future legislation was scary. The Colville reservation occupied some of the poorest land in northern Washington state, between the Columbia River and the Cascade mountain range, where eleven tribes, some ancient rivals, had been dumped. Here the Nez Perce war chieftain Joseph and 150 survivors of his 1877 retreat had been exiled on unfamiliar, nearly barren ground, forbidden ever to go home.

Tribal management on the Colville reservation was contentious, a mirror of its mixture of languages and cultures. Congress intended to restore 818,000 acres of public domain (forfeited in 1891) to the Colville confederation on condition that the business council submit a plan for termination within five years, and that the Colvilles work out a contract to pay lump sums annually to two counties in lieu of property taxes. Noting this arrangement, the acting commissioner of Indian affairs commented, "This type of legislation, if enacted, would invite several hundred other counties to demand the same type of treatment, and eventually the Federal government would be committed to making payments which would be extremely difficult to terminate." [13]

The use of land concessions as a carrot to entice tribes to consent to termination appalled the NCAI. The Indian congress resisted taxation of Indian lands in any guise. Furthermore, the Yakima bill limited per-capita payouts to enrolled tribal members of at least half-blood. Since members of many tribes possessed less than half-blood, they might press for termination before a blood requirement could be written into a model bill.

To forestall adoption of the Yakima or Colville bills as models, the NCAI publicized the agony of the Menominee and Klamath terminations. Cutting loose from the government was going badly for both tribes. At the Omaha convention, both Menominees and Klamaths warned other tribes "not to take termination."

Garry, in fact, called on Congress to repeal the Klamath act, even though the Klamaths were not NCAI members. He telegraphed their negotiators in Washington, D.C., advising them to ask for repeal, and he and Peterson appeared before the tribal council to plead with Klamaths to call off termination. But rumors that each Klamath would receive $50,000 upon sale of their forests enticed a majority to vote for it.

As for the Menominees, attorney Glen Wilkinson described their termination as "pilot legislation which will probably be the basis for a historical measurement of the manner in which the government discharged its responsibility" toward Indians. The Menominee experience so devastated the tribe that Congress would eventually vote to restore tribal status. As historical measurement, the Menominee disaster offered no consolation to Congress or Indians.

As pilot terminations floundered, Helen Peterson wrote the Colville chairman, "I wonder how you are feeling about all of this by now. . . . The clear mandate of the Convention was to try to slow down any kind of termination . . . unless it had the clear consent of the tribes."[14]

The sentiment on the Colville reservation was volatile—doubly troubling to Joe Garry because Colville disputes echoed in affairs of the Affiliated Tribes of Northwest Indians, and Frank George, an old friend, was in the middle of ugly confrontations. Moreover, the Colville situation worried the NCAI because Albert Grorud, no longer a congressional staffer, showed up to advise those Colvilles who favored termination.

To McNickle, George wrote: "The chairman of the business council is in favor of termination as are about four other members. The other nine members have been timid in making a stand." Timidity was not a George characteristic; he held off termination with bulldog tenacity, relying on Rep. Walt Horan's pledge to oppose termination without tribal consent. The Colville tribal chairman wrote to the commissioner that the "overwhelming majority of the Confederated Tribes are not in favor of combining restoration [of land] and terminal legislation . . . and they are not inclined to plan for termination until they get back their 818,000 acres."[15]

About half of the enrolled Colvilles lived off the reservation, and its preservation meant little to them. An appraisal of the reservation by Stanford Research Institute intimated that liquidation might result in a per-capita payout of about $30,000. That they wanted, and that they demanded to vote for.

Garry offered the Affiliated Tribes' view of the Colvilles to a House subcommittee: House Resolution 6154 "is opposed on the grounds that the bill contains three provisions—restoration or quieting title to tribal lands, payment of money to counties, and termination of Federal supervision— each of which involves a matter of serious policy which properly should be considered separately. It is quite evident that these three provisions are grouped together in one bill because the major objective of the Indian Bureau is termination of Federal trusteeship which the Indians are being forced to accept in return for the restoration or quieting of title to the tribal lands."[16]

Garry's home tribe, the Coeur d'Alene, declared itself "fundamentally and historically opposed to the Colville type of termination bill. It is a meat cleaver approach." If termination had to be accepted at some future date, the Coeur d'Alene tribe wanted it to be "gradual and natural." By natural, the tribe meant that "the tribal rolls would gradually deplete themselves" through intermarriage between Indians and whites.[17]

It was by no means certain then that Frank George, Lucy Covington, and others would noisily—in the courts, by voting out council members, and with propaganda—stall termination of the Colvilles while gradually building a constituency to defeat it. But that defeat finally came, in 1971, sixteen years after termination was first proposed.[18]

With Klamath, Menominee, and Colville prototypes before them, the NCAI solicited public statements against termination. On her way home from Omaha, Ruth Bronson had called on Harold E. Fey, executive editor of the *Christian Century,* a weekly magazine widely circulated among Protestant denominations. She urged Fey to write "articles explaining what is wrong in Indian affairs and what needs to be done [to] help mold public opinion more favorably toward the Indians." Fey agreed to publish a series.[19]

Peterson urged leaders of Indian coalitions and pivotal tribes to welcome Fey's inquiries and to speak frankly. His articles, in her opinion, would be a "fine opportunity for Indians to reach a great segment of the American public."

Fey wrote eight "eyewitness" accounts, published from March through June 1955, uniformly sympathetic to Indians. Tribes of the Northwest, he observed, believed that Indian affairs were in acute crisis; those of the Southwest "realize they must make common cause or be overwhelmed." The Indian, he wrote, "is buried up to his neck in legal paper." Fey commented that Indians did not understand civil government and needed training in the ordinary conduct of economic life.

In addition to his articles, Fey published editorial comments and news of Indian activities. He also attended the 1955 NCAI convention in Spokane, reporting that "appreciation for the necessity of cooperation is growing steadily among Indian tribes," and he quoted William Zimmerman's assertion that the "NCAI is coming to be recognized by committees of Congress as the responsible Indian voice." The Spokane delegates saluted Fey for his "courageous and penetrating analysis of vital issues affecting Indians."[20]

Lacking money for a staff publicist, Peterson circulated reprints of Fey's articles widely among tribes, members of Congress, foundation managers,

and others. As a way to spread the Indian story, she looked for other articles to reproduce and mail, giving them a wider audience. (Fey, inciden-
tally, soon after coauthored a book, *Indians and Other Americans,* with
D'Arcy McNickle.)

Garry, meanwhile, stirred tribes with visits, writing ahead for permis-
sion to talk to tribal councils. In February 1955 he spoke to the Confederated
Tribes of the Umatilla Reservation (Oregon); in April he appeared at the
five-day NCAI-Arrow planning institute of the Arizona Inter-tribal Council
(where Peterson served as consultant); a few weeks later, he conferred with
the Federated Indians of California on the potential effects of Public Law
280, and gave the opening address at the California Indian Congress. "You
know the best ways to pep them up," Peterson told him, "and that is what
you are supposed to do." [21]

Joe took part in the Yakima Treaty Centennial on June 9, 1955, which
dedicated a monument to Yakima warriors and commemorated a treaty
forced on the Yakimas and others in 1855 by Territorial Governor Isaac I.
Stevens. The ceremony seemed hollow to Garry, and he remarked privately
that "whites got the best of that deal." In the lobby of the Marcus Whitman
Hotel in Walla Walla, Leona Garry fell into conversation with an army engi-
neer who was then negotiating to flood the great fishing site at Celilo Falls
on the Columbia River. He observed that "it seems heartless that in this
great country an act of Congress can destroy a culture and traditions built
up over generations," adding that "it is impossible to appraise in dollars
and cents a way of of life, a God-given primitive economy." [22]

The Garrys then went on to Pine Ridge, Leona's home reservation, for
the annual Sun Dance celebration and a session with the council; and following that, they traveled to the Fort Peck reservation for a meeting with
the tribal executive board. Since Garry arrived late, the board reassembled
after dinner to hear him. "The BIA is not our friend any more," he averred.
"They are acting as a conqueror. Hang onto your lands. Kick and scratch
if you have to, but hang onto your lands." And he concluded, "I am here
to instill courage. Don't sit back and let things happen to you." It was the
message he carried everywhere. [23]

When he was not on the evangelical trail of Indian unity, he wrote let-
ters, such as this unvarnished epistle to Quinault Indian Frederick W. Saux:
"While the pressure from Congress has somewhat eased . . . House
Concurrent Resolution 108 is still in existence and the Indian bureau . . .

is still trying to use this means by which Federal supervision can be lifted. . . . Their basic intent is that they want to *free the government* from its obligations to Indians." He listed the congressional bills "that caused the greatest concern" to the NCAI, adding that "all these bills had the same purpose . . . to liquidate all Indian lands and assets and then to disintegrate the Indian people [so that] . . . any further claims against the government would be impossible. The joint sub-committee under Senator Watkins attacked furiously at hearings. . . . As a counter measure, NCAI called an emergency conference."[24]

Perhaps it was the tenacity of the National Congress of American Indians that compelled Congress to pay as much attention to Indian affairs as it did during the mid-1950s. Certainly the NCAI stalled hasty termination. "Whatever may have been the policy of the 83rd Cong. evinced in HCR 108, no similar policy has been followed by either the 84th or the 85th Congress," Peterson was able to observe in the NCAI *Bulletin* of May 1958. "Neither has passed a bill to 'terminate' without the consent of the tribes affected; nor has either Congress pressured tribes."[25]

Congress had much else to occupy it during these years: a president who left leadership of the nation largely in Congress's hands; cold war, with the threat of atomic extermination; the Soviet Union's launch of a space rocket; a U.S. secretary of state advocating brinkmanship—"the ability to get to the verge without getting into the war." And that was not all: Fidel Castro overthrew Cuba's regime and declared himself dictator; the United Arab Republic seemed bent on conquest of the Middle East by assassination; and Latin America clamored for economic perquisites.

In domestic affairs, Congress debated sixty-three days before passing a new civil-rights bill intended to assure minorities the right to vote; Eisenhower launched a national highway construction program; and so on. Members of Congress had plenty to do, as both House and Senate permuted from Republican to Democratic majorities.

Indians could not match the high visibility of African American civil-rights marches, boycotts, and passive resistance. They hewed to the Garry line—assertive lobbying—and thus hectored, the men and women of Congress concerned themselves with Indian affairs. Yet the Bureau of Indian Affairs aggressively dealt away Indian lands in supervised sales, under a "liberalized" policy promulgated by memo on May 16, 1955. The sales, supposedly made whenever an Indian owner asked, were castigated by Indian supporters in Congress: "Thousands of Indians have been forced by poverty to sell their landholdings, which all too frequently constitute their only source of income." Garry called the sales policy "termination in fact."[26]

Commissioner Emmons defended the sales. In answer to a letter of protest, he explained, "The present policy is not . . . directed toward the sale of any Indian land unless the individual owners request such sale. . . . We believe that an Indian who has an allotment should have the same right to dispose of it as any other landowner." And while Emmons defended the policy in his address to the NCAI's Spokane convention, he promised elsewhere: "I won't let the tribes be dissolved or destroyed. By all means we want to preserve the Indian culture."[27]

Such promises did not mollify Joe Garry. To the NCAI 1956 convention in Salt Lake City, he emphasized: "Your land, whether it be individually or tribally owned, is . . . your share in the United States. It is not our purpose to retain the land merely for sentimental purposes, but . . . the land is the very basis of the economic and general welfare of the Indian people. . . . To raise a family, we must first have a home, and in order to have a home, we must have land."[28]

The Salt Lake City delegates called for a new statement of national policy: "A plan of development for each reservation or other place inhabited by a recognizable group of Indians, the plan to be developed with Indian cooperation and consent and with federal technical assistance . . . the ultimate purpose of such planning to be growth and development of the resources of the people rather than the heedless termination of federal responsibility."[29]

Taking their cue from President Truman, who in his inaugural address in 1949 had outlined a "Point Four" program for economic assistance to the world's undeveloped areas, the Indians called their program "Point Nine." They asked that "Indians be consulted *prior* to the passage of laws or the enactment of regulations affecting them and given full opportunity to present their views." They also requested the Bureau of Indian Affairs to "stop immediately the sale of trust land to non-Indians without first giving the tribal governing body of each reservation a prior right and opportunity to purchase same and make funds available for such purposes."[30]

The Indians urged especially that the government not sell "key tracts," those central to consolidating Indian ground. As Senator Murray put it, key tracts were those "Indian trust lands which, if sold, would reduce the value and use of surrounding Indian trust land." But with most tribes the rub was money; they did not have funds to compete in the bidding on tracts for sale.[31]

The Point Nine program, consequently, asked Congress to authorize money for planning and for "an adequate revolving credit fund," to be reimbursed "on terms at least as favorable as those accorded farm tenants." Keeping the land, holding on to federal funding, and providing training "comparable to the GI training programs" were the core principles of Point Nine. It was, said an NCAI press release, "the first time in history that the Indians have proposed a formal plan of constructive action to halt their steadily worsening economic and social situation and to build for a brighter future . . . a plan of action they hope to undertake for themselves."[32]

Helen Peterson made a formal presentation of Point Nine to the chairs of the Senate and House Committees on Interior and Insular Affairs and their subcommittees. Murray soon offered a resolution for long-range technical assistance and community development for Indian tribes, an initiative Garry called "the single most important measure to encourage the Indians to work on their own behalf."[33] McNickle wrote Joe a Christmas letter: "After so many years of waiting for the organization to grow up, it looks as if it has. . . . You and Helen have made the difference."[34]

Murray also persuaded the outgoing secretary of the interior, Douglas McKay, to suspend land sales until the committee could study the true situation and offer legislation. "The major apprehension," Senator Murray explained, "is that decreases in the Indian land base will seriously impair the effective use of Indian tribal and individual trust land in terms of economic land units."[35]

Thousands of Indians, Murray declared, had been forced by poverty to sell their landholdings, which all too frequently constituted their only source of income. He read into the record a letter from a Crow tribesman: "I am an old man, and as you know that very seldom an old man can get a job. . . . I have been compelled to put up as security all of my beaded buckskin outfit, war bonnet and my saddle and bridle in order to get something to eat.

"I don't know how I am going to get more money for my living expenses. So I thought it possible the quickest way is to try and get a fee patent on some of my inherited land. If I ask to put some of my land in the supervised land sale it would take too long to wait."

Garry wrote to congratulate Murray, pointing out that the commissioner's memorandum liberalizing sales "disqualified . . . tribal councils from any further authority or veto power on Indian land sales . . . [and] likewise stripped the tribal councils of any and all authority over individual allotted lands of its members." He went on to charge that the bureau "has been diminishing the remaining land holdings of the American Indian people at a very alarming figure," and that Indian regional councils and individual tribes had protested vigorously against the sales.[36]

Along with McKay's departure, Albert Grorud left the Senate staff. James Gamble, also committed to termination, but less hostile to Indian interests, succeeded him. But the Indians were not rid of Grorud: He set about the country organizing "Indian associations," largely off-reservation Indians and tribal factions who favored termination.[37]

Murray's committee sent questionnaires to fifty-two bureau offices and to tribes. A compilation of the replies, published by the committee as *Indian Land Transactions,* showed that tribes were active within their means in acquiring lands, and that individual tracts were being sold rapidly, especially in Montana, Nebraska, and the Dakotas.

Between 1948 and 1957 tribes added 1.2 million acres to their land bases, but individual Indians sold more than 3.3 million acres. Between 1953 and 1957, under Emmons's "liberalized" program, sales of individual Indian tracts doubled over the previous five years. Murray mildly scolded the Bureau of Indian Affairs for claiming, in press releases, that its policy rested on "intensive study." The returned questionnaires, chided Murray, "indicate that very few studies have been or are being made" by the bureau.[38]

A number of tribes with money hired real-estate specialists to extend and manage their lands, and to find business uses for their holdings. Many farmed, a few had attracted industry to their reservations, and others—through "enterprise" programs—hoped to apply their land to uses that would support their members.

The reports of transactions largely confirmed Garry's views on land. He was, of course, not the only prominent Indian advocating land reforms. In a blunt, eloquent speech to an Arizona industrial conference, Clarence Wesley, then president of that state's Inter-Tribal Council, declared: "Only about 100 of the tribes today have significant land holdings or other property rights, and they are located largely in the Western half of the United States. . . . Many of our Indian reservations and Indian communities are extremely poor and it is true that they are sometimes referred to as 'rural slums.' But it is important to remember that land grows more valuable with the months and years and the resources of minerals, timber, water, fish, and game are just as valuable and important and possible of development among Indian people as among other citizens, and we feel very strongly that to develop our own resources is a proper beginning point."[39]

Garry echoed Wesley in testimony before the Senate Sub-committee on Labor and Public Welfare: "It is an established fact that the greatest problem confronting American Indians on reservations is poverty and, of course, the lack of employment opportunities in vicinities of their established homes. . . . This poverty has not only been the source of many social problems, but it is also a blight on the national conscience. It is repeatedly stated that American Indians are the poorest, least educated, least healthy group in our nation." He urged that a pending bill (Senate Bill 2663, Eighty-fourth Congress, second session) to relieve depressed economic areas be amended to include Indian reservations.[40]

Garry stressed land again in a welcoming letter to the new secretary of the interior, Fred A. Seaton. So did Oliver La Farge, president of the Association on American Indian Affairs. Both men urged a fresh look at the plight of tribes working to establish economic development programs "at the very same time that the communities are being sold away from under their feet," as La Farge phrased his appeal.[41]

Garry wrote, in his letter to Secretary Seaton: "Indians are seriously concerned" that "[federal] actions . . . are constantly initiated and even completed without notice to the Indian people or any occasion for the expression of their views." As "matters of great urgency," he listed land sales, heirship, an adequate credit program extending to all tribes, land-purchase funds, and "overhaul" of procedures for adopting bureau policies. Helen Peterson mimeographed the letter for circulation among Indian tribes.[42]

The Indian community, however, was of different minds on land. The Navajos, for one, regarded attacks on Emmons's policy as "misinformed and in some cases malicious criticism. . . . The storm aroused over his memorandum . . . was all out of proportion to its limited recognition of Indian rights; and judging by some of the personalities who led the attack, it was neither disinterested nor free from political motives."[43]

Garry discussed Indian lands face to face with Commissioner Emmons, who toured Indian country for "social and economic improvement conferences." The commissioner met tribal representatives in groups and private sessions on a four-month junket. Garry saw him in Boise, where he again urged Emmons to support "a general bill to loan money on a long-term basis to tribes to buy land," the loans to be repaid from income obtained from the land. Any legislation should stipulate, he proposed, that a tribe could purchase a given tract by meeting the highest bid for that tract.[44]

As an example of the Indian plight, Garry offered a down-home instance. On his reservation—the Coeur d'Alene—Garry said, lessees once paid one-third of gross crop income to an owner; but as farming fell on meager times, the owner's share shrank to one-fourth. The tribal council voted to enforce one-third payment in lease contracts, but its resolution "didn't pass the bureau."

Many Coeur d'Alene landowners had never farmed because their superintendent, at the time of allotment, "recommended to the Indians to rent their land to . . . white people and live from the income." Lena Louie, Coeur d'Alene tribal secretary, who joined Joe in his talk with Emmons, spoke up: "We farmed until the cost of machinery and everything just completely overbalanced our income from farming so then in order to keep from getting further in debt we just sold out."[45]

Following his meeting with the commissioner, Garry complained that bureau publicists misrepresented Indian courtesy as endorsements of Emmons's program.[46] Then the Indian leader resumed his punishing schedule, dashing from state to national capital, from the annual salmon festival at Celilo Falls to the Indian Exposition at Anadarko, Oklahoma, and on to an Indian Institute at Fisk University, a small African-American college in Nashville. At Fisk, Garry gave the opening address wearing his beautiful white Indian regalia. Surrounded by news photographers the next day, he posed obligingly in buckskin for families who wanted snapshots.

After Anadarko, Garry visited the governing bodies of all the Oklahoma tribes. He impressed nearly everyone who heard him. "Congratulations on a great speech at Anadarko," wrote the secretary of the Cheyenne and Arapaho tribes. After Garry's address to the annual Cheyenne and Arapaho Pow-wow, a tribal officer told him: "The enthusiasm which you aroused is a great asset to your membership campaign for NCAI. . . . You can well be proud of your record of sound and constructive leadership."[47]

Helen Peterson wished, she confided to a benefactor, that the NCAI could afford to send Garry "to talk to the people in small groups, in meetings, in their homes, etc. He is very effective in explaining . . . issues, and he is deeply respected by Indians of the Northwest as he is indeed everywhere." At the same time, Sister Providencia gently teased Joe, calling him "Joseph Butterfly Garry—flitting around helping everybody."[48]

Garry was, indeed, trying to be everywhere at once, traveling on skimpy funds, staying with friends, a mendicant in a business suit proclaiming his Indian gospel of unity, land, self-help, and governance by consent. In one typical three-week period his schedule took him from Cherokee (North Carolina) to Osage (Oklahoma), Oklahoma City, Taos (New Mexico), Colorado Springs, Stillwater (Oklahoma), and again to Pine Ridge (en route to Idaho). Sometimes he was hard to find. When Joe scooted from tribe to tribe, recruiting for the NCAI, Peterson bundled his business correspondence (penning her comments in margins or typing long advisories) and sent it to Leona in Idaho, counting on her to locate him. And when a telegram or letter demanded fast action, Peterson (and sometimes Leona) answered as she thought Garry would, and signed his name.

In addition to selling the NCAI, Garry tinkered with its administration. He had not been in office long before he proposed changes in bylaws and rules. A revised constitution, much of it his doing, passed the twelfth convention, in 1955, providing for an executive council of one representative from each member tribe and an executive committee of eight elected by the council. Both changes were intended to give the tribes more control. In the original constitution the president appointed an executive committee and executive director. The council now chose the executive director and treasurer by secret ballot.[49]

Garry's constitution established five categories of membership: individual, tribal, Alaskan, individual associate (non-Indian and nonvoting), and organizational associate (non-Indian and nonvoting). It defined "Indian" as "a person who is recognized as a member by a bona fide Indian tribe." In further amendments, the NCAI designated area liaison officers and added the temporary office of convention manager.

Garry and his advisers—John Rainer, Clarence Wesley, Paschal Sherman, and others—toiled to devise funding plans, and finances came abruptly to the fore with the resignation of Ruth Bronson as treasurer. Believing that the members must know the true situation, Sherman persuaded her to comment on the NCAI's financial condition. She did so reluctantly. There were no rules, Bronson observed. "Too much is left to chance and to the demands of the moment. . . . The budget which the Executive Council has annually approved at past NCAI conventions has in reality been only a dream budget, because it has been based on funds NCAI hoped to get. Very often, we have not got nearly the amount hoped for."[50]

Bronson recommended that a finance committee be empowered to write a budget, reserve monies for fixed expenses ("so that our employees may be relieved of the harassing worry that next month their salaries might not be paid"), and set criteria for expenditures. And she closed: "I constantly rejoice at the maturity and progress that NCAI has shown in these recent years. Under our current leadership, the organization . . . has made amazing growth in prestige, influence and income. Our business procedures must reflect that maturity."

Part of the burden of raising funds fell to Arrow, the tax-exempt affiliate. As partner with the NCAI, Arrow had secured foundation and individual grants and managed several projects—the Crown Point health-education experiment among the Navajo, directed by McNickle; tribal leadership training; citizenship schooling at Pine Ridge; voter education for New Mexico Indians; and others. But Bill Short, when he had been president of the NCAI, questioned Arrow's effectiveness, and Garry followed suit, concluding that "Arrow did not have a proper, qualified staff," and was in debt. After he closed Arrow's New York office, Joe put Helen Peterson in charge, rewrote its constitution, and lured new board members. Then "some misunderstandings appeared," Garry told his executive council, and the demands were smothering Helen.[51]

When Arrow hired its own executive and moved into separate offices, Garry concluded that the corporation, "since early 1956 has gone increasingly in an arbitrary and independent direction." He and the Arrow staff met in long sessions without agreeing. Garry finally realized, he wrote his council, that "whatever 'affiliated' relationship may have meant in the beginning seems not to exist any longer." He recommended ending the partnership.

Garry called for a mail ballot of council members on the Arrow compact, expressing again his conviction that affiliation "has no meaning." The council voted to divorce Arrow, and at the next convention the members balloted in favor of a new NCAI unit, a tax-exempt NCAI Fund. [52]

Garry's travels slowed in the first months of 1957, as he was mired in Boise when the Idaho legislature convened. On his second try, Garry had won a seat, the first American Indian elected to the state's house of representatives, an intractable body for generations made up of white farmers and ranchers. On one of Peterson's letters forwarded to Joe, Leona penned a sharp reminder: "Don't let her think you are neglecting NCAI while you're in the legislature."

With the house session ended, Garry was on his way again, first to Washington, D.C., where the National Congress of American Indians and the Association on American Indian Affairs sponsored a conference to rally tribal support for Senator Murray's Senate Concurrent Resolution 3 (Eighty-fifth Congress, first session). Murray's resolution restated congressional intent, and it was, in the words of Oregon senator Richard Neuberger, "a backfire to termination . . . to reverse the termination policy." Overturning House Concurrent Resolution 108 had long been one of the NCAI's objectives, and the Indian Congress had pushed hard for introduction of Murray's bill.[53]

Hearings on Senate Concurrent Resolution 3, scheduled on short notice, were combined with a bill to provide economic aid to tribes (Senate Bill 809) and another to amend Public Law 208 to require consent of tribes before extending state jurisdiction to reservations (Senate Bill 331). Garry testified, of course, and a large troop of tribal spokesmen, drawn to the capital with their attorneys, endorsed the three bills. There were supportive statements from the Montana Intertribal Policy Board, the Affiliated Tribes of Northwest Indians, the Idaho Inter-tribal Council, the North Dakota Intertribal Council, the All Pueblo Council of New Mexico, the Arizona Inter-Tribal Council, the South Dakota Intertribal Council, and the Five Civilized Tribes of Oklahoma. Their common theme, however stated, was that Indians wanted to manage their own affairs.

In Helen Peterson's words: "It has been our understanding that many members of Congress would not be willing to support just an outright repeal of the termination policy. We are always urged to be constructive and spell out what we mean. Our support of this particular resolution is because we hoped it spelled out in a little clearer terms constructive proposals, many of which could be undertaken by the tribes themselves with their own resources."

Owen Panner, attorney for the Warm Springs Tribes of Oregon, reviewed the NCAI resolutions calling for tribal plans of development with federal assistance. He summed up: "The Indians want to solve their own problems. I think they want to make their own plans with the assistance and, of course, the concurrence of the government, but they want to solve their own problems and get at them."

John Cragun, attorney for the NCAI, testified: "Above everything else, the Indians have wanted their wishes taken into account. . . . The first thing that the Indians have wanted to say to Congress and to have Congress act upon is to require that their consent be obtained."

At another juncture in the hearings, Cragun contended: "If the Indians did not have to labor under the great pile of regulations which now afflict them, and be bottlenecked first at the reservation and be bottlenecked at the area office, and finally have to go to Washington anyway with all of that duplicate structure that they now suffer with," appropriations for Indian administration and health would be "trimmed way down."[54]

Garry, in the first of several appearances during the three-month course of hearings, introduced himself as president of the NCAI and of the Affiliated Tribes of Northwest Indians, a member of the Idaho legislature, chairman of the Coeur d'Alene tribal council, and a veteran of World War II and the Korean campaign. He called Senate Concurrent Resolution 3 a "constructive measure to restore confidence to Indians and motivation to renew and increase their efforts in their own behalf."

House Concurrent Resolution 108, he maintained, "created confusion, chaos, unrest, and fear. Oldtimers, non-Indian lessees, neighbors of Indians . . . began to put pressure, not only on Indian allottees and tribal officials, but on the Federal Government to buy Indian land. . . . More greedy non-Indians began to paint pictures showing liquidation of reservation property to be consistent with progress, freedom, equality, and first-class citizenship." Bills to carry out the intent of House Concurrent Resolution 108, he went on, "kept the Indians so busy defending themselves they had no time or even energy for constructive planning or action." Murray's resolution, Garry concluded, "will be a meaningful, effective, and long step toward solving the Indian problem and restoring dignity and justice in dealings of the United States toward the first American trust beneficiaries."

In answer to a question about blood quantum, Garry responded that defining an Indian "should be left more or less up to the tribe," and he volunteered that his people, the Coeur d'Alenes, since 1940 had enrolled no one of less than one-fourth Indian blood. Subcommittee members murmured approval.[55]

Although Congress did not vote on Senate Concurrent Resolution 3 in this first session, and the Bureau of Indian Affairs opposed it, the hearings persuaded many that coercive termination was losing adherents. As Peterson observed, in her draft report on legislation, "Several members of Congress appeared to be genuinely concerned to know [the] Indian viewpoint." But Indian legislation bogged down in wrangles over the president's Middle East agenda, budget appropriations (especially for foreign aid), and civil rights.[56] And Arthur Watkins, galled by the direction the hearings were taking, cut them off by invoking a prohibition on subcommittee hearings while the Senate was in session.[57]

Summing up in her report, Peterson wrote: "From the correspondence, resolutions, and minutes received from tribes and inter-tribal groups, from field visits to reservations, and from talk with official delegations in Washington it seems clear to the NCAI Washington office that Indians in general still want: "1) Repeal or drastic modifications of the termination policy in HCR 108; 2) a constructive and large-scale approach by the federal government in helping the tribes to develop their human and natural resources; and 3) legislation to keep and conserve Indian land in Indian ownership."[58]

Shortly after the hearings, Peterson underwent surgery. Paschal Sherman, who worked for the Veterans Administration, ducked in several times each day to look after the NCAI office. Much of the preliminary planning for the 1957 convention fell to him. The executive committee had voted to hold the meeting in Claremore for cheaper hotel rates and promises of free meeting space. The elegant beggar, Garry, could honestly tell a prospective donor that "the NCAI has grown from fourteen-tribe membership in 1953 to fifty tribes," but "to keep alive as of now we must continue the unpleasant task of begging from door to door."

Sherman exhorted Garry to make money a major part of his presidential address to the 1957 convention. "I would like to suggest that you as President dwell at some length in your address at opening ceremonies on the approaching crisis in NCAI finances," he wrote. "Your putting the convention on notice will smooth the way toward . . . calling on all members to do something substantial to help." Knowing that Joe was on the run and overburdened, Sherman closed: "Joe, please, I want an answer from you WITHOUT FAIL—and soon. I know you are busy but I am, too, and we do have a mutual interest in NCAI's future."[59]

Peterson mused on the possibility of hiring a professional fund raiser but knew that the NCAI's dilemma would be hard to dramatize: The NCAI did not have national figures to list on its letterhead, a base of large contributors, or "sharp, clear-cut dramatic issues. . . . One fund-raiser told me if Linda Darnell or Gary Cooper actually identified themselves with Indians and if they would let us use their names these would be sufficient to get real support and recognition," she told Sherman. Instead of drama, she added, "we have a tremendous volume of chronic, localized problems and issues, except for House Concurrent Resolution 108, and that is extremely hard to explain in dramatic, general terms to the public."[60]

An audit of NCAI records showed that in the past full year, the congress had taken in roughly $31,475 from all sources and had spent $31,689. In the first quarter of the current year, income amounted to $5,701 and expenditures $5,523. At this pace income would not equal that of the previous year, and the Robert Marshall Civil Liberties Trust, which had contributed approximately half of the income for several years, notified the NCAI that its grant would be cut to $10,000 on a matching basis. Garry had hoped that a proposed meeting between the Marshall trustees and the NCAI executive council might raise the trust's support to $30,000 a year, but the meeting never took place.[61]

Hilda Henderson told Joe she had not ordered new letterheads because the NCAI did not have the necessary forty dollars. She chided him for turning in expense accounts without charging the NCAI for taxi fares and telephone calls, simply to save the organization a few dollars. And so the NCAI scraped along on little economies and volunteer labor. Letters of appeal went out, and plans for Claremore went on: Who should speak? Should the NCAI give a blanket to Bill Short (as it had to Napoleon Johnson) as a token for his services? Who was writing resolutions? And should Joe present "some kind of award" to an eighty-year-old lady who contributed to the NCAI and Arrow? They were off to Claremore with nits to pick and a great deal at stake.

5 Roots: The Coeur d'Alenes

*J*oseph Garry descended from a mixed lineage of Kalispel, Spokane, and Coeur d'Alene Indians. And Irish. He could have settled among any of them—perhaps not among the Irish—but he was raised in the fertile Lovell Valley in the southernmost reaches of the Coeur d'Alene reservation, and considered himself a Coeur d'Alene.

The reservation, as Garry knew it, had shrunk in size and spirit from the aboriginal territory of the Coeur d'Alenes. Joe drove on highways, visited towns and cities, swam in waters, and saw farms and windmills and fences and railroad tracks on the earth that belonged to the Coeur d'Alenes two generations before him. The misadventures of the Coeur d'Alene tribe at the hands of the U.S. government were virtually a paradigm for the experiences of other western tribes.

The government prattled for decades about turning this tribe into farmers and herders, but never set aside enough arable land for the whole tribe to farm. Each time the Feds squeezed the Coeur d'Alenes into successively smaller areas, some Indians were left out.

Joe Garry knew this story and stories of a more distant past; he had heard them from his family and tribal elders: who the Coeur d'Alenes were, and what it meant to be one—the rubric of an honorable heritage. He could see Steptoe Butte in the distance from Lovell Valley, its name a reminder of his tribe's woeful encounter with the army. And he learned the tenets of the Catholic faith, infused with the Indian sensibility that the earth, and all that lived on it, were part of his soul. He would be proud all his life to be a Coeur d'Alene.

By Joe Garry's time, the Coeur d'Alenes were chastened and beggared, their ancient means of survival taken from them. Nobody knows how long the tribe had occupied and used their homeland of lakes, rivers, mountains, and prairies—perhaps thousands of years—but nobody could deny that they had adapted admirably to what they found around them.

A large Coeur d'Alene community clustered on the north shore of Lake Coeur d'Alene; another near the mouth of the Coeur d'Alene River and upstream; and another at the mouth of the St. Joe River and along adjacent beaches of the lake. Coeur d'Alenes also occupied an area near modern Wardner, Idaho; a rich camas ground along upper Latah Creek; the Spokane River valley almost to the great falls; and ground near modern DeSmet. These settlements might number 200 or more inhabitants during the winter; fewer during hunting-and-gathering seasons. Major villages were governed autonomously by a chief and a council of men and women. Anthropologists think that after the tribe acquired horses, their political organization may have become more centralized, but their cohesive territory did not demand the protection of warrior cults typical of Plains tribes.[1]

The Coeur d'Alenes baffled white fur traders, who invaded early in the nineteenth century, by their casual response to offers of beads and mirrors. The tribe bartered furs at Spokane House and Fort Colvile for guns, knives, tools, and woolens until they had what they needed, and then traded little more. Their homeland already supplied them well. They resisted traders who beckoned them, and the traders—who hung descriptive French tags on many of the tribes—named this people for hearts as hard and sharp as awls: Coeur d'Alenes. No trader married a Coeur d'Alene woman.

On the currents of trade came missionaries. They hitched rides with trading caravans and learned about tribes from the trappers. The Jesuit missionary Peter John DeSmet, foremost among them, captivated the Coeur d'Alenes. In 1842 he paused at Chief Stellam's village at the Spokane River outlet of Lake Coeur d'Alene. Like several tribes, the Coeur d'Alenes embraced a prophecy that black-robed men would come to teach them. In DeSmet they saw myth materialize before their eyes. They implored God's salesman to teach them prayers.

Seating young men in a circle, he taught each a line of the Lord's Prayer in English before hurrying on to survey his mission field. Upon his return, DeSmet found that several of the men now knew the whole prayer, and he, in his turn, was charmed by the Coeur d'Alenes' "unmistakeable proof of true conversion." Like every other white man who met Indians, DeSmet saw what he wanted to see, and in his view the Coeur d'Alenes were vessels to be filled with the truths of Christianity.[2]

DeSmet sent Father Nicholas Point and a Jesuit brother, Charles Huet, to minister to the Coeur d'Alenes. In 1843 Point and Huet established a rough-hewn, leaky-cabin mission about a mile up the St. Joe River from

the southern shores of the lake, and Huet scratched the soil for a rude garden. Huet meant eventually to show the Indians how to farm, but for the
time being he and Point ate what the Indians ate.

In the Coeur d'Alenes, Point found a people united by territory, customs, language, and dependence on lake, rivers and surrounding mountains. "Their country, dotted with lakes and interlaced with rivers," he
observed, "abound in fish no less than in game animals."

From the start, this was a mission of improbabilities. The site flooded
in spring, washing out the garden. Point found Coeur d'Alenes living in
twenty-seven (by his count) family villages around the lake, moving with
the seasons to hunt, dig roots, pick berries, and revel in the great salmon-
fishing camps on the Spokane and Upper Columbia rivers. It was more
than unlikely that Point could ever collect the tribe in one place for instruc-
tion, and equally improbable that he could reach all of the villages in timely
fashion. But DeSmet, the cheerleader, urged him on.

Curiosity may have held the Coeur d'Alenes to the faith at first, for Point,
a primitive artist who amused them with pictures, was moody and
unhappy. He once huffed off as if to abandon his waterlogged mission.
DeSmet sent a new man—the short, headstrong Swiss, Joseph Joset—to
move the mission and replace Point. Joset came to stay: Despite brief assignments elsewhere, he always returned, and he served the Coeur d'Alenes,
as their confessor and champion, for more than half a century. The Coeur
d'Alenes' Catholicism fused with their ancient practices; they blended the
white religion with their native songs and ceremonies. Joset died before
Joe Garry was born, but it was Joset's continuity of faith that permeated
the tribe, and that Garry eventually embraced.[3]

Joset moved the mission in 1846 to a knoll beside the Coeur d'Alene
River. There, tutored by the remarkable Jesuit Anthony Ravalli—physician,
architect, sculptor, and musician—the Indians built a church of logs, straw,
and mud, today the oldest extant building in Idaho. Joset named it Sacred
Heart. The new location was more central to the tribe, and it allowed room
for a larger mission farm.

The role of Jesuit missionaries extended to the material concerns of
Indians. They were available, if not ideally prepared: The clerical corps of
the Rocky Mountain missions (as the Missouri Province termed them) consisted largely of sons of wealthy families in Italy, France, and the Low
Countries, recruited from novice houses. They spoke and wrote English

Indians flocking to Mass at Sacred Heart Mission, DeSmet, circa 1900. (Dellwo collection)

with varying skill, and some never mastered Indian dialects (although Joset was noted for his facility in the Coeur d'Alene tongue). They kept mission records in ecclesiastical Latin, framed official correspondence in Latin or English, and wrote to their parents in French, Italian, or Dutch. As citizens of monarchies, they grew up accustomed to arbitrary and perfidious government.

The U.S. Army and civil officers used missionaries as intermediaries with Indian tribes, since they were trustworthy men who frequently spoke and wrote English. In turn, Indians relied on Jesuits to convey their views. When

The Coeur d'Alene tribe celebrates the Feast of the Assumption each year at the old Sacred Heart Mission church, the oldest building in Idaho. (*Spokesman-Review*)

Isaac Stevens, the first governor of Washington Territory, commenced negotiations with interior Indians to cede some of their aboriginal lands for
white settlement, he called on Father Adrian Hoecken to convene the
Flatheads, and Father Ravalli to suggest to the Coeur d'Alenes that they
share a reservation with Flatheads, Pend Oreilles, and Kutenais.

The thirty-five-year-old Stevens, small of frame and large of ego, had
come west in 1853 with three objectives: to form a civil government for
the new Washington Territory, to investigate possible routes for a railroad
from St. Paul, Minnesota, to the Pacific shores, and to learn the disposi-
tions of Indian tribes toward railroad and settlement. Commissioned by
President Franklin Pierce to negotiate treaties with Indian tribes, Stevens
imposed heartless contracts on those of the Pacific Coast, then moved inland
in 1855 to bargain with Nez Perces, Cayuses, Umatillas, Walla Wallas, and
Yakimas. Most interior tribes sent observers who were dismayed by
Stevens's demands for huge cessions of aboriginal lands. The Indians signed
his treaties with reluctance, and Joset, who attended the Yakima negotiations at Walla Walla, saw in their capitulation "a mock treaty, in order to
gain time and prepare for war." [4]

Stevens then headed east to parley with Indians in what is now Montana.
En route he paused at Sacred Heart Mission, where he naturalized the
priests and told the Coeur d'Alenes he would return to "see if we cannot
make an agreement for you to sell your lands and live on a reservation."
This was perhaps the first time the Coeur d'Alenes heard directly that the
government meant to reduce their customary range.

While the governor waited for supplies for a Blackfeet treaty council,
the war that Joset foresaw erupted. Provoked by prospectors invading their
territory, combined Indian war parties, led by Yakimas, swept across the
Columbia Plain attacking lonely farms above Walla Walla and gold prospectors near Colville. Stevens abandoned bargaining to rush to the territorial capital, Olympia, to take charge of civil defense, railing at the army for
its failure to protect isolated farms. When he stopped breathlessly to tell
Spokanes and Coeur d'Alenes that their treaty council would have to wait,
both tribes begged him not to send troops north of the Snake River into
camas fields, "our garden . . . [where] our women dig the roots on which
we live." The Indians never supposed that Stevens would neglect to relay
their appeal to the army. [5]

For the elders of Garry's time, men who had been young at midcentury, Stevens's words tolled like a funerary bell over the lakes and prairies to signal the end of Indian times. Stevens meant to open the lands for settlement. "There is much valuable land and an inexhaustible supply of timber east of the Cascades," he told the territory's legislators. "I consider its speedy development so desirable that all impediments should be removed." Among impediments, of course, were Indians. This brusque little man, dusty and trail-worn when the Coeur d'Alenes met him, proposed to herd the tribes east of the Cascades onto two reservations beyond the path of immigrants and railroads.[6]

As Stevens sped on to Olympia, news of army forays against the warring Yakimas and their allies distressed the Coeur d'Alenes, who heard rumors of a planned attack on them. Joset tried to calm them. "Several times they questioned me as to whether the troops should come," he would recall. "I told them always that I considered it an idle tale."[7]

But troops did come into Coeur d'Alene country. In May 1858, as muddy trails dried to dust in spring sunshine and camas colored the prairies blue, an awkward train of 152 soldiers with officers and Nez Perce scouts plodded north from Fort Walla Walla toward a confrontation that no one understood, then or since.

Col. Edward J. Steptoe, a West Pointer promoted for bravery in battle, governor-to-be of Utah (until Brigham Young refused to vacate the capitol), was in command. The marchers strung out in ragged order (Steptoe would explain that many were raw recruits), dangerously vulnerable to attack. When Steptoe's column crossed the Snake River, Stevens's undelivered caution to avoid the camas fields bore violence. The Indians assumed that Steptoe had come to fight. Coeur d'Alenes, Spokanes, and Palouses painted for war.

Steptoe's men were ill equipped, infantry armed with smoothbore musketoons, scorned throughout the ranks (soldiers joked that they could throw rocks straighter and farther), and cavalry with carbines difficult to load at a trot. To lighten his pack load, Steptoe left boxes of ammunition in Walla Walla. He himself seemed on holiday, dressed in civilian jacket and breeches.

This oddly nonchalant horseman unwittingly pulled the trigger of momentous change; he dislodged a stone that tumbled a wall. Had he been ready to fight, Steptoe's expedition probably would have passed as a minor frontier episode. As events turned out, life for the Coeur d'Alenes, after Steptoe, would never again be as it had been.

Joset tried to shame young Coeur d'Alene hotheads from fighting, but they would not heed him. The priest rode to Steptoe. Where was he going? The colonel mentioned Colville. If so, he was far off the route. Then a Coeur d'Alene called Joset away, and as the priest reined his mount, a confused, swirling battle broke out: Whooping Indians dashed close to fire; troops shot back and strained to control panicked animals. The soldiers began a slow retreat over open, grassy, treeless terrain. The day might have lived in Indian memory as ludicrous, if its consequences had not been so dire.[8]

At dusk, Steptoe's men dug in on a low hill. Surrounded by Indians, short of ammunition and water, they expected to be overrun when day broke. But in the night the soldiers slipped out of their death trap. How? A battlefield monument near modern Rosalia, Washington, credits an Indian, Timothy, and Nez Perce Christians with guiding them. True or myth? More likely the Coeur d'Alenes, hoping to seize the lion's share of abandoned military equipment, ushered the troops through the Indian line. Steptoe's ragged command fled back to Walla Walla.

Warriors—old, arthritic, and bent by the time of Joe Garry's youth—had celebrated their victory; they had whipped the white army. Now cocksure and boastful, they would drive out the white settlers. The news that Indians had nearly wiped out an army column resounded in official Washington, D.C. Feathered savages shooting arrows from half-wild ponies? General of the Army Winfield Scott forwarded Steptoe's account to the secretary of war, endorsed as "a candid report of a disastrous affair."

Isaac Stevens, who had moved to the nation's capital as Washington's territorial delegate, blamed Steptoe's defeat on "the temporizing measures of the military." Temporizing no longer, the army determined to inflict a hard lesson on the Coeur d'Alenes, Spokanes, and Palouses. For a punitive strike, headquarters of the Pacific designated as field commander Col. George Wright, a veteran of clashes with Seminoles and Yakimas. Western garrisons were reduced to give him 570 regulars, almost one-fourth of the army strength in the Pacific Northwest. A disciplinarian and skilled strategist, Wright encamped his troops at Walla Walla for six weeks of drill in maneuvers and marksmanship.

Army orders to Wright were forthright: "You will attack all the hostile Indians you may meet, with vigor; make their punishment severe, and persevere until the submission of all is complete."[9] Wright moved north from Walla Walla in late August, posting guarded supply caches along the trail in case he had to fight his way back. He half expected the Indians to mount a guerilla campaign—ambushes and raids over terrain they knew well—to whittle his column and exhaust his supplies without a decisive meeting.

But the warrior coalition, confident and bold, meant to separate Wright from his supply train by breakneck forays erupting from the hills. They would capture and share his supplies and equipment. Wright deployed troops to protect the train and kept it tight to the main column, and the Indian strategy failed.

About fifteen miles south of the Spokane River, at Four Lakes, Wright ran into a large force of mounted Indians, armed with muzzle-loading muskets, bows and arrows, and lances. They attacked, eager for war. Wright had equipped his infantry with new .58 caliber Springfield long-range rifle-muskets and Jaeger rifles that fired a minie ball, deadly at 600 yards. Indians fell before they could dash close enough to shoot, and when they backed away to reconnoiter, Wright's howitzers scattered them. Astounded, whipped, the Indians withdrew at dusk, carrying their dead and wounded. Wright had not lost a man.

The colonel rested his troops for three days, then marched toward the Spokane. Warrior parties set prairie grasses ablaze, and in a boulder-strewn draw chosen to impede troop maneuvers, they attacked again. Wright pushed his men onward through embers and smoke. Again the long-range guns held the Indians at a distance. A running battle lasted seven hours and covered fourteen miles, as the Indians slowly backed away.

The war chiefs deliberated far into the night: Should they try again? scatter to wage guerilla war? surrender? Joset apparently sat in, for it was he who sent a message to Wright: The Indians "are down and suing for peace."[10]

Wright proceeded to the Coeur d'Alene mission, leaving behind him burned lodges of stored grain and slaughtered Indian horses. Under a leafy bower, he negotiated a preliminary peace treaty, which required the Indians to return captured military property and to allow whites henceforth to travel through their territory unmolested. The Indians refused, however, to turn over for punishment the men who led them in war. They had seen Wright's grisly hangings—the Indian standing on a wagon with rope thrown over a tree limb, the wagon pulled away, the dying man jerking and kicking in the air as he strangled, eyes protruding and tongue thrust out. Sometimes the soldiers left a rotting body hanging as a warning.

"Sir: the war is closed," Wright reported to headquarters. "Peace is restored with the Spokanes, Coeur d'Alenes and Pelouses. . . . The Indians have been entirely subdued, and were most happy to accept such terms of peace as I might dictate." [11] On his way back to Walla Walla, Wright imposed agreements on the Spokanes and Palouses. In a tree-shaded, grassy valley of Latah Creek, he hanged Palouses and Yakimas as instigators and murderers. From that time, the stream would be known as Hangman's Creek. To Spokanes and Palouses, Wright gave a terrifying warning: If they warred again, he would return to wipe them out. DeSmet, authorized by the army to visit the Coeur d'Alenes, was directed to tell them that "they can only expect to exist by implicitly obeying the commands they receive." [12]

Steptoe's outing started all of this. Consider that the Jesuits imposed notions of western European culture and Christian conduct on the Coeur d'Alenes, who nonetheless mixed Catholic with native exercises. Frustrated by continued traditional practices and their patent inability to settle the tribe in one place as a Christianized nation, on more than one occasion the priests questioned whether they should stay on. The man in a hurry, Stevens, lit a candle of uncertainty with his talk of reservations, then went his way. But Steptoe brought tangible disaster. If not for Steptoe, Wright would not have come. Wright's terms ended forever the Coeur d'Alenes' secure tenure in their own country, binding them to admit strangers. After Wright, the Coeur d'Alenes knew they would not survive a future war. The certainties that had regulated their lives for centuries blew away with the battlefield smoke, their present severed from their past.

The government advanced no permanent peace treaty, and Wright's terms stood as merely the first of a sequence of affronts that stripped the tribe of its domain. The Feds left them, as a congressional paper put it, "under the impression that the Government would . . . act justly and fairly toward them, so far at least as their lands were concerned." That hope for justice is all the Coeur d'Alenes had. The future lay not in what they would do but in what would be done to them. Many drifted into supine resignation. To Joe Garry, a century later, would fall the task of reviving their independent spirit. [13]

Despite Wright's brutal show of military superiority, the United States prepared for more Indian wars. To move men to future trouble spots, Congress authorized building a military road between Fort Benton, on the Missouri River, and Fort Walla Walla. Capt. John Mullan, who had surveyed possible railroad routes for Stevens and mapped for Wright, commanded the road company, and the route eventually bore his name: the Mullan Road. His crews started in 1859 on a line projected directly through Coeur d'Alene country, over the mountains to the Coeur d'Alene mission, thence southwest along the east shores of Coeur d'Alene Lake and across the St. Joe. The Indians honored their agreement to allow whites to cross their lands.

Reports from his surveyors and builders ended the hope that a railroad could use Mullan's route. Maintaining even this wagon road, with its fallen trees, earth slides, bridge washouts, and steep grades, was impractical. One of his crew leaders told Mullan in disgust, "If all the Americans work here a thousand years they could not make a road." Mullan finished his work in 1862—after scraping an alternative route that bypassed the most tortuous mountain terrain to run north of Lake Coeur d'Alene.[14]

While Mullan toiled, gold seekers found color in the Hoodoo Hills not far south of Latah Creek. In search of metal farther south, they overran the Nez Perce reservation and spilled into Clearwater country and the Boise Basin. By the fall of 1861, Orofino alone throbbed with perhaps 12,000 rambunctious prospectors.

This rowdy populace in a few months tilted the distribution of citizens in Washington Territory eastward, threatening the political power of coastal settlements and the capital, Olympia. Ten years earlier, coastal settlers north of the Columbia had protested their distance from Oregon's Salem to lever Washington Territory into being. Demands now rose for a capital closer to Boise and the Clearwater—Lewiston or perhaps Walla Walla.

The newcomers succeeded in dividing Washington in 1863 to form Idaho Territory, with the border drawn north from Lewiston to balance the population between the two territories. The Coeur d'Alenes now resided almost wholly in Idaho. For the time being, that did not much matter, since nobody was paying attention to them.

The federal government had put the tribe on the shelf: "These Indians have never been collected on a reservation nor brought under the immediate supervision of an agent," the secretary of the interior remarked in 1860. "So long as their country shall remain unoccupied, and not in demand for settlement by whites, it will scarcely be desirable to make a change in their location; but the construction of the Northern Pacific Railroad, which will probably pass through or near their range, may make it expedient to concentrate them."[15]

For a decade after creating Idaho, the federal government was engaged elsewhere: with Civil War and Reconstruction, with the Chinese in California, with impeaching a president, with cornering the gold market, and with the trial of New York's Boss William Tweed.

In 1864 Congress authorized the northern railroad, and by 1870 the company formed to build it began construction. To assist in financing, Congress granted the Northern Pacific the odd sections of public land in a ten-mile strip on both sides of the track. If title to these grant lands already belonged to someone, the railroad might then choose other sections (in-lieu lands) in a thirty-mile corridor, creating the possibility of a railroad swath sixty miles wide through part of its route. That positively would trample on Indian claims.[16]

Settlers in number would surely come with the railroad. The government, apparently willing to exterminate the natives, ruthlessly drove Indians away from railroad routes and declared the land on which the Indians depended to be public domain. States and territories, eager for settlers and economic development, demanded that Indians be confined to reservations—by military force, if necessary. When Indians defended their lands, they were branded as aggressors who brought bloodshed on themselves.

In 1867, responding to calls from the territorial government, President Andrew Johnson set aside a reservation for the Coeur d'Alenes on the west side of the lake, in the Latah Valley. The Coeur d'Alenes paid no heed. In 1872, President Ulysses S. Grant ordered formation of a Colville reservation in the northeastern corner of Washington, to collect the interior tribes, including the Coeur d'Alenes. Roughly three months later he reduced the area of the Colville by a second order. No Indians moved there.

Clearly the Great White Father meant to push Indians off their ancestral lands. Rumors spread that Nez Perces, Yakimas, Palouses, and Umatillas would resist by arms, and that smaller bands would join them. War songs and drums echoed from the canyons. A shaman sect, the "dreamers," passed among the tribes, foretelling miraculous events that would wipe away the whites.

Buoyed by some sensible talk from the Jesuits, the Coeur d'Alenes ignored the dreamers. The tribe's headmen considered what they should do. Joining a war coalition was out of the question. They concluded to

Andrew Seltice, chief of the Coeur d'Alenes
during the time of aboriginal land cessions.
Seltice died in 1902. (Dellwo collection)

petition the president directly for a reservation in their familiar territory.
Evidently Father Joseph Cataldo, a Sicilian Jesuit who had worked six years
on Indian missions, translated their wishes into English. Dated November
18, 1872, the petition set out the Coeur d'Alenes' request for "a part of our
land . . . for our exclusive use," to include the mission church "built with
our own hands," and traditional fishing, hunting, and gathering grounds,
"from old our habitual residence." [17]

The petition asked the president to send a negotiator, reminding him
that the tribe had lived up to its treaty with Wright and now felt entitled
to consideration as reliable men. Cataldo and Fathers Gregory Gazzoli and
Joseph Joset signed as witnesses to the marks of nine chiefs. The first chief
was Andrew Seltice, emergent over Vincent, whose prestige waned after
the encounters with Steptoe and Wright.

As tribal spokesman, particularly with white men, Seltice was a fortu-
nate choice. He herded horses and cattle near Saltese Lake (now drained,

it was on the Washington side of the territorial border, south of Liberty Lake), and once a year he invited the tribe there for a day of picnicking and racing. He had counseled the Coeur d'Alenes against attacking Steptoe.

Erect and dignified in carriage, Seltice wore his hair at shoulder length rather than braided, and he dressed in white men's clothing for comfort, not as symbol. For business he customarily donned a suit coat and hat, with shaped crown and broad brim. He was intelligent, a shrewd bargainer, and not inclined to hasty judgments; he solicited counsel from the elders, acted from consensus, and dedicated himself to doing his best for his people.

To support the Coeur d'Alenes' petition, Father Cataldo wrote to the commissioner of the Bureau of Catholic Indian Missions, Charles Ewing, who in turn addressed the secretary of the interior: "When they [the Coeur d'Alenes] have the guarantee that their reservation, as they want it, is secured to them, they are disposed to relinquish all their lands. . . . They want schools and a saw and grist mill. But the Indians say that this settlement must be a permanent one." Ewing added that the Indians wanted to negotiate with a federal agent "whose report will be respected at Washington, so that what he says will be law, permanent law, unchangeable law."[18]

The commissioner of Indian affairs, Edward P. Smith, was considering an inquiry into Idaho's Indian situation, largely to quiet the territory's carpetbag governor, Thomas W. Bennett. When Ewing's letter reached him, Smith acted: He named Bennett, Rep. John P. C. Shanks (chairman of the House Indian committee), and Indian agent H. W. Reed to a special commission. One of their purposes would be to "visit the Coeur d'Alenes, to hear complaints, with a view to their cure or removal, and to induce them to abandon a roving life and consent to confine themselves to a reservation."[19]

Unaware that the government agent assigned to the Nez Perce (that skinny bundle of Christian righteousness, John B. Monteith) had already worked out a tentative pact with the tribe (at Smith's behest), Shanks and Bennett went with Monteith to talk to the Coeur d'Alenes. They found there was really nothing to talk about. The tribe wanted the reserve already negotiated with Monteith. Shanks and Bennett, the two grumbled later, "joined Mr. Monteith as there seemed to be a necessity for it at the time."[20]

In due course, on November 8, 1873, President Grant signed an executive order creating the reservation Monteith had agreed to. Described by natural features and landmarks, the reserve extended westward from the mission to the territorial boundary (taking in the southern half of the Spokane River), followed the border south to a ridge between Latah and Pine creeks, then bent eastward to include the lower St. Joe River, and finally traced the Coeur d'Alene Mountains northeastward to the place of beginning, the mission. It embraced the lake entirely, although a government survey later sliced off a wisp of the northern end.

And so the Coeur d'Alenes had their reservation. Would it be, as they hoped, permanent and unchangeable? In the opinion of settlers, it was too big. Bennett, in a letter to the *Idaho Signal,* protested that "the Indians *demanded* an extension of the [1867] reservation so as to include the Catholic Mission and fishing and mill privileges on the Spokane River." Then Bennett departed for Washington, bearing a fraudulent certificate as territorial delegate.[21]

About three weeks before Grant's order, the banking house of Jay Cooke and Company collapsed in New York, precipitating a national panic. Cooke's fall bankrupted the Northern Pacific Railroad, and construction stopped. For the time being, the government no longer needed to move the Coeur d'Alenes from the railroad's route, and except for a trickle of settlement seeping north from Walla Walla, homesteading slowed nearly to a halt.

Ten years passed before the government got around to surveying the Coeur d'Alene reservation. In those ten years, the Coeur d'Alenes saw the tendrils of settlement inch toward them, patchworks of fields fenced amid log barns and houses. By 1870 a trader had set down a store at Spokane Bridge, at the territorial border crossing of the Spokane. By 1872 postal service had come to Spokane Bridge and Spokane Falls.

Settlers preferred bottomland, and as the nation's financial panic eased, more claimed it. This rolling, grassy country, the Palouse, was as good as Walla Walla for growing, but it was farther from the river landings, the commercial transportation network of the interior. A government land office opened at Colfax in 1876, sparing homesteaders the trek to file their claims at Walla Walla (although most still went there once or twice a year for supplies).

Seeing the land seekers and calculating that a railroad north of the lake would bring more hundreds, the Jesuits in 1876 moved the Coeur d'Alene mission south of the lake into Hangman Valley. A slow passage began to the new place, named DeSmet. Some Coeur d'Alenes refused to follow, and even Seltice held back for a time. Five years went by before a majority of the tribe relocated. The Jesuits leased their abandoned mission grounds and buildings to Matthew Hayden, an Irish immigrant who would become Joe Garry's great-grandfather.

At DeSmet, two days' journey from the older mission, the Jesuits and Indians built a new church, laid out a village of streets and log huts, and opened schools. The Jesuits taught the boys, and in 1878 three Sisters of Providence would come to teach the girls. Indians from many tribes would flock to this mission.

The vanguard of Coeur d'Alenes was barely settled at DeSmet when the nontreaty Nez Perce, under Joseph, resorted to war to hold their ancient lands in the Wallowa country of northeastern Oregon. Fearing a general Indian rising, settlers fled to fortified villages as the army chased the Nez Perce across Idaho into Montana. Seltice steadfastly refused to join in the war, and even sent Coeur d'Alene men to guard white homes whose owners had fled. With Joseph's surrender and exile, the Coeur d'Alenes could then ponder what their fate in war might have been. Immigration resumed.

A small flour mill started grinding at Spokane Falls, a village grown to eighty-one houses on the flat above the Indians' great salmon resort. In all, the 1880 census counted more than 7,000 white souls in the Palouse. Under Congress's edict to build the railroad or forfeit its land grant, the Northern Pacific resumed construction in 1879. The rail line would run south from Lake Pend Oreille toward Lake Coeur d'Alene, before bending westward to Spokane Falls, there crossing ground the Coeur d'Alene Indians had regarded as theirs for millennia.

Persuaded that a sweeping Indian war might still be possible, the army in 1877 sent Generals William T. Sherman and Phil Sheridan on a tour to recommend new military posts. The two old officers chose three sites: Fort Missoula, Montana; Fort Spokane, at the confluence of the Columbia and Spokane rivers; and Fort Coeur d'Alene, on the north shore of the lake, at the outlet of the Spokane. After the general's death, this last fort would be renamed Fort Sherman. It was built and garrisoned in 1878, and quickly a small town, Coeur d'Alene City, sprouted beside it, mainly for the recreation (and fleecing) of the soldiers. James Monaghan, an Irish immigrant who held contracts to supply Forts Colville and Spokane, also provisioned Fort Sherman. The town was largely his, shared with a partner C. B. King. Fort Sherman lay only eight miles south of Rathdrum, a town-to-be on

Facade of Sacred Heart Mission church, with convent of Mary Immaculate beyond it. (Author's collection)

the Northern Pacific main line, and it arrogated one of the Coeur d'Alenes' main village sites, where traditionally a fish-snaring weir spanned the Spokane.

An Idaho surveyor, Darius F. Baker, showed up in 1883 to map the reservation. His survey matched Grant's order, except on the north, where Baker overstepped to include Indian farms in the reserve, a deviation of 67.30 chains. Nor did he survey eight miles east from the Spokane River, but merely estimated, because the line ran in lake water. The General Land Office, when the north line was challenged later, refused to correct the discrepancy, since other properties rested on the boundary as mapped and it "was satisfactory to the Indians."[22]

Baker's surveying monuments, widely spaced, did not delineate an unmistakable border, and trespasses—deliberate and accidental—were frequent. "We hardly had our day of rest," Seltice observed.

The Northern Pacific hammered its ceremonial golden spike in September 1883, marking a completed track from Lake Superior to the Pacific shore. All that summer platoons of knowing prospectors had headed into the mountains east of the old mission. First there were whispers, then shouts: Gold discovered on the north fork of the Coeur d'Alene River! In deep snow a stampede overran this old Coeur d'Alene hunting ground, crossing the reservation with hardly a nod to its occupants, rushing pell-mell to nuggets that "fairly glisten" in streams.

But there were few nuggets to be plucked, and the rush soon subsided. However, in 1885 Noah Kellogg, a veteran prospector with a grubstake and a borrowed mule, located lead-silver ore on the south fork of the Coeur d'Alene, at Milo Creek (now Wardner). Two miners staked lead-silver claims on Canyon Creek by the trail from Thompson Falls, Montana. On their heels others filed hundreds of claims in a few weeks. Coeur d'Alene City swelled with men on their way to the silver. A few Indians made quick wages packing in supplies and mail.

Monaghan and King launched two steamers on the lake to haul men and supplies from Coeur d'Alene City to Old Mission, whence riverside trails led to the mining claims. When a Portland company with a fancier steamer decided to compete, Monaghan connived with his old friend, Matthew Hayden, to deny it the mission landing. The Portlanders sold their fine boat to Monaghan and King, giving the two a monopoly on the lake's commercial traffic.

Treaty negotiators in 1887 when a number of Spokanes agreed to move to the Coeur d'Alene reservation. Back row, left to right: Robert Flett, a noted Salish interpreter; R.W. Gwydir, Colville agent under whose jurisdiction Coeur d'Alenes fell; and James Gibson, agency clerk. Middle row: Billy Mason, a Spokane; Andrew Seltice, Coeur d'Alene chief; Spokane Garry, chief of the upper Spokanes; and an unidentified nephew of Seltice. Front row, left, is Nellie, daughter of Garry, Pier Bartholomew, a Spokane. Others not identified. (*Spokesman-Review*)

In 1886 Daniel C. Corbin, a partner in a smelter at Wickes, Montana, laid down one railroad from Old Mission to the mines, and another between Coeur d'Alene City and the Northern Pacific main line. Connected by steamers on the lake, Corbin's two railroads were soon busy hauling in supplies and carrying out sacks of ore from mills at the mines. Although he passed through Coeur d'Alene Indian aboriginal lands, to which title had not been extinguished, the General Land Office assured Corbin that his track from Old Mission lay wholly on public domain.[23]

Thus a busy commerce plied the northern waters of Lake Coeur d'Alene in 1887 when Congress dispatched the Northwest Indian Commission, a team of three, to persuade tribes, including the Coeur d'Alenes, to cede their traditional lands. The commission, in discourse at DeSmet, contracted with the Coeur d'Alenes to give up their aboriginal lands outside the reservation of 1873.

Why did the Coeur d'Alenes agree to this? The northern sector was lost, preempted by the Northern Pacific, Fort Sherman, the mines, and steamboats on the lake; to the west, the city of Spokane Falls surrounded the Indians' main source of salmon; and settlers pressed on Indian root fields from the south. The Coeur d'Alenes, in fact, had nothing to yield that had not already been taken away.

But the Indians' evident doubt that Washington would keep a promise induced the commissioners to pledge that "no part of said [1873] reservation shall ever be sold, occupied, open to white settlement, or otherwise disposed of without the consent of the Indians residing on the reservation." The Feds offered $150,000 for the ceded lands.[24]

In the nation's capital, however, Congress had already begun undoing the pledge of a permanent, secure reservation. It had passed the General Allotment Act (usually called the Dawes act) in 1887, and allotment meant dividing Indian reservations into individual tracts to destroy tribal unity.

While Corbin invaded Indian haunts on the north, the Union Pacific, building through the Palouse from the south, applied for authorization to cross the reservation. It proposed a route from Farmington (population 418, with bank and newspaper) across the St. Joe, along the east lakeshore to the Coeur d'Alene River, and from there, up the river valley to the mines. Seltice thought a railroad on the reservation would be good for his people, and he gently prodded the Coeur d'Alene elders to approve it. As the Washington and Idaho Railroad, this branch of the Union Pacific was authorized by Congress on May 18, 1888.

Congress, on the other hand, delayed ratifying the 1887 compact with the Coeur d'Alenes. The committee considering ratification was frank: The reservation, the lake, the mineral mountains, and the root fields, "while of great value to the Indians, yet are of greater value, if not inestimable value, to the citizens of the United States." The committee also noted that the previous Congress had deferred ratification "for sundry reasons, among which was a desire on the part of the United States to acquire an additional area." In its appropriations act, Congress directed the secretary of the interior to bargain for more—whatever "the tribe shall consent to sell." So much for a permanent reservation.[25]

A generation had passed since Wright's punishment. Veterans of that adventure neared middle age, hair graying, a little paunchy in the belly. Coeur d'Alene horsemen no longer sashayed at will across an open landscape. The Indians adopted western white-men's clothing—jeans for men, skirts for women—usually embellished with native ornament, their native finery of white deerskin, beading, and feathers stored for ceremonial occasions.

Several Coeur d'Alenes operated showplace farms, but most of the tribe fished, hunted, and gathered in familiar environs that shrank each year, and augmented their diets from garden plots. White businessmen did not encourage Indians as entrepreneurs; Indian farmers were unwelcome in granges and cooperatives, reminded of their place sometimes by a town's vigilantes, operating below the calm surface of village life.

The Indians stood on the threshold of an era when they were to be curiosities at county fairs and icons for civic ceremonies—people walled off from participation in American life by silent segregation. This was the milieu into which the Garrys were born. Perhaps reservation boundaries were hard to see, but whites erected social barriers impossible to mistake. To settlers, the notion of Indian sovereignty was a mere legalism, and the government increasingly treated Indians as business to be dispatched.

And the government's main business with the Coeur d'Alenes was to pry away more land. Another commission showed up in 1889, and the Coeur d'Alenes courteously talked. The tribe consented—only if their 1887 compact were ratified—to sell 184,960 acres of lake and land north of a line drawn west from the mouth of the Coeur d'Alene River, for $500,000. To hold it was, in any case, a forlorn hope: The waters churned with steam-

Costumed for drumming and dancing. Tensed, Idaho, 1907. (Dellwo collection)

boat traffic, and more than a thousand squatters fastened on tracts they expected would soon be public domain. The *Spokane Falls Review* described the cession as "the choicest portion of the reservation . . . most of the reservation land lying around Lake Coeur d'Alene."

There would be one more sale, that of 320 acres, including the townsite of Harrison. Located at the mouth of the Coeur d'Alene, Harrison, founded by squatters and served by the Washington and Idaho Railroad, was rapidly becoming a lumber-mill town. Consummated in 1894, the Harrison strip would be the last ceding of reservation land to which the tribe consented.[26]

Congress ratified the 1889 sale, and with it the 1887 compact, on March 3, 1891. In the meantime, both Idaho and Washington, frontier no longer, had become states—Washington on November 11, 1889, and Idaho on July 3, 1890.

The federal Indian office considered the Coeur d'Alene tribe a prime candidate for allotment. For years field agents, eager to show progress in turning Indians into farmers, had penned glowing descriptions of Coeur d'Alene farms for Washington, D.C. There were a few truly fine farms, since after payment for the forfeited northern lands, Indians had improved homes and bought farm equipment. A month after passage of the Dawes act, the commissioner of Indian affairs observed, in a letter to the agent responsible for the Coeur d'Alenes: "From your annual report, it is believed that the Indians upon the Coeur d'Alene Reservation . . . are prepared to take allotments in severalty. . . . It is expected that you will do everything in your power to encourage the Coeur d'Alenes to take allotments."[27]

The Coeur d'Alenes resisted allotment; they were, in fact, appalled by such a prospect. The Indian office suspected that prosperous reservation farmers led the opposition to allotment because their properties, each 700 acres or so, would be reduced in any equal division of lands among members of the tribe.

Perhaps half a dozen Coeur d'Alenes at that time produced commercial grain crops and owned equipment, homes, and barns. They sold in a local market, and the Washington and Idaho Railroad cut their profits by importing grain products. Dry years of low crop yields cast them in debt. A Spokane newspaper commented, "A large amount of land on the Indians' domain is not naturally adapted to the growth of wheat"; another article stated, "Their town residences at DeSmet mission . . . are nothing more than huts, many containing but one or two rooms." Oswald George, a contemporary of Joe Garry, remembered that "certain families fairly prospered. . . . The lakes and streams were plentifully supplied with fish." And many Indians lived on fish. As allotment would eventually demonstrate, the reservation did not contain enough tillable acreage to sustain the tribe.[28]

To Congress, the "logic of events" dictated absorbing Indians into the national culture by allottment. Within two years of implementing the Dawes act, however, allotment was an acknowledged disaster: Two-thirds of the Indians allotted in the West had lost their lands to white buyers.[29]

Ignoring the early evidence of cataclysm, a freshman congressman from Idaho, Burton L. French, in 1903 called on the secretary of the interior to allot the Coeur d'Alenes, alleging that 240 adult Indians occupied 404,480 acres—figures pitifully distorted. Doubtless his constituents were pleased, for French succeeded in putting the resistant Coeur d'Alenes on track for allotment.[30]

During this critical time, the tribe lost its most experienced leader: Andrew Seltice died, blind, aged ninety-two, in 1902. Peter Wildshoe, who succeeded him, died in 1907, and the mantle then fell to Peter Moctelme, an unyielding foe of allotment. But in letters and trips to Washington, Moctelme failed to hold off the inevitable. Congress had voted on June 21, 1906, for allotment of the Coeur d'Alene reservation, stipulating that each man, woman, and child receive 160 acres. To Moctelme's protest that the tribe had been promised their reserve forever, the commissioner of Indian affairs answered indifferently that the government made a reservation by one law and could unmake it by another.[31]

The choosing of tracts and the surveying began in the snow on January 16, 1908. About 270 Indians selected acreages near DeSmet; thirty others, in Mission Valley. "About 100 . . . were compelled to take sparsely timbered land," according to the allotting agent, William B. Sams. In all, 638 allotments were recorded. The new agent, Charles O. Worley, who had been the reservation miller, advised Indians to rent their land to white farmers rather than farm it. When allotting ended, lands not chosen were opened for settlement.[32]

"The Indians who received . . . trust patents were undoubtedly unaware of the legal consequences thereof," an educated Coeur d'Alene pointed out later. "They either did not know how to read or write, or knowing how, they were too young to appreciate such consequences. . . . Those trust patents were . . . vague and ambiguous."[33]

Within twenty-four months of allotment, 370 Coeur d'Alenes had leased their land. By 1912 only sixty-six tilled their own acreages. Twelve years after allotment, an inspector found that "the allotted land retained by the Indians aggregates 73,194 acres distributed over a large area intermingled with patented homestead land," a checkerboard of Indian and white farms. "Most [Coeur d'Alene] Indian acreages "are . . . leased to white men for sufficient revenue to permit the owners to live without work," the inspector added. He counted only fourteen Indians working farms large enough to support themselves and their families.[34]

By Garry's time more than half the owners of allotments lived off the reservation; their interest in Coeur d'Alene affairs was limited to the rent they realized.

6 Boy to Man

*J*oseph Richard Garry was born as the sun broke over the forested hills to light the patterned fields and pastures of the Coeur d'Alene reservation on the crisp morning of March 8, 1910. Glancing at the rose-streaked sky outside her tepee, his mother named him Dawn Light.

The child came from an illustrious line. His father, Ignace, was a son of Annie, daughter of Nellie, whose father, Garry, was the melancholy chief of the Spokanes in treaty-making days. Ignace's father, Antoine, was the son of Matthew Hayden. Born in County Wexford, Ireland, Matthew migrated to the United States, moved west with the army in the field against Indians, and when his enlistment ended, settled to farm near the center of Indian-white trading, Fort Colville. Later he moved to Idaho, where Hayden Lake was eventually named for him.[1]

Joseph's mother, Suzette, a Kalispel, descended from Michel Revais, the noted blind Flathead interpreter for government emissaries seeking concessions from tribes of the interior Northwest in the mid-nineteenth century.

At the time of Joseph's birth, his father's tribe, the Coeur d'Alenes, was in the last galling stages of allotment. Joseph arrived too late to be allotted as a Coeur d'Alene. But to assure his son of land, Ignace enrolled Joseph with the Kalispels, and the boy received allotment 31, forty acres on the Pend Oreille River in northeastern Washington, where the Kalispels were squeezed onto 4,629 acres in 1914.[2]

Just east of Tekoa, Washington, at the edge of the Coeur d'Alene reservation, lay a sublime bowl of fertile land, the Lovell Valley. There blind Nina, Spokane Garry's widow, had moved after his death in 1892, and there her daughter, Nellie, received an allotment of 160 acres. As a child, Ignace had witnessed the death of Spokane Garry. Soon after, Nellie took Ignace to the Coeur d'Alene reservation and changed his name from Hayden to Garry, so that the name would not die out. Determined that he would be taught in both Indian and white cultures, she packed Ignace off to Alpine, a white school near the farm town of Fairfield, Washington.

Joe's mother died when he was eight, and Ignace remarried. In his youth Joe lived much of the time under Nellie's watchful mothering. She and Ignace imbued the boy with love of family, a sense of duty, and pride in his heritage. He heard the old men's stories of times past and of Spokane Garry's struggles to teach his people.

Taken by the Hudson's Bay Company as a boy to be educated and Christianized at Fort Garry (Winnipeg), Spokane Garry had returned in 1832 determined to educate and Christianize the Spokanes. Nellie schooled Joe with her father's dreams, and Joe, in later years, spoke with pride of his link to Spokane Garry. Indeed, in Joe some would see the fruition of Spokane Garry's hopes.

Surrounded by the spirit of ancestors, Joe lived among family and tribe who were proud of him and expected great deeds from him. From his roots he drew strength. "Strong people come from strong families," says one who knew the Garrys well, "and Joe Garry came from a strong family."

Joe Garry's childhood shines through a moving memoir of Ignace written by a daughter, Celina: "I never knew Dad to be bored. His fellow man was pure entertainment." Ignace loved the ancestral drums and chants, and "he loved sitting cross legged . . . with a circle of Indian people exchanging stories." [3]

When his family traveled by automobile, Ignace took the prettiest route, usually one where the children could picnic and swim. And when they went north to the Kalispel reserve, past his wife's childhood home near Lake Pend Oreille, he stopped at Trestle Creek "so Mama could . . . walk around and reminisce. When she got back in the car she would cry" until the lake was out of sight.

"Dad believed in Indianness stemming from his heart instead of the long braids, a beaded belt buckle, or a big hat. When he dressed in his [Indian] regalia, it was white and spotless. . . . He believed in looking his best out of respect to his fellow man," Celina wrote. Ignace, a practicing Catholic like most Coeur d'Alenes, honored the customs of his people: Indian foods, spiritual powers, sweats, chants, and other traditions. "He taught us to be accepting of the movements of the Great Spirit." Joe Garry thus absorbed the customs of his ancestors as part of the fabric of everyday life. All his life Joe Garry relished the drumming and the chants and treasured his heritage.

At the same time, Ignace was determined that his children would be

The Garry family about 1920. Left to right, front: Joe, Annie (Joe's grand-mother), and Helen Kamiakin. Rear: Alice (Joe's sister) and Ignace (Joe's father). (Arlene Owen family collection)

Ignace Garry at Coeur d'Alene powwow in the twenties. (Arlene Owen family collection)

educated to live with assurance in the white culture that surrounded them. Thus he planted his children's feet in both worlds. So, too, would Nellie, who, bearing the sobriquet "Indian princess," regularly attended Spokane City's pioneer picnics and spoke an invocation in Salish. She dispatched Joe at age nine to the DeSmet mission boarding school for boys, where he studied lessons much like those of a city parochial school.

In Coeur d'Alene finery; left to right: Susan Mechel, Joe Garry, Ignace Garry, and Annie Garry. (Arlene Owen family collection)

Alice Garry, Joe's older sister, Miss Indian America
of 1927. (Arlene Owen family collection)

But Joe saw a different way of living when Ignace took his family to
Spokane's Davenport Hotel to perform in welcoming ceremonies for dig-
nitaries visiting the city. W. Harry Wraight, who arranged these appearances for the hotel, drove to the reservation to outline the program and,
as Celina remembered, "to buy a pair of beaded buckskin gloves that Mama
had made."

For the ceremony, "Father dressed in his finest buckskins and headdress."
He spoke a greeting in Salish. Joe interpreted, and "Dad would then 'adopt'
the visitor into the tribe, give him an Indian name"; sister Alice, a beau-

tiful young Indian girl, would present the gloves. "There was always some white woman that our mother would dress in one of our costumes [to] sing 'Pale Moon' or 'Indian Love Call.' We didn't know such 'Indian' songs."

At banquets the Garrys sat at a front table "so the people could watch us as we ate in our buckskins and feathers." Guests "filed by to shake hands with the Indians" and slip them coins.

"It was the treat of treats to go to Spokane," in Celina's memory. "We would take in a show and shop," and the hotel manager would give the children Davenport cookies as the bellhops loaded their suitcases into Ignace's old truck for the return. "When we got home, Mama would get busy with another pair of gloves for another 'adoption'" the next time the hotel called.

At nine, Joe Garry was a year or two older and had seen more of the interior Northwest than many of his reservation classmates at the mission school. The Garrys passed back and forth among the Spokane, Coeur d'Alene, and Kalispel tribes, and Joe learned the dialects of each. And he bore the burden of his father's reputation: He was expected to behave and perform like a chief's son.

Joe Garry remained at the mission school until 1926 when, at sixteen, he enrolled at Gonzaga High School in Spokane, also run by the Society of Jesus. The school operated in a four-story brick building on Boone Avenue that contained a university, a high school, a law school, and a Jesuit residence. Classroom lectures paused for the whine of saws and the steam whistle of the nearby McGoldrick lumber mill.

After a year Joe returned to Nellie's allotment in the Lovell Valley and transferred to the public high school in Tekoa, a two-story brick building with a gymnasium attached. Joe played on the basketball team, which won the county championship. Celina remembered her brother's school days: Joe rode horseback to Tekoa, through rain, snow, and freezing weather, wearing a sheepskin coat and carrying "pancake" sandwiches in his pockets for lunch. (Rural schools then provided sheds and hitching racks for students' horses.) Joe did not casually miss classes. When the roads or the weather seemed too bad, his father sometimes drove him by wagon. Often the boy rode his horse on the hard gravel between the railroad tracks to avoid muddy, neglected reservation roads.

During summer vacations, Garry worked at farm jobs: One summer he drove a neighbor's team carrying grain bundles to a threshing machine;

Joe Garry (back row, far right) as a freshman interclass basketball player at Gonzaga High School, Spokane. (Arlene Owen family collection)

Joe Garry's Gonzaga High School graduation picture, which he used for some years on employment applications. (Family)

another summer he sold wood for winter fuel, grossing $350 from June to September; and another, he drove a four-horse team hauling water tanks for a thresher steam engine. In those days grain farmers threshed with stationary steam engines connected to threshers by huge leather belts. They were noisy, hot, and potentially dangerous. To get jobs each summer during the twenties, Joe must have been known as a hard, productive worker, for inland farmers were pinched in those times.[4]

When Joe was about to begin his senior year in high school, his aunt Sabine Polotkin insisted that he finish at Gonzaga. He went back to Spokane, made the track team—he won the broad jump in the city meet—and graduated in May 1930. With the other seniors, he sat on a temporary stage in the gymnasium, wearing mortarboard and gown, and when his name was called, he crossed the platform to kiss the bishop's ring and collect his diploma. Of course, the Garry family attended.

Garry hauled wood again in the summer of 1930, leaving his valley at the end of August to enter the Haskell Institute, the Indian school in Lawrence, Kansas. Haskell was properly a business college, offering a two-year program. (So many of its graduates entered the federal Indian Service that, for a time, they held sway in the agency's field offices.) Joe Garry—known as Geary throughout his Haskell days—was not enthusiastic about clerking. He really had not yet settled on his future.

Almost immediately upon graduation from Haskell, however, Joe found a place as a lifeguard and instructor in Indian lore at Gridley, a boy's camp near Knox, Indiana. When the summer ended, he moved to the Fort Apache Indian agency at Whiteriver, Arizona, to work in the commissary, and he soon advanced to office work.

In the summer of 1934, Joe Garry landed a post as counselor and woodcraft instructor at Pokagon, a boys camp near Angola, in the lake country of northeastern Indiana. The camp director, Hermon Phillips, was also track coach at Butler University, a private coeducational institution affiliated with the Disciples of Christ Church, located on a 280-acre campus in Indianapolis. Phillips encouraged Joe to enter Butler and turn out for the track team. The university awarded Garry a half scholarship, and the coach found him a room "for about 10 minutes work each day."

Garry enrolled in preforestry, intending to study forest biology, and he trained with the freshman track team. But taking up books again was daunting, and Joe was mindful that he was three or four years older than most of the students. He apparently expressed doubts to his father, Ignace, who sent him a money order to pay his way back to the Coeur d'Alene reservation. Joe returned the money, writing to Ignace, "I plan to stick like a man."[5]

"This is my only and last chance to go to school," Joe wrote in a long, earnest, affectionate letter. "If I went home now and be a clerk that's all I'll ever amount to. There is no future in it." Hundreds of Indian boys and girls were in colleges, he went on, and the best jobs would go to those who earned degrees. "I want myself, your son and only son, to be among the leading ones." In time, he hoped, he would buy Ignace "a fine ranch at Cusick." The students at Butler "want me to go on and are back of me in everything. I am at present under the best track coach in the country." So he would stay at Butler.

The university's student newspaper pictured Joe in "the white buckskin costume made for him by his father," and remarked that "the business of being a college freshman is entirely to the liking of Joe Garry." He was studying to be a forest ranger, the newspaper said, and Coach Phillips thought that he showed "much promise" as a distance runner. His Indian name was "Little Eagle," and he descended from a famous chief, Spokane Garry. "Indians are not 'vanishing Americans.' . . . There will always be Indians," the student paper explained. Obviously most of the story came from Garry. It was perhaps his first conscious attempt to shape his image.[6]

He spent another summer at Pokagon camp, telling the boys about Indian life; but in the fall, without money to continue college, he returned to the Fort Apache agency at Whiteriver rather than to Butler. In Arizona he lived with relatives and worked in an agency warehouse. Garry was now twenty-five years old, five-feet eleven-inches tall, and weighed 168 pounds. He was handsome, likeable, and a cousin thought him "quite a ladies man."[7]

Early in 1936 the Northern Idaho agency in Moscow hired Garry as a clerk for roadwork accounts. By automobile Moscow was only about one and one-half hours from the Lovell Valley. Garry could go home to visit old friends anytime he could hitch a ride, and he could attend Mass at DeSmet. Soon after settling in Moscow, Garry went home for a few days. Celina "saw him enter the church and kneel. I recognized the back of his head. In my happiness and excitement at seeing him for the first time in two years, I ran down from the choir loft and did the unforgiveable. . . . I sat with him on the men's side. I was proud and happy to be a part of him."

Joe Garry, age twenty-four, in ceremonial dress at DeSmet. (Arlene Owen family collection)

Garry could even find time to play the role of an Indian chieftain in a historical pageant, with a cast of fifty Coeur d'Alenes, in Coeur d'Alene City on July 4, 1937, a spectacle witnessed by a patriotic crowd of 8,000.

At Moscow, Joe took the noncompetitive civil-service exam twice before passing, and then he became what he did not want to be: a clerk. But if he had not by then scaled great heights, he had learned—from the Davenport Hotel, Gonzaga High, Pokagon, and Butler University—that he liked to be the Indian among whites; he liked to portray his Indian heritage and customs; he enjoyed telling of Indian ways and showing Indian finery; and he liked to sing Indian chants and to recount the legends of his people. In all these Joe found a role he could play exceedingly well.

Garry moved in 1937 to Lapwai, Idaho, a few miles outside of Lewiston, when the Fort Lapwai sanitarium and the agency combined. The Coeur d'Alene tribe tried to keep Joe closer to home, urging the commissioner of Indians affairs to open a subagency on the reservation, with Garry in charge. But the commissioner refused. There would be no agency and no Garry, the commissioner concluded, for such an appointment "requires an older man of extensive experience."[8]

Joe clerked in the Northern Idaho agency approximately four years, making small advances. Although he was stuck in a rut, in the depressed thirties one did not heedlessly quit a job, no matter how dreary. Garry's evaluations generally praised his personality and cooperativeness. "Efficiency fair, endeavors to do good work but is slow," read one, which added the compliment: "A Spokane Indian boy of very fine personality." He was overloaded with work for a time, because a vacancy went unfilled. Another evaluation observed: "This employee . . . desires to give satisfactory service, but requires plenty of time be allowed him." One supervisor marked two plus signs by the phrase "ability to work with and for others" on an evaluation form.

The tribe again attempted to boost Garry by recommending that he be employed at the Golden Gate International Exposition in San Francisco in 1939 as salesman of Indian arts and crafts. Congressman John Tolan wrote to the commissioner of Indian affairs that "Garry has a fine reputation for honesty and sobriety, and all the leaders on the reservation desire that he be employed" as salesman. But the sales position in San Francisco fell through because the Indian Service would not grant Joe a leave of absence. He would have to take his chances on getting a job when the exposition ended.[9]

Joe Garry, in ceremonial dress, shortly before his call to military service in World War II. (Arlene Owen family collection)

After four years as a clerk at Lapwai, stifled by the fussy paternalism of the Bureau of Indian Affairs, Garry could imagine himself growing gray at his ledgers. He was dispirited, unsure of how to approach his future. He knew that he had not lived up to the high expectations of his tribe and family. Neither had he met his own resolve to be more than a clerk. He was not doing what he did best: represent his people, showing pride in his Indian heritage by using his gifts of speech and personality. At least he could now decide to leave the Indian Service: He resigned for a clerical job with the navy in Washington, D.C., at the same pay, $1,440 a year.

In less than a year, Garry quit the navy to take odd jobs for Congressman Tolan. One of those jobs was to organize an exhibition of buckskin goods made by nine Northwest tribes and the Kateri Guild (a sodality on the Coeur d'Alene reservation), for display in the House Indian Affairs Committee room of the capitol. Eleanor Roosevelt mentioned the demonstration in her newspaper column, "My Day."[10]

But his life continued trackless. He returned to Idaho to marry Frances Waukeshan, a Menominee secretary in the Lapwai sanitarium. Father Cornelius Byrne celebrated the nuptial Mass, and the couple breakfasted with the DeSmet nuns. It was an unhappy match that ended when Joe discovered his wife in a liaison. She soon accompanied the body of a deceased friend to her former home in Kenosha, Wisconsin, never to return. But the marriage was binding in the Catholic canon: That he could not marry again in the embrace of his church weighed on Joe for the rest of his life.[11]

Garry turned to farming in the Lovell Valley but had hardly settled in before he was called to military service. Inducted on July 25, 1942 — and, despite a defective right eye, classed as a rifleman — he rose to the rank of staff sergeant, a platoon leader in the Three-hundred Fourteenth Infantry. After duty in Germany, he was mustered out two days before Christmas in 1945. At age thirty-five, he went home again.

He found his people in political ferment. The superintendent of the Northern Idaho agency, Archie Phinney, had scolded the Coeur d'Alenes for selling or renting their allotments. He urged the tribe to "go back to farming their own lands" as the first step in rehabilitating a poor reservation that was becoming more fragmented each year. But many Coeur d'Alenes, particularly elders, had neither the equipment nor the business experience to farm successfully.

Phinney could see the Coeur d'Alenes' economic base slipping away,

Garry (left) in his infantry uniform, with an unidentified buddy. Joe rose to platoon leader. (Arlene Owen family collection)

and with it, the old ways that emanated from the earth. He encouraged a coterie of younger and better-educated Indians gathered around Lawrence Nicodemus and Paschal George—the progressives—to elect a council to handle the tribe's business. Father Byrne, whose influence went beyond spiritual ministry, lent his voice to change. "Our village . . . is in great need of a governing body," he declared. "The time has come that there should be a permanent body to lead our people."[12]

Home again, perhaps to stay, Joe Garry was inevitably thrust into the ceremonial and political life of the tribe. He was a frequent speaker at holiday observances, he was prominent among eulogists at funerals, and, shiny and smart in his reserve uniform on Memorial Day and at military funerals, he was in charge of soldierly ceremonies at the mission cemetery, where graves of three Coeur d'Alenes killed in World War II were marked with stones painted red, white, and blue.

Ostensibly he studied to be a cattleman, learning animal husbandry by special arrangement with Washington State College. But Coeur d'Alene leaders wanted him to work for the tribe. In November 1947 the Coeur d'Alenes sent Garry as their delegate to a meeting of inland Northwest tribes called by the Colvilles to consider united political action. The Yakimas, Kalispels, Umatillas, Warm Springs, Nez Perces, and Flatheads sent representatives. Work together, "make history with this meeting," John B. Cleveland, Colville chairman, exhorted them. He called for selfless dedication to fulfill their "duty as educated Indians to help the older faction. Forget about personal gain [and] . . . personal prejudices." Hold onto the land, for Northwest Indians "are not ready for liquidation of their reserves," Cleveland declared. The time had come to "bring our problems together."[13]

To Garry, Cleveland's words sounded as a summons to serve. Two years later these tribes, with others, would formally band as the Affiliated Tribes of Northwest Indians (working through the National Congress of American Indians), and they would elect Garry their president. This call to serve would springboard Joe Garry into a larger political arena.

The Coeur d'Alenes elected tribal council members for the first time on May 27, 1948. Joe, with the highest number of votes, was elected chairman and council member for a three-year term.[14]

Garry began to speak out beyond the reservation. At a Tekoa Kiwanis Club luncheon he joshed with pioneers about the old days of rutted streets and hitching posts, where he would tie his pony borrowed from the mission. His message was an appeal for support of the reservation. Indians should not be "emancipated" before they were ready, Garry told this friendly gathering, and he emphasized that Indian peoples, long tyrannized by government, wanted a voice in their affairs.[15]

He said much the same on the reservation. At a general meeting of the tribe, Garry promoted a resolution to bar a Coeur d'Alene from selling trust land to a non-Indian without tribal approval. At Phinney's urging he led the tribe to its decision to sue before the Indian Claims Commission for lost aboriginal lands. And as fund raiser to defend Indian exemption from income taxes on profits from trust land, he expanded his arena to much of the West.

Garry issued a call to "all Indians of the Northwest" to join a delegation to Washington, D.C., to combat taxes (a cause that would surely spread to other tribes) and to oppose reorganization of the Bureau of Indian Affairs. Seven tribes responded, and four brought white attorneys with them. Garry had "thus far nobly engineered" the protest, commented an Indian writer.[16]

The delegates' mission drew no sympathy from members of Congress, but it was a first stroke in the united action that John Cleveland had called for. The Associated Press filed a jocose report on the hearing: "The chief complainer was chief of the Coeur d'Alenes . . . Joseph Garry, a handsome gent in a pin-striped blue suit with a matching figured tie. He could talk lickety-split, and did." The report quoted Garry: "I venture to say that 80 percent of all the money spent by the Indian affairs bureau goes for paper work. Fellows, the Indian cannot progress on paperwork." And the story concluded: "By now, they [Indians] must have learned that it's hard to hurry the United States government."[17]

If he and the other delegates had not yet convinced the Washington lawmakers to do something for them, Garry nevertheless perceived that going directly to Congress got him a hearing. And though he had not anticipated a foray into politics—neither his experience nor his education pointed that way—he now realized that, for the moment, his personal future lay in politics.[18]

He had taken to wearing white shirts as part of his public image, much as Ignace had worn spotless buckskin. And he had written for himself a sort of political primer on a three-by-five index card: Don't criticize, con-

Sergeant Joe Garry, an army portrait mailed
to his family. (Arlene Owen family collection)

demn, or complain; give sincere appreciation; arouse in others a sincere
want; become genuinely interested in other people; smile (underlined
twice); remember a man's name is most important; be a good listener; and
let the other man give his opinion. By and large, he would follow these
simple precepts for the rest of his career.[19]

But then his career was suddenly on hold. When President Truman
ordered mobilization for a "police action" in Korea, Sgt. Joe Garry was
the first reservist called to duty from Benewah County.

When he returned home with a medical discharge in the fall of 1951, he
was immediately deputized by claims attorneys to survey Indian timber-
lands in the Northwest. Garry traveled with a Wyoming forester, who, at
the end of their tour, wrote to his supervisor: "I am taking the first opportunity available for the purpose of saying that I enjoyed the trip with you

and Joe Gary [*sic*]. . . . I was . . . impressed with our mutual friend Joe Gary. Joe is a well-rounded individual, a splendid traveling companion, including among other accomplishments being quite a humorist." [20]

Once back in Idaho, Garry threw himself into Indian politics and the Democratic party. Encouraged by the party, he ran for the Idaho legislature and lost. In 1956, however, he ran a second time and won.

Consequently, in the first week of wintry January 1957, Joe Garry set out on Interstate Highway 95 for Boise to represent Benewah County in the Idaho house of representatives. Highway 95 is a winding, hilly two-lane roadway, treacherous in places. It is almost a historical boulevard, leading southward past DeSmet, the venerable Jesuit mission and school, through the university city of Moscow, thence to Lewiston, birthplace of Idaho statehood and pivot of the Weyerhaeuser Company's invasion of Idaho's white pine forests. It meanders through the Nez Perce reservation, descending in great loops into Whitebird Canyon (where Nez Perce warriors smashed the U. S. cavalry in 1877), and follows the Little Salmon River past national forests. There the direct route to Boise jogs into state Highway 55 near Meadows, which then twists down valleys to the fertile Boise Basin and the capital city. Gold was the siren for settlement all along this route.

As the highway descends toward Boise, the land flattens into broad valleys. Larger towns appear. Idaho's population, economy, and political strength cumulate in the southern counties. Its northern panhandle—once characterized by white pine and minerals that, by Garry's time, were already near-spent—tags along as hinterland. Garry understood that, as representative of a northern county, he was not likely to play a significant role in the coming session.

As he traveled to the legislative session, Garry must have reflected that he was going to Boise not as a supplicant but as a participant. He had observed legislative bodies for years; now he was part of one. He had campaigned using an act borrowed from his days at the Davenport Hotel: He piled nieces and nephews in Indian dress into his car, drove to a fairgrounds or meeting house, and thumped a tom-tom while the children danced, capturing the audience's attention. Then Garry spoke a sentence or two in Salish, paused in mock embarrassment, and continued his campaign speech in English to the bemused listeners. In his talks Garry did not promise great deeds; he spoke simply for education and youth opportunity. [21]

Democrats controlled the Idaho Senate for the first time since 1946, and a ten-year Republican majority in the house had shrunk to five members, when the thirty-fourth biennial legislature convened on January 7, 1957. Garry's victory restored Benewah County's seat in the house to Democrats, who had lost in the two previous elections. All of the members knew they would have to raise taxes during the session, and Democrats resolved that Republicans would be blamed for it.

Once sworn in, Garry seemed almost to disappear from public view, as if he had sunk beneath the political surface. He received workaday assignments to committees for fish and game, reclamation and irrigation, and state affairs. In an assembly notably short of lawyers, Garry was one of twenty farmers and ranchers among the fifty-nine members. In his own friendly way, he fit in, and he more or less attached himself to a veteran of the house, Clarence H. Higer (Democrat from Gem County), as his mentor on protocol and form. Garry sat near the back, at one of the desks scarred from long use, in a house chamber turning tagrag although it had been dressed up with bright new draperies. He joined legislative colleagues trooping down marble stairways for coffee and rolls at "the pit," Casey's Corner, in the statehouse basement.

Even at the start of his first session, he could not give his entire attention to Idaho. As president of the National Congress of American Indians, Garry ought to have been in Utah supporting the Utes' campaign for the right to vote. John Rainer reported a balance of $176.83 in the NCAI treasury, and clearly Garry ought to have been on the road raising funds. Helen Peterson sent Garry business mail, and in a letter to Leona remarked, "We hardly expect to hear from Joe now that he is in the Legislature, but would appreciate a note from you." Twenty-two days after he reached Boise, Garry bolted for home at the news that his beloved daughter, Cubby, was ill. This would not be merely a temporary emergency, for Cubby—Ursala—was afflicted with asthma, which gradually grew worse. (In fact, she turned out to be both autistic and developmentally disabled.)

But Joe was soon back in Boise, resuming his role as a legislator who was rarely quoted in the newspapers and who generally voted with his party. But he was not always silent. From notes on a legal tablet, he spoke for a bill to extend increased bonding limits to Idaho's hard-pressed school districts, and the bill passed. He supported salaries for then-unpaid county officers, he favored exempting household goods from an *ad valorem* tax,

High jinks in the Idaho legislature. When a good-natured argument broke out over apple quality, Garry posed for the photographer in the act of "scalping" Clarence Higer, Gem County. (Family)

and he came out for allowing women (including tavern owners' wives) to tend bar. These were all concerns his constituents had written to him about.

As the legislature deliberated on a budget and the means to finance it, Garry voted against a higher tax on beer and against a state sales tax; he voted to ban sale of salacious comic books to persons under eighteen; he opposed outlawing the "closed shop" in Idaho; and, in the waning days of the session, when the thirty-fourth legislature had run longer than any since the first in 1890, Garry voted against higher income taxes to balance the largest general budget in Idaho's history. He was one of three in the house to vote against an appropriation for schools (Senate Bill 290), because he considered it too small, leading the Idaho Education Association to commend him in its newsletter for his "protest."[22]

All was not business. When Higer bragged that Gem County grew the best apples in the state, a newspaper photographer posed Garry, wearing feathered bonnet and waving a tomahawk, in the apparent act of threatening to "scalp" the bald Higer unless he delivered enough apples for the entire house. And Garry sat for a formal portrait, in native bonnet and tunic, by Boise photographer Virgil Parker. The portrait, shown in the 1957 exhibition of the Photographers Association of America, was subsequently adapted by the NCAI for its letterhead.[23]

For a day, the legislators debated the licensing of rainmakers—those seeding clouds from airplanes—and a Pocatello newspaper ran a cartoon of a sad Indian (no likeness to Joe) contemplating the headline, "Legislator Demands Rainmakers Register."

Meanwhile, as the U.S. Congress deliberated on extending the period for Indians to claim income-tax refunds, Garry actively advised tribal spokesmen to lobby for the bill's passage. When the Idaho legislature wearily adjourned on March 16, Garry scurried to his neglected precincts: the tribal business of the Coeur d'Alenes and the NCAI. Helen Peterson had been hospitalized for a month; the executive committee fretted over Arrow; an annual convention had to be planned; and the organization was painfully short of operating funds. Garry spent April in Washington, D.C., and New York talking with prospective contributors and restoring momentum to congressional lobbying.

Then he embarked on a tour of tribes to solicit memberships in the NCAI and to raise funds: In June he scoured the western Washington and Oregon tribes (taking time to return home when Cubby's tonsils were removed on June 18); in July he covered Montana and spoke at a government conference at the University of Washington. He received notice on July 19 that he had been chosen Outstanding Indian of North America for 1957. He hurried to Sundance and Pine Ridge in August, and to Anadarko, Oklahoma, for his award ceremony. Then he was on the road again to Colorado and southern Idaho. So it went. At tribal councils Garry pleaded with tribes and individual Indians to join the NCAI and contribute to it.

Some of Garry's visits stressed local tribal matters. For example, Arrow had handled citizen participation clumsily at Pine Ridge, and the tribe now mistrusted the project. When the Cheyennes and Arapahoes received 3,900 acres back from the federal government, the NCAI sought to impress members of Congress with the notion that a precedent for returning Indian lands had thereby been established. And the Zunis lobbied Congress to protect them from fake jewelry makers.

Congress deliberated on relocation (assisting individual Indians to move from reservations to cities), turning tribes over to state jurisdiction, termination, and other issues that the NCAI regarded as threats to Indians. Some idea of the volume of Indian legislation may be grasped from the fact that hardworking Frank George, secretary-treasurer of the Affiliated Tribes, filled thirty-two single-spaced mimeographed pages with a digest of Indian bills then before Congress.

Despite his merciless schedule, Garry was not yet ready to turn the National Congress of American Indians over to someone else. Helen Peterson wanted him to stay on. Consequently Garry ran for a fifth term as president and was reelected. Likewise, Benewah County Democrats urged him to seek another term in the legislature. He would do that, too.

Garry believed the Indian congress was making progress. When the government returned 10,260 acres to the Crows, Garry pointed out that the NCAI "had a very large hand in this restoration." And while he criticized the Bureau of Indian Affairs for "hiding behind the 'mandate'" of House Concurrent Resolution 108, he observed that recent Congresses "have shown no eagerness to carry out" the policy set down there. In March, Garry headed a fourteen-member commission to study Puerto Rico's economic resurgence. He returned with new enthusiasm for a program of public relations and economic development for American Indian tribes.[24]

Garry's campaign for a second term in the legislature was modest. Labor unions and educators supported him on his record. He had been speaking to civic and service clubs when occasions offered, and although he invariably talked about Indian rather than state issues, he felt voters had come to know him better. In the last weeks before election day, opponents of Ernest Gaffney, veteran senator from Benewah County, tried to make an issue of improving the St. Joe River road between St. Maries and Avery, a useful local route. Gaffney and Garry, working with Idaho's congressional corps, had succeeded in having the road added to the Idaho forest highway system, which meant the federal government would pay for improving it. In full-page newspaper advertisements, Garry—who admitted to "being somewhat of a 'silent man'" in the legislature—reviewed his and Gaffney's work. Both Garry and Gaffney were reelected.[25]

The thirty-fifth legislature, convening on January 5, 1959, immediately faced Idaho's recurring need for higher revenues. The capitol did not look much changed from two years before, with file boxes piled in office corners and worn desks. As a now-seasoned legislator in a house controlled by Democrats, Garry's committee assignments gave him a persuasive voice. He chaired the fish and game committee and the select committee on minority groups and Indian affairs, and he served as well on state affairs, aeronautics, civil defense, military and veterans' affairs. The fish and game committee set out to overhaul licensing laws, and the state affairs committee sought to write a new insurance code. Both tasks promised long hours of discussion.

Garry again warranted little notice in news reports of the session, although his impress was evident in two joint memorials addressed to the U.S. Congress: One urged repeal of House Concurrent Resolution 108 and petitioned Congress to adopt an approach to Indian administration that "did not destroy native culture and life"; the other recommended federal fiscal aid to local school districts where nontaxable trust lands hobbled a district's ability to raise construction funds. And Garry again played Indian with Clarence Higer, staging their apple buffoonery. This time Garry set an apple on Higer's head and drew an arrow in his bow to shoot it off. House members watched in awe until they realized that Garry did not really intend to shoot. "Horseplay about Gem apples," Joe noted in his diary. The prank yielded a picture for the newspapers.

Garry was on hand when the personable young senator from Massachusetts, John F. Kennedy, stood for introduction in the legislature and spoke at Boise's Jefferson-Jackson Day dinner on March 7. The next day was Garry's forty-ninth birthday, and he addressed the breakfast meeting of the Boise Holy Names Society. The legislature had almost finished its work. Garry joined five others to introduce a bill that removed doves from the migratory game list, and his fish and game committee offered several bills, all defeated except an increase in resident license fees. He advocated legalizing interracial marriages, a cause sponsored by the Japanese American Citizens League, and he offered a bill (drafted for him by Higer) to require restaurants to serve minority patrons. But when the restaurant bill failed, he confided to a constituent that he "had never taken this problem too seriously." Garry voted for an unsuccessful proposal by Higer to limit primary runoff voting, supported county option for parimutuel betting—which the governor vetoed—and again opposed antilabor legislation.

He had been present for most of the session, slipping away for a few days to move Leona and Cubby from Spokane back to Plummer, and to chair Coeur d'Alene tribal council meetings. He spent a day arranging loans with a finance company for travel and living expenses. One day he drove to Twin Falls to speak before the Federation of Women's Clubs there. When they adjourned four days beyond the session's limit, the legislators had raised income-tax rates (Idaho's main source of revenue) and imposed a surtax on tax returns. Garry voted for both.[26]

Four days after adjournment, Garry took the "red-eye" night flight to Washington to attend the NCAI executive council meeting. Then he was off to New York to appear on television with Dave Garroway, a popular broadcaster. Back in Washington, he closeted himself with Sen. Frank Church, and the two were photographed together in front of a statue of Charlie Russell, the cowboy artist. Garry's calendar was full of NCAI business.

7 Toward a Victory of Sorts

October 28, 1957: More than 200 delegates from eighty-six tribes crowded into Claremore over the weekend before the fourteenth annual convention of the National Congress of American Indians. They found the resort town of 6,000, site of an old Cherokee trading post, awash with visitors, hotels and boardinghouses crammed, and knots of men and women hailing old friends on Main Street.

In a holiday mood, Oklahoma celebrated the fiftieth anniversary of statehood. Banners flapped in the streets. Will Rogers Day—commemorating the late cowboy humorist's birthday with parading bands, wild-buffalo and mule riding and roping, and a barbecue for a thousand—would follow the convention. The eighth annual All-Oklahoma Hereford Show opened at the fairgrounds on the last day of Indian sessions. And there were mineral baths, an Indian hospital, and a gun museum to see. Delegates were invited to take them all in before turning for home.

The convention started with a short procession along Main—delegates bearing placards with the names of their tribes—to the Oklahoma Military Academy auditorium, where general sessions met. Next to the academy stood the Will Rogers Memorial, which includes a heroic bronze statue of Rogers and a museum. On this Monday morning, after a chilly weekend, the weather warmed enough for marchers to shed topcoats. A newspaper reporter who expected Indians in blankets, with hair braided, saw instead Indian men wearing business suits and woman delegates comprising "a neatly dressed group such as one might meet at any convention." The *Tulsa Tribune* pictured Joe Garry and Helen Peterson on its front page.[1]

Garry's presidential address struck at House Concurrent Resolution 108 and legislation resulting from it. The crowd listened respectfully, for they knew how far the NCAI had progressed under his leadership. With his trademark gleaming white shirt, and with his hair now graying, Garry showed a little paunch from banquet meals. The president called on delegates to resist termination and preserve Indian landholdings: "I think to retain our identity as Indian people, we should hold onto everything we have, to every square inch of land that we still hold. That's one of the surest ways, I think, to retain or continue our identity and to eventually achieve some of the goals that we are fighting for."[2]

He implored delegates to support the NCAI financially: "When I come around asking you for measly dues, maybe a hundred and twenty-five dollars a year, you're afraid because your tribe is going to criticize you—spending money foolishly. Stand up and tell them the NCAI is the organization. . . . We need that office open in Washington. We need our lobbying groups. We need attorneys. . . . NCAI is your salvation. . . . We want to build the greatest NCAI ever in the next twelve months!"

Garry served on the altar the following morning at a Roman Catholic Mass celebrated by the bishop of Oklahoma City. Women of Christ the King Church served breakfast. (Later in the week, delegates breakfasted with the National Indian Committee of the Boy Scouts and the ladies of the Methodist church.)

Then delegates heard Paschal Sherman and Helen Peterson report on the state of the NCAI. Peterson reiterated Garry's appeal for financial support, and summed up congressional actions with her impressions: "A significant and increasing number of members of Congress were very firm in insisting on the consent principle and in acting on legislation in such a way as to protect the best interests of the Indians." While that trend was encouraging, there had been no action on any major Indian bills in the first session of the Eighty-fifth Congress.

Congress was mucking through a periodic pruning of government costs, Peterson pointed out. The NCAI had written to the House Indian Subcommittee to ask that members of Congress "concentrate on certain bills requiring no appropriations" and act on tribal requests to return Indian lands.[3]

The evening before, Congressman Ed Edmonson of Oklahoma had spoken on federal Indian policy as the convention keynoter. Now, when Sherman's turn came, he was fiery: "We want the Indian to cease being policy. We want him to be accepted as a person with rights to life, liberty, and the pursuit of happiness like anyone else.

"This may sound fundamental, quite obvious to everyone, but it is in fundamentals that the Indian has been misgoverned for a century and a half!" The slender Colville's earnest manner betrayed how hard he had worked for the NCAI since its founding.

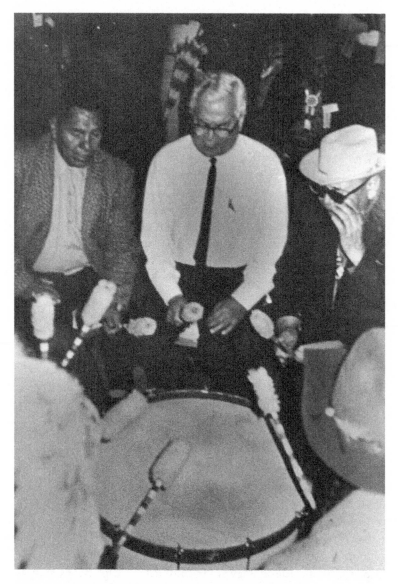

Garry drumming after the business session of a National Congress of American Indians convention. (Arlene Owen family collection)

"We like to think of the NCAI as an encampment of Indian tribes, in a circle of tipis, for a historical purpose," Sherman went on: "Our meeting here at Claremore is faced with issues which, while not of war or peace, threaten our very existence as a distinct ethnic group. . . . The policy for termination . . . and the laxity of government attention to Indian health, to Indian education, and to Indian rehabilitation in home communities are far-reaching in their destructive effects. These are among the burning issues on which we must take our stand!"[4]

With Sherman's challenge to ponder, delegates bussed fifty miles north to the noted Woolaroc ranch near Bartlesville for a picnic hosted by William W. Keeler, principal chief of the Cherokee nation, and Phillips Oil Company. On the border of the Osage nation, near the place where oil was discovered in Oklahoma, Woolaroc had become more museum than ranch, with western paintings and sculpture on display and pioneer and Indian artifacts on the grounds.

There the crowd listened to Glenn Emmons, Commissioner of Indian Affairs — aware of his doubting audience — deliver a wary "progress report" on the Indian Service. Emmons touched on none of Paschal Sherman's burning issues, but noted that more Indians now went to school, that Indian health had improved, and that the bureau had launched adult vocational programs and encouraged industry to locate near reservations to hire Indians. Nonetheless, he offered the bureau's dispiriting opinion: "We have to face the fact that the population on most reservations . . . has already outgrown the resource base and is getting bigger all the time."[5]

The Indians noted that, besides Emmons and Edmonson, who did not linger, no one from Congress or the Bureau of Indian Affairs observed or took part in convention sessions. All the members of the Fund for the Republic's new Commission on the Rights, Liberties, and Responsibilities of the American Indian attended. Wheaton College, the National Council of Churches, the Indian Rights Association, the Association on American Indian Affairs, the Boy Scouts of America, and others sent emissaries. And Gardner Jackson, a trustee of the Marshall Trust, and Sol Tax, chair of the Department of Anthropology at the University of Chicago, were there. Tax joined Garry and the noted psychiatrist Karl Menninger in a panel on the future of Indian policy.

"I want to speak very frankly," Tax told his listeners. "The present Indian policy of the United States Government is bad. I shall also say that the policy of the National Congress of American Indians as presented in the resolutions of last year is infinitely better." [6]

Leona Garry, registered as a delegate of the Kalispels and more and more stepping out of her husband's shadow, was a panelist for Sherman's session on NCAI finances. She had asserted herself in Democratic party and tribal politics, and now she carved her nitch in the National Congress of American Indians. During the closing ceremony, she was awarded a concho belt "for her work in behalf of the organization."

The "infinitely better" NCAI policy (to which Tax referred) resounded as the first of sixty-one resolutions passed in the last two days of the convention. Two days remained for resolutions, committee and tribal reports, and elections. The policy statement (for that is what the resolution amounted to) called for each tribe to prepare a plan for using its resources, for federal appropriations to assist tribes in carrying out their plans, for Indian input and agreement to federal or state decisions affecting them, for an information system to notify tribes of pending legislation, and for "a concentrated effort . . . to retain, rather than dispose of, Indian lands" as economic units. [7]

Resolution one demonstrated a maturing of the NCAI's agenda from the tumult of the emergency conference of 1954. It no longer merely resisted; it offered its own alternatives, as Garry intended. Helen Peterson pointed out that the NCAI now put forth its own positive program of "what most responsible Indian leaders want the government to do . . . a sincere attempt on our part to spell out to Congress a constructive policy to supersede the termination policy." [8]

The NCAI was also saying that its people wanted to continue to be Indians. As Garry phrased this resolve, "Retaining the lands means keeping our tribes together. I'm not against integration, but I do not believe we should have legislation to force integration. If we are going to have integration with the rest of the population of this country it should come natural and it should come gradual."

Of course, many resolutions opposed pending bills or called on the government to do what it had promised to do. One pleaded for an extended moratorium on the sale of Indian trust (or restricted) lands, for regulations giving the tribes first right to buy, and for federal funds to assist tribes in land purchases. Another urged the government to live up to a restriction on the sale of Crow reservation lands under the 1920 Crow allotment

Senator Frank Church of Idaho presents the prize-winning Garry portrait to Helen Peterson and Garry. The picture, by Virgil Parker of Boise, was adapted for the NCAI letterhead. (*Spokesman-Review*, May 25, 1957)

act. Others asked for more money for Indian health services and education, and for confirmation of Indian water rights and title to tidelands or submerged lands adjacent to reservations.

Eighteen resolutions expressed NCAI support for specific tribal concerns: For example, neglected Washington state tribes wanted rural electric services extended to them. Furthermore, the NCAI reiterated its opposition to the Colville contract to pay counties in lieu of taxes, and it protested the state's intention to tax the Yakimas' per-capita compensation for lost fishing rights on the Columbia River as a result of the building of

The Dalles Dam. One resolution reminded delegates that the Marshall Trust would reduce its matching funds and urged tribes to vote higher dues and donations to the NCAI.

In the deliberations the *New York Times* saw "a wistful quality. . . . Many of the Indian protests were offered with the defeated air of a batter already called out on strikes." It described the convention as "a modern day council of war. . . . As they once did when they camped in teepees instead of hotels, the Indians felt they were fighting for preservation. Instead of bows, they brought lawyers. Instead of arrows, they fired resolutions." This was more attention than news media had given the NCAI in the past. A number of newspapers sent reporters, and so did *Time* magazine. The NCAI had finally moved beyond two inches of type dropped among movie ads on an inside page.[9]

Joe Garry was reelected president for a fifth term. A Southwest cabal proposed Clarence Wesley for the post, and a noisy faction backed Walter "Blackie" Wetzel, Blackfeet chairman, who openly grumbled that Garry's views carried too much weight. That was an objection to which Garry disdained a response; he was patient with dissenters.

At the close of the meeting, William W. Short tearfully accepted an Indian blanket as a symbol of appreciation for his service as the second president of the NCAI. His friends joked that he received it "in Indian time—four years after his retirement from office."

Convention adjourned, the National Congress of American Indians went back to the daily business of lobbying. The bureau, meanwhile, continued selling lands needed for an Indian economic base and expanding its program to relocate individual Indian families in cities, a policy Garry condemned as termination in another guise.

The federal Department of Justice conducted a baleful campaign of misinformation: It alleged that the Indian Court of Claims threatened 70 percent of the nation's land, and that Indian compensation for lost aboriginal territories would amount to "a staggering total of several billions of dollars." Oliver La Farge, president of the Association on American Indian Affairs, retorted that the Justice Department "had been lobbying . . . to frighten members of Congress about the 'immense problem' and the vast sum . . . which the Indians might collect." John Cragun caught a rumor that Justice Department officials had approached members of Congress to support a ban on all claims based on aboriginal occupancy. La Farge declared that the Feds "fought hard" against Indian claims, but the Justice Department, in fact, delayed its effort, failing to assign enough government attorneys for an expeditious hearing schedule.[10]

An article in *Reader's Digest* magazine, entitled "Must We Buy America from the Indians All Over Again?" spread the Justice Department's fabrications: The article, echoing Ralph A. Barney, chief of the Indian claims section of the Department of Justice, alleged that Indians, hiring adroit lawyers to press their claims, would collect "fantastic" sums for lands the nation had already paid for. The polemic also called for a new look at the Indian Claims Commission, which Congress had studied carefully only two years earlier.

The National Congress of American Indians had been a leader among those calling for extending the commission's life until all legitimate claims were adjudicated. Hoping to offset any damage to public opinion from the *Reader's Digest* article, Helen Peterson distributed reprints of newspapers and magazines rebutting the article's distortions, including an editorial in Harold Fey's *Christian Century:* "Is it any wonder that Indians and the growing number of other citizens who are coming to understand their problems are concerned over what new direction injustice may take when the magazine with the largest circulation of any American periodical speaks in this way?"[11]

In his annual report for the Association on American Indian Affairs, La Farge departed from his usual review to decry "the assault now being carried on against Indians by our federal government. . . . In a bitter, shocking example of man's inhumanity to man, the 'Indian problem' is to be erased by liquidating the Indians."

La Farge offered examples. The northern Cheyennes of Montana, he said, had spent tribal money to keep their lands intact by buying allotments offered for sale. While their funds were tied up by audit, 10,000 key acres in the heart of the reservation came up for sale. The tribe petitioned for postponement until they could bid, but their request was ignored. The bureau rationalized that the tribe was not using the land before the sale, and if they weren't using it, they didn't need it.

When the Blackfeet of Montana and the Midwestern Intertribal Council of North and South Dakota and Nebraska protested land sales, the Department of the Interior refused to halt them, setting the right of individuals to sell above tribal exigency. "We have the case of a poor old Blackfeet woman whose land was sold for her," La Farge recounted. "She was then persuaded to spend the greater part of what she received . . . for an automobile. She cannot drive it. To date she has not even got to ride in it. She continues in her poverty."

La Farge branded these sales as "creeping termination," concluding: "Indians and non-Indians must join in insisting that Congress cancel that declaration of policy [House Concurrent Resolution 108] by adopting, instead, Senate Concurrent Resolution 3, with its positive, constructive policy, and back it with sound, working legislation to solve the Indian land problem."[12]

Publicity had been hit or miss for the National Congess of American Indians, mostly a limited circulation of reprints when Peterson had time and money to mail them; but in the face of persistent canards, Garry, Peterson, and the executive committee agreed that a systematic public-relations program was imperative. A former newspaperman, James H. Hayes, had handled press relations for a time as an intermittently paid staff member, but he had gone to Arizona as business manager of Hualapi enterprises. (In starting a cooperative association for Maricopas in New Mexico, Hayes would soon go on to the hard physical labor of clearing land for farming.)

As usual, the stumbling block was money. Helen Peterson set about writing a grant proposal to the Marshall Trust and other foundations for support of an information and education program, a "broad and sustained public information campaign." Tribal public relations committees and an Indian press association would be organized. The NCAI would contract with a professional public-relations firm, Sontheimer-Runkle, which represented the Commonwealth of Puerto Rico in the United States, and Jim Hayes would eventually come back. In the first year the project would cost an estimated $24,000.[13]

To Garry and Peterson, it also seemed imperative that the NCAI stage another splash like the emergency meeting of 1954 to draw new attention to Indians. An on-site study of Puerto Rico's dazzling economic transformation—"Operation Bootstrap"—appealed to them as a potential catalyst for American Indians. (Perhaps Puerto Rico was suggested by the professional publicists who, without charge, occasionally counseled Peterson.) Expense money for the public-relations junket was donated by the Association on American Indian Affairs, the Indian Rights Association, and the Phelps Stokes Fund. The trip would be publicized as a case study for American Indian tribes striving to improve the economy, health, and education of their people—an inspiration for the NCAI's Point Nine program.[14]

In Helen Peterson's words, the tour was "possibly the most timely, worthwhile, meaningful, promising activity that could be planned at this time to bear on several of the most pressing problems of the Indian people, not the least of which is their frustration, discouragement, and need for how-to-do-it ideas. Indians, at this time, are in need of a 'shot in the arm'—I can think of no better way to bring this about."[15]

The Association on American Indian Affairs, in signing on for the excursion, advised Peterson: "It so happens that we have been thinking of asking Mr. Joseph Garry, NCAI president, to spend some time consulting with us on program development. . . . He would consult with us either before or after the tour." The association would pay Garry's way.[16]

The Puerto Rico excursion would be timed to end with a report to the NCAI's executive committee, who were not all enthused about it. Garry, Wetzel, and James Frechette (Menominee) endorsed it; C. C. Victory (Cherokee) remarked that it would be a wasted effort "for the reason that no matter what we learn, I do not think our recommendation would be followed"; Robert Burnette approved on condition that no NCAI funds were used; and three—including Frank George—did not comment. But with Garry and Peterson behind it, and with contributed funding, the trip was scheduled.[17]

Puerto Rico, indeed, offered a dramatic paradigm of progress, "a tribute to both American generosity and to Puerto Rican gumption," as a *Washington Post* writer phrased it. The commonwealth had become "a magnet for curious visitors from 99 different countries and territories . . . to see whether what the Puerto Ricans have done cannot help them in the development of their own homelands. Often it can." Ironically, Puerto Rico's development nest egg had come from excise taxes on rum sales during World War II.[18]

After the war, densely populated Puerto Rico fostered an economy based on diversified manufacturing, with the United States providing technical assistance and tax exemptions for investors. By 1957, 450 factories had sprouted, employing more than 40,000. Manufacturing overtook agriculture in volume of income. Average family income rose from $660 to $2,400 (still far below the poorest levels in the United States). A middle class emerged. Medical expansion cut Puerto Rico's death rate in half and extended life expectancy. Education and housing made parallel strides.[19]

Newsweek magazine was enchanted by Puerto Rico's low-cost housing: "A mutual-aid plan provides building materials and an experienced foreman, all for $300 [the builder paid it off over ten to twenty years]. The man who is going to live in the house must provide most of the labor." There were, in fact, only about 3,700 such houses on the island. Public housing sheltered thousands more at low rents based on income.[20]

And so a delegation of fourteen, headed by Garry and Peterson, was off for a speedy inspection. Tribes sent their own observers: In the party were Frank Walker (White Mountain Apache), Allen Quetone (Kiowa), Walter Vorhees (Confederated Tribes of Nevada), and Clarence Wesley (San Carlos Apache), among others. The *New York Times* pictured the delegation, with the Empire State Building in the background. Garry, "a 47-year-old smiling Coeur d'Alene," wore an Indian feathered bonnet.

The touring party gathered in New York City at the Sheraton-McAlpin Hotel, and the next day sat for introductions and a talk by Clarence Senior, of the Puerto Rico department of labor, who was in charge of the tour. Then they boarded a night coach for an eight-hour red-eye flight to San Juan, Puerto Rico's capital, where they slept until midafternoon. They were roused for a guided tour of the palm-lined streets and a greeting by Gov. Luis Munoz Marin, pictured in Indian headdress with Garry on the front page of *El Mundo*.[21]

On Wednesday, their first full day of inspecting, the NCAI party toured industrial plants near the capital and visited the economic-development office for interviews and mimeographed data. Obviously their tour took them to showplaces to chat with Puerto Ricans accustomed to visitors. The next day they saw canneries and farms, and they bussed along the island's northern shore, to Arecibo, to look at low-cost private housing and talk with homeowners (often through a government interpreter who accompanied the Indians). Then, the party returned to San Juan for a cocktail party with participants in a teacher-development workshop for Central American educators.

Friday they saw a large public-housing project in nearby San Jose, inspected Rio Piedros vocational school, and passed a formal hour with the woman mayor of San Juan. Garry slipped away long enough to spend $46.85 on Puerto Rican clothing for Leona and Cubby.[22]

The touring Indians saw for themselves Puerto Rico's crowding (pop-ulation density twelve times that of the United States), and by contrast the mountains and streams of Garry's Coeur d'Alene reservation seemed spacious, indeed. They saw, too, that women continued to be restricted in public by the old customs of male priority. Garry traded impressions with visitors from other countries: To one, he wrote in the margin of a housing authority press release, "Are you Catholic?" then, after a nod, wrote "So am I." Despite the commonwealth's progress, the tourists learned that Puerto Ricans continued to migrate to the United States seeking work, because their island offered too few jobs.

By the end of their lively week, the NCAI visitors had also spent a day with the community-development office, and had separated into pairs to sit in on community meetings. They were excited by leaders who read "prac-tical books on practical problems" to resident groups each evening, and charmed by the university chancellor's candid remark that devising an edu-cational system amounted to "creative fumbling." The island's informa-tion system of bulletins, large-type how-to books, and instructional films impressed them. Even lowly citizens seemed informed about current events in Puerto Rico.

The Puerto Rican news service distributed press releases daily about the touring Indians. And the island's English-language newspaper noted their stay, reporting that Garry's Indian name meant "Son of the Sun." By Monday a tired band of inquirers was en route by air to Washington, D.C., to report to the NCAI executive committee.[23]

So what had they learned? This, of course, was the first question from the committee members. They had seen "all kinds of efforts to improve housing, education, health, industrial development, and community rela-tions . . . and there has probably been more success in a shorter length of time than in any area in the world," replied Helen Peterson. John Rainer spoke up: He felt that those who took the trip "came back feeling more humble, more eager to serve their people." In Puerto Rico, he said, there "is an atmosphere of faith and trust among the people . . . especially in the community meetings."[24]

But these were first impressions. On reflection, the lesson of Puerto Rico seemed to be that, with planning and capital, many Indian tribes could improve the lives of their people. The tour sharpened the perception that Indians needed to be free of the fusty paternalism of the Bureau of Indian

Affairs. If the Puerto Rican jaunt had not produced a publicity splash for the American public, it had caught the interest of tribal councils. Robert Burnette summed up, "Motivation! It is needed on reservations; it is the key to everything."

Puerto Rico's handling of its scarce land suggested a model for tribal councils: The commonwealth limited the acreage anyone could hold, redistributed land among families, and set aside land for business, leasing it to private operators. By redistributing lands, "families, by the thousands, have been moved out of unspeakable slums onto half-acre tracts with sanitary, decent houses."

The committee moved on to the continuing sales of individual lands by American Indians, agreeing that tribes needed capital and experienced management for land programs. Burnette outlined the Rosebud Sioux enterprise under which the tribe took over tracts when the number of heirs reached fifty, and issued share certificates to their owners for purchase of other tracts with fewer heirs.

While reports of the Puerto Rican tour occupied the first day of the meeting, the discussion inevitably moved to finance. Garry justified tribal support of the NCAI by a brief reprise of what it had done. The minutes of the executive committee, at this point, read: "President Garry spoke with a great deal of feeling on what NCAI means and does and emphasized that it protects what you have (your property), your pride (whatever of it you have left), your rights (including claims)."[25]

Gardner Jackson, a trustee of the Marshall Trust (and a Washington, D.C., resident) who attended the meeting, "spoke on the great importance of NCAI and his hope that it could be adequately financed and staffed." But Jackson warned privately that the trust would not continue grants to the congress if NCAI members did not provide its major support. He would repeat his warning in a telegram to Garry later in the year: "Please tell your fellow officers and council members that they must get their tribes to give greater support to NCAI if my fellow trustees are to continue their backing much longer. I know you feel as strongly as I do that NCAI provides the best instrument for the Indians to attain fair treatment."[26]

The committee adjourned briefly to troop to a congressional hearing on a bill to preserve boundaries of Indian reservations and deter trespassing. Frank George testified on behalf of the Affiliated Tribes. Garry, whom the congressional committee members knew, spoke in favor of the bill and introduced his group. Then they went back to struggling with financial realities—how to raise money.

A fiscal subcommittee headed by Paschal Sherman had disbanded, and Garry appointed Forrest Gerard (Blackfeet) as temporary chair of a new one. (Gerard had taken the post of tribal affairs officer for the Indian division of the Public Health Service a few months earlier.) The group adjourned. They had not solved their money dilemma, for there still was not enough anticipated income to cover the costs outlined on the yellow sheet—their projected budget—that passed among them.[27]

Helen Peterson mounted her own campaign to raise money. She sent, over Garry's stamped signature, more than 2,000 form letters to anthropologists urging their support of the NCAI; and she composed a form letter for 400 locals of the International Union of Electrical, Mechanical and Radio Workers. The Washington headquarters of the union had contributed $500, and three locals had also given funds.

"With two years of sustained financial help from all the locals," she wrote, "we could expand our staff in a way . . . that is essential if whole Indian tribes and communities are not to be wiped out in the next few years, and new ghettos of Indians added to city slums." She asked each local to pledge only twenty-five dollars a year. But the letter was never sent out: The union resisted canvassing its locals. And few anthropologists responded.[28]

Garry appealed to the Crow tribal council to raise its dues to the NCAI by $1,000 when the tribe received title to 10,260 acres restored by Congress, reminding them that the "NCAI had a very large hand in this restoration." Garry wrote: "In foreign countries where I served in the army, like Japan, I have seen how precious every inch of land is. . . . We put the land restoration bill ahead of nearly everything else on our legislative concerns." Similar letters would go out to other tribes who had benefited from the NCAI's lobbying.[29]

The restoration bill, which the NCAI *Bulletin* termed the "NCAI land restoration bill," returned approximately 70,200 acres to five tribes, lands ceded many years earlier but never homesteaded or sold. (NCAI convention resolutions since 1955 had called for restoration.) In addition to the land returned to the Crows, titles to land previously owned by the tribes were restored to Fort Peck, Klamath River (California), Garry's own Coeur d'Alene, and Spokane tribes.[30]

The restoration stood as a modest victory for the National Congress of

American Indians—one of the few scraps of pro-Indian legislation so far in that session. Congress in 1958 showed little disposition to press tribes for termination, and even less to help Indians. In the muggy heat of May and July, Garry testified twice at hearings on federal Indian policy, conveying his message that Indians wanted to manage their own affairs.

In his testimony the previous year before the Senate Committee on Interior and Insular Affairs, Garry emphasized the pernicious effects of House Resolution 108, which, he said, "created confusion, chaos, unrest, and fear" among Indian peoples. Now the House committee asked for detailed reports from the field on Indian relations with the federal government, and for profiles of Indian advocacy organizations.[31]

In his letter transmitting the National Congress of American Indians' response, Garry pointed out again that "our organization is the only one of Indian tribes and Indian individuals exclusively on a national basis; while we have a very few non-Indian associate members, they have no voice or vote in the organization." He went on: "In its relations with Congress," the NCAI "strives to maintain an organizational reputation that Members of Congress can trust."

Garry offered a report prepared by Peterson. Among the NCAI's accomplishments, it noted efforts to assist Colorado, Arizona, and South Dakota Indians in asserting water rights; aid to Indians in Arizona, New Mexico, Idaho, and South Dakota in registering to vote; vigorous lobbying to extend the life of the Indian Claims Commission; and other activities. Approximately thirty tribes paid dues to the NCAI, and a number of others made financial contributions. "Many more tribes than the dues-paying members," Garry's report said, "use the organization as though they were members."[32]

Garry's appearance before the committee was only one of many obligations that drove him; he was sprinting to keep up with his varied offices. In his role as chairman of the Coeur d'Alenes, he had learned late in December that the government might negotiate the tribe's award from the Indian Claims Commission, a development that would require conferences with attorneys and votes by the tribe. These took time.

In another role, as president of the Affiliated Tribes of Northwest Indians, Garry made last-minute preparations for the group's annual convention, which he hoped would sound a battle cry for Senate Concurrent Resolution 3. To Forrest Gerard he wrote: "We have decided to call this meeting earlier than usual this year with the hope of mustering greater support and pressure to make possible the passage of Senate Concurrent Resolution 3 . . . together with the idea of setting the stage for the National Congress of American Indians convention." [33]

Garry simultaneously campaigned for reelection to the Idaho house of representatives, trying to snatch a day here and another there to appear and speak in the towns of Benewah County. He squeezed in a dinner address to the Idaho State College Institute of Government. And as president of the NCAI, he was cajoled by Peterson (who could be insistent) to appoint committee chairmen and solicit speakers for the NCAI convention. [34]

Garry's call to the Affiliated Tribes convention, which like the NCAI meeting would be in Missoula, Montana, urged "every Indian in the Northwest to attend. . . . You will hear an objective analysis of what is going on. We operate a dedicated and unremitting campaign of persuasion to point out to the Congress of the United States and the Public in general what is good for us and what is bad for us."

Three days of discussion concerned largely Northwest topics. In resolutions the tribes commended the Fort Peck tribes who bought food for destitute Rocky Boy Indians, and they challenged the authority of the Colville business council to pay taxes to counties or to proceed with termination. The Colville resolution underscored the influence of Frank George in the Affiliated Tribes. The delegates reaffirmed their opposition to House Resolution 108, and their support of Senate Concurrent Resolution 3, as Garry intended. Every Indian in the Northwest did not attend, of course; neither did the convention attract wide public notice. But it did put the eminent Affiliated Tribes solidly behind Garry's agenda for the NCAI.

In the weeks after the meeting, Walter McDonald, Flathead chairman, lobbied the Montana delegation in Congress. He became convinced that not much could be done quickly on Senate Concurrent Resolution 3, and he was told that if it got to the Senate or House floor, "it would be butchered up so badly that it would not be of much value to Indians." McDonald added: "Tell the tribes we all have to pray that next session of Congress there will be a change of attitude." [35]

But Sister Providencia thought the Affiliated Tribes conclave went well. "Still a-glow over the good meeting," she wrote Garry. And when Walter "Blackie" Wetzel, whom Joe had named general chairman for the coming NCAI convention, asked for her help with the program, she offered the theme "The Federal Indian." She had been impressed by Rep. E. Y. Berry's recent speech at the Institute of Indian Studies at Vermillion, South Dakota, in which he described the Indian predicament: "A home land which is both part of the United States and *not* a part of the United States. A home land which makes him [the Indian] both a citizen and a quasi-foreigner. A home land having the right of self government and yet lacking in authority to make that government effective. . . . A home land which is neither fish nor fowl, which he cannot understand and others cannot comprehend. A home land situated in the heart of a free nation, founded upon the rights of the individual but which is shackled and bound by bureaucratic regulations and control."[36]

The nun sent Garry a typescript with a letter: "Here is the basis for your convention speech—by the opposition itself, Congressman Berry!"[37] Her suggestion was timely, with the House and Senate both deliberating federal Indian policy. Wetzel adopted Sister Providencia's idea enthusiastically. The notion of emphasizing the special status of Indian peoples struck him as promising a clearer understanding of Indian legislation and administration. He had thought for some time that Indians spun their wheels when they criticized congressional actions without stressing their special condition, and he persuaded himself that Garry neglected the political reality of Indian status. Wetzel also considered the advantage to his own ambitions of introducing a new motif for the NCAI. It could be his platform in a run for the presidency.

Garry had called the Affiliated Tribes convention early to kick off a new drive for Senate Concurrent Resolution 3, and he had set the NCAI meeting for September to avoid conflict with the national elections. The compressed schedule made for a busy summer. He was in and out of Washington often, and when he was out, Peterson sent Leona urgent messages to track him down.

The NCAI office was crowded with visiting delegations. A Klamath team missed Garry when they came to the capital hoping to convince Congress to extend the deadline for termination or to repeal it altogether, questioning both the fiscal prospects of termination and voting within the tribe. The delegation alleged that about a hundred votes were cast for people who were dead, and they complained of the sales tactics of government management specialists advising the Klamaths.

The Senate Committee on Appropriations recommended an increase

Opening the Missoula National Congress of American Indians convention. Left to right: John Rainer, Joe Garry, Leo Vocu (Oglala Pine Ridge), and Lester Oliver (White Mountain Apache). (From NCAI's *Pictorial Highlights*)

in Indian health funding that fell below Congress's own estimates of the cost of an effective program. Garry and Peterson lobbied the committee chair jointly, urging a "level of operation required to deal effectively with Indian health problems." No amendment. It was hard to sway members of Congress on a downhill rush to adjournment.

Garry was in Spokane on August 12 to ride as grand marshall of the city's Diamond Spur Rodeo parade, wearing Indian regalia, and he stayed to lead the nightly grand entry of rodeo contestants. A conspicuous role in a Northwest event a few weeks before election day seemed useful. The rodeo was publicized in newspapers and on television stations that reached Idaho voters.

Garry had gone back to Washington by early September when President Eisenhower vetoed the area-redevelopment bill, a bipartisan make-work and training bill, which the NCAI hoped might create jobs for Indians. Garry had spoken in favor of the legislation at a Senate committee hearing: "A bill of this kind in which the Indian reservations would be included would do much to relieve many bad conditions now existing on many Indian reservations. . . . Poverty and want created by unemployment has forced many Indians to sell their lands." Garry had also telegraphed the president urging passage. A special counsel to the president sent Joe a copy of the president's memo of disapproval from the White House.[38]

Garry was still in the capital when he received a rousing letter from Sister Providencia, with her favorite salutation: "Joseph Butterfly Garry— flitting around helping everybody! You sit down and write the speech of your life on the federal Indian. This is the moment to run with the ball. . . . Don't let any picnics or dances fritter away the time of advantage. I really feel that the Indians are at the point of initiative now. . . . The worm is turning. This is the high point of your career. Don't muff it for lack of preparation!"[39]

Garry was still in Washington four days before the opening of the 1958 convention in Missoula, telling reporters that although recent Congresses had not imposed termination on any tribes, Indians were under "heavy administrative and psychological pressure" to end wardship. The NCAI convention, he said, would consider "the urgent need for a redefinition of United States Indian policy."[40]

Garry's call to the convention: "We must think through our problems together. We must plan jointly. . . . We must speak with a strong, united voice." The NCAI is growing in strength, prestige, and effectiveness, he added, but "it needs the best thinking and planning and work of all of us."

Approximately 200 delegates from twenty states came to Missoula's aging Florence Hotel. They opened with a traditional procession through the streets. This fifteenth annual convention, advertised as a federal-bashing festival, would have a surprise climax. It opened as expected: Montana congressman Lee Metcalf, in his keynote address, charged that the Bureau of Indian Affairs applied "duress, blackmail and pressure" to force tribes into termination, and he forecast that Congress would reverse House Concurrent Resolution 108 in its next session.[41]

In his presidential speech, Garry again attacked House Concurrent

Resolution 108 as coming "nearest to spelling disaster for us than any other legislation in our nation's history." If Indians were consulted on bills and policies affecting them, and mutual confidence established, "we could then toss out of the window all out of date arbitrary regulations . . . and the much talked about integration would be but a natural event." Go home, he urged his audience, with a resolve to overturn the termination policy in the next Congress. Plan a tribal program of self-help. Remember that we need one another. "We can and we will win our point."[42]

While the convention was in session, Secretary of the Interior Fred Seaton, talking with tribal leaders of the Southwest, broadcast a statement of his policies on Arizona and New Mexico radio stations. The assistant secretary, Roger L. Ernst, read part of Seaton's statement to the NCAI delegates at their closing banquet: "My own position is this," Seaton declared: "No Indian tribe or group should end its relationship with the federal government unless such tribe . . . understands the plan . . . and concurs in and supports the plan proposed. . . . It is absolutely unthinkable to me as your Secretary of the Interior that consideration would be given to forcing upon an Indian tribe a so-called termination plan which did not have the understanding and acceptance of a clear majority of the members affected."

Ernst did not quote all of Seaton's policy statement, which continued: "Under no circumstances could I bring myself to recommend the termination of the Federal relationship with any tribe in this country until the members of the tribe have been given the opportunity of a sound and effective education."[43]

Seaton's message electrified the NCAI. "This is an historic occasion," declared Garry. "[It] could reverse the trend of headlong termination . . . by administrative action."[44] It was a victory of sorts.

8 The Garry Era Ends

*H*olding the Missoula convention in September put the National Congress of American Indians on record before the 1958 elections in November, and the early date also gave Joe Garry and his executive council a little more planning time before the next annual meeting. The council earnestly discussed changing the convention program structure—perhaps dividing delegates into working groups—to give everyone a chance to be heard.

"The main criticism of previous convention programs seems to be that there is not enough opportunity for participation by enough people," Helen Peterson advised the planners. "I have opposed dividing the convention into groups because a considerable number of people have opposed this. But the number who are asking for more participation by all delegates is growing each year, and it seems clear now that the overwhelming sentiment is for some such arrangement as this." [1]

Planning a convention had to be crammed into Garry's and Peterson's schedule. There was so much to be done. The National Congress of American Indians foundered in its success. Tribal lobbyists crowded its offices; they flocked to Washington to speak out at hearings on Indian bills; they expected Peterson to shepherd them to their congressional representatives and guide them through the warrens of government offices. "NCAI became the central headquarters and the work place" for tribal delegations, Peterson would remember later. "Our role was mainly helping them prepare their testimony, getting them to the Hill, getting them around, finding information, producing their testimony—getting it in writing and making copies." [2]

Major tribes—Navajos and Yakimas among them—had not joined, but Indians showed up at the NCAI offices whether their tribes were members or not. (Even some Indians appeared from tribes unrecognized by Congress.) The executive council debated whether to serve them.

Allen Slickpoo, a Nez Perce, argued that Peterson "should not help nonmember tribes—if all tribes were helped, there would be no need to join and pay dues." Yet some tribes, the council knew, were too poor to pay. Paschal Sherman suggested that the council leave the decision to help nonmembers to Peterson, to "her discretion in coming to the aid of a non-member tribe where the question involved may be of paramount importance to all tribes." John Rainer proposed "working with non-member tribes to make them want to join NCAI."[3]

They agreed at last to leave the choice to Peterson. But the debate epitomized the evolution of the NCAI under the Garry-Peterson regime: Five years earlier the NCAI had seemed to be made up largely of Oklahoma politicians angling to curb a Congress bent on shedding Indians. In Garry's years it had ripened from opposing to proposing: It proclaimed its own agenda for Indian people, and Senator James Murray adopted the Indian program as Senate Concurrent Resolution 3. The National Congress of American Indians had courted advocates in Congress, and bits of its program turned up as "NCAI bills." There was no question that now the NCAI was the agent that most nearly spoke for all Indians in the United States.

How much strength Indians showed at the polls remained a question. Peterson attempted to measure Indian voting for an article in a scholarly journal. The government estimated about 143,000 Indians of voting age. Helen could only surmise that "in some districts and in close races the Indian vote could be . . . a decisive factor." She speculated that Indian ballots "could have" swung an election for Montana's Murray, who won by a margin of 1,728 votes, and "might" have elected Idaho's Frank Church, who ran only 170 votes ahead in his 1956 primary race.[4] (Indians would have been delighted to think they contributed to the defeat, in 1958, of Sen. Arthur Watkins, who, ironically, was appointed to the Indian Claims Commission.)

But without reliable statistics on Indian voting, Peterson's article dealt mostly with process. "The greatest factor in getting Indians to the polls has been the development and growth of their own organizations, tribal and intertribal, and finally the National Congress of American Indians," she wrote. "These groups have been able to interpret the issues confronting Indians, to offer information about candidates, and to explain the mechanics of voting."

Within the NCAI, Garry, in an effort to close the gate against non-reservation Indians, had pushed through an amendment to the constitution requiring delegates to conventions and nominees for committees to be credentialed by their tribes. Yet free lances, who were difficult to squelch without appearing to discriminate, showed up each year, wanting to be heard. In his presidential address of 1958, Garry reminded his listeners that "we must discipline ourselves so that we shall never undermine each other. Remember, the common enemy is outside—not within our organization."[5]

Dissent was symptomatic of the Indian community—scattered, generally poor, clinging to old ways. Not only did reservation clash with non-reservation Indians, but elders often differed with the newly elected young bigwigs conducting tribal affairs through a business council, with parliamentary rules of order. Many elders shrank from such doings. In his home tribe Garry confronted all these conflicts.

The National Congress of American Indians strove to give these divergent elements a unified voice. Garry, Peterson, and the executive council understood the reality: The NCAI lacked both money and votes to be a major force on election day, and Indian issues rarely aroused a wide non-Indian public. Too many Americans still thought of Indians in terms of western movies and wagon-train fiction. On the broad canvas of the nation, the National Congress of American Indians represented a reservation constituency of perhaps 435,000, but its business weighed heavily on the American conscience.

Garry continued to push for Indian legislation to advance the NCAI's slate of issues, and he cajoled sympathetic members of Congress to go along with him. At the third annual NCAI banquet for congressional representatives, their spouses, and aides, held at the Sheraton Park Hotel in Washington, D.C., Garry assured his guests that "we appreciate what you accomplish for us. . . . Our purposes in NCAI are constructive purposes. We have always contributed to American society. We want to develop our resources, improve our conditions, and maintain the values and beauty in our culture, not only because we are proud of them but also for all America to enjoy."[6]

He deplored an "Indian" demonstration at the White House led by a retired brigadier, Herbert Holdridge, who called himself a spokesman for the Iroquois. Holdridge also led a "march" on the Bureau of Indian Affairs. "I want to make it crystal clear that the general does not speak . . . for *the* Indian people in America," Garry told his banquet audience. The National Congress, he went on, has won gains, "not by rabble rousing, but by legislation, with the help of you, the members of the United States Congress."

The Eighty-fifth Congress would consider 113 bills dealing with Indians in its first session. That was a remarkable number for a Congress in turmoil over a national minimum wage, civil rights, medical care for the aged, and escalating expenditures for foreign aid, among other issues, and a citizenry learning piecemeal of U.S. clandestine operations in Southeast Asia and the Middle East. Of the bills, seventeen were reported out of committees and fourteen enacted. Two of these extended the deadlines for termination of the Klamaths and the Menominees. One, intended to initiate economic development, transferred surplus federal lands at McNary Dam, Oregon, and in Pickstown, South Dakota, to tribes. The Umatillas rented their 344 acres at McNary Dam to a California manufacturer of mobile homes, who employed forty Indians. (Subsequently, the Oregon attorney general investigated a charge that the company discriminated against non-Indians!)[7]

The bureau's economic-development program for reservations was doing poorly. In hearings the bureau identified seven industries near reserves employing Indians. Only one was actually in operation, a maker of fishing gear and wooden souvenirs at Lame Deer, Montana, near the home of the Northern Cheyennes. Prospective manufacturers included a maker of mocassins and other leather goods in North Carolina, a children's furniture company in New Mexico, and manufacturers of electrical components, children's clothing, ceramics, and house trailers in Arizona, New Mexico, and South Dakota.[8]

Bureau officers struggled against past national policies—giving Indians the bleakest, least promising lands and removing them from the routes of railroads—that had created reservation sites least likely to support industry. The bureau's James Lowe told the NCAI executive council that "there were many practical difficulties in bringing about industrial development," and "in his opinion very little had been done . . . and he doubted that much could be done." [9]

Murray's Senate Concurrent Resolution 3, disclaiming a policy of termination, made no headway. Asked why this was so, John Cragun blamed "the unspoken prejudices of men on the Hill." Congress grows more frustrated each year when it appropriates more money and sees no progress, Cragun added, but it does not understand that Indians feel the same way. Many members of Congress, he warned, feel that unless Indians are moving toward termination, Congress should abandon its trust relationship.[10]

Cragun predicted that neither Senate Concurrent Resolution 3 nor the
NCAI Point Nine program would pass Congress, and he urged the NCAI
executive council to back, instead, Murray's Senate Concurrent Resolution
12. The latter, he maintained, echoed the policy position of Secretary of
the Interior Seaton that no tribe should end its relationship with the government unless it clearly understood and accepted its termination plan.
Simpson Cox, attorney for the Gila River Pima–Maricopa tribes, seconded
Cragun's view. Both attorneys predicted that any Indian legislation seriously considered by Congress would include termination as an eventual
outcome, and on this score Senate Concurrent Resolution 12 offered the
best prospect.[11]

Yet Congress had not forced termination on any tribe in two and a half
sessions. Its mood was changing. The NCAI could hammer at such issues
as economic development, saving the land, education, and vocational training. If such a package was unlikely to pass Congress, Indian lobbyists could
work to pass it in bits and pieces in other bills. To this end, Joe Garry testified
on general-welfare, federal-loan, area-redevelopment, and other related bills
to plead that Indians not be left out; and he added his voice on such legislation as wilderness areas, irrigation and power projects, and others to
caution that Indian lands not inadvertently be jeopardized or taxed.

On his home reservation Garry could sway the Coeur d'Alene tribal council to adopt resolutions that were forwarded to congressional representatives. The Coeur d'Alenes, for instance, sent forward a resolution endorsing
Senate Concurrent Resolution 12, with the comment that Secretary
Seaton's policy statement "has already brought about marked improvement in the Bureau of Indian Affairs' relationships with any number of
tribes, particularly, with those of the allotted reservations."

Over his signature as tribal chairman, Garry mailed copies of the resolution to members of Congress from Northwest states, with the comment,
"The Coeur d'Alene Tribal Council does not especially like SCR 12 and
believes that a better policy resolution at some future date could be passed
by Congress, but that for the time being it would be a considerable improvement over HCR 108 . . . and hence urges the adoption of SCR 12."[12]

While Garry worked for the NCAI program, Congress authorized funding for the Coeur d'Alenes' award from the Indian Claims Commission.
The appropriation language required the tribe to submit a program for
using the money. The ensuing conflict over the money would grind Joe

Garry with the bitterest attacks of his career and stir animosities within the National Congress of American Indians. "It has happened on other reservations," Leona Garry wrote to Helen Peterson sorrowfully, "but somehow no one thought it would happen on the Coeur d'Alene."[13] Garry, realizing that a split in his tribe at this pivotal time could sap his credibility within the NCAI, did not respond publicly to the carping of fellow Coeur D'Alenes in northern Idaho.

Moreover, too much work demanded his attention. By the time the Idaho legislature adjourned and Congress wound down, the year was half spent, and it was time to plan another NCAI convention. And since none of the schemes to raise money for the NCAI had yielded the operating funds needed, Garry again took to the road, selling the NCAI to tribal councils. He was a persuasive salesman and congenial companion; he relished the drumming and traditional singing that often followed his talks.

The executive council laid out its legislative concerns as a framework for planning the 1959 convention, scheduled for early December in Phoenix. The council's targets did not differ much from those of previous years, and Congress now seemed to be listening. That, as much as anything, testified to the progress made by the National Congress of American Indians during Garry's six years as president.

Looking back thirty-three years later, Helen Peterson recalled: "What I think we did in those six years was firmly establish NCAI as *the* national Indian organization." And she added: "I've thought a good deal in the past few years about our era in the fifties. I keep coming to the same conclusion, that if I had to describe the most important thing we did it would be providing the vehicle for Indians to recognize the importance of organizing, learning how to be lobbyists. . . . Indians had it tough because of a vast body of law, and there were so few of them and they were so scattered."[14]

A shift in Congress, however modest, toward the NCAI's position was evident in 1959. With Garry's persistent warnings that the tribal land base was eroding rapidly, the Senate Committee on Interior and Insular Affairs, chaired by James Murray, sent questionnaires to bureau field offices and selected tribes in search of detailed information on Indian trust lands.

The NCAI executive council had criticized the bureau for precipitous sales, for "failure to see that often lands are pressing on the market because their owners need money to live. . . . The Council is convinced that on many reservations the further loss of land should be stopped."

Murray's report confirmed the council's worry: "An alarming acreage of individual Indian trust land has been removed from that category. . . . The magnitude of these removals raises a question as to whether the Indian Bureau has exercised its authority wisely in granting so many applications for sales and patents. . . . Bureau field officials do not follow uniform procedures in passing on an application for sale or fee patent. . . . This is not in keeping with the position of the Federal Government."[15]

Meanwhile, a study of the costs of federal wardship, compiled for the House Committee on Interior and Insular Affairs, summarized eloquently some of the reasons Congress did not move faster on Indian legislation. It was all very well to pan "unspoken prejudices of men on the Hill," in Cragun's phrase, but the report asserted that Indians could not be treated as a single group because of huge variations in reservation size, in tribal assets, in educational levels, and in other characteristics. Congress was troubled by unreliable statistics and bureau bookkeeping: "It is not only impossible . . . to study a reservation or jurisdiction over a period of years to ascertain the adequacy of funds and progress, but it is apparently impossible for the Bureau of Indian Affairs to do the same. . . . Government financial and personnel contributions to the various [bureau] administrative areas seem to have little relation to the local Indians current economic conditions."[16]

Congress was puzzled by the growth in Indian appropriations without visible results. In a six-year period (which coincided with Garry's six years as president), Bureau of Indian Affairs expenditures rose from $81.5 million to an estimated $158.5 million per year. Why had so little been accomplished?

"Tribal assets and liabilities as compiled . . . cannot be considered accurate or conclusive," the report went on. Bureau statistics "are incomplete and widely varying on the same reservation." Fort Berthold, as an example, counted 472 resident families on one line of its answer sheet and 400 on another. (The bureau recorded the Coeur d'Alenes' population at 469; the health service listed 380.)

Congress wanted a definition of "Indian," in order to identify whom the government served as Indians. (The NCAI held out for defining Indians as enrolled members of tribes.) As for honoring promises of the past, the committee realized that "many items in Indian affairs stem back to the treatymaking period," and it requested "some clear statement of remaining obligations," only to discover that "the Department of the Interior does not have these facts."

Lacking reliable data, Congress and the NCAI laced deliberations with anecdotes and personal observations. Speaking of health services, Garry told a committee that his reservation had had no contract physician since the last one died in 1951. To an Indian denied welfare assistance, the Fort Belknap superintendent wrote: "Your desire to remain with your family is not an acceptable reason for not finding employment." With six children, the Indian stayed home to pick up rocks for a Montana farmer.[17]

Sen. William Langer of North Dakota published his impressions in the *Congressional Record:* Scouting in four states, he found Indians living in primitive conditions: "Imagine a mother and father and 13 children living in a one-room cottage with no flooring, no utilities, no water, and no sanitation." Sen. Barry Goldwater of Arizona observed wryly, "We ought to find out why the Indian Bureau has not been able to do more good for the Indians with a billion dollars. If you gave me a billion dollars, I could help 400,000 Indians in this country. So help me, the better off the Navaho Tribe gets, the more white people go to work for the Indian Bureau."[18]

Yet anecdotes and personal impressions were not the hard data Congress wanted. As members of Congress and lobbyists bobbed together in a sea of Indian regulations littered with a flotsam of contradictory information, the National Congress of American Indians pleaded the Indians' obvious exigencies.

Not only must Indian land sales halt, the NCAI executive council submitted, but federal loans for economic development must be authorized. The bureau insisted that Indians "have access to the same sources of credit as non-Indians, but [the council] is concerned because such sources frequently may impose conditions which are a step towards termination." Without consulting Indians, the bureau worked out an agreement with the Farmers Home Administration for Indian loans that required an Indian borrower to mortgage his trust property.[19]

The council expressed concern over closure of Indian hospitals and schools as the Public Health Service took over Indian health and the bureau shifted Indian children to public schools. (In 1952 the bureau had closed down federal schools in Idaho, Michigan, Wisconsin, and Washington, discontinued loans to Indian students, and in the next year began closing Indian boarding schools.) "The Indian population is not as mobile, generally, as its white neighbors," the council pointed out, "and it is still important that medical and school facilities be as close as possible to the Indian home. . . . The Indian community would prefer to keep the children in government schools, both because they are nearer home and because teaching methods and standards are better suited to Indian children."

Both the health service and the bureau denied medical care and education to Indians who did not live on trust lands. The council believed this "deprived many Indians, who had lost their land or had not owned any land, of services which the Congress of the United States intended them to have. The effect . . . is to terminate individual Indians by administrative orders."

For all the publicity claiming improvement in Indian health services, the NCAI took a view similar to that of Sister Providencia: "You know, the offshoot for Res. 108 in the PHS [Public Health Service] is an attitude that the Indians have already been fully assimilated, that the means-test should be applied, that understanding about group insurance, for instance, is the same as whites, that Indians are on their own, emergency or no emergency." When polio broke out in Browning, Montana, in Blackfeet country, she observed tartly: "It will be a neat question . . . how an epidemic can be controlled by stone-age thinking."[20]

With the executive council's concerns as his mandate, Garry continued to lobby and to travel, urging tribes to unite behind the NCAI and contribute to its support. But he remained strapped for money, and on the road he usually stayed with friends.

The days sped toward the 1959 NCAI annual convention. It would be the sixteenth (and the fifteenth-anniversary) convention, and the Indians wanted it to be a special celebration of the NCAI's progress. There was much to be done, and the NCAI grapevine murmured that this year would offer serious competition for the office of president.

Garry was like a juggler with too many balls in the air. Nonetheless, he tossed up another: He announced that he would run for the U.S. Senate. The idea had grown on him as he made the rounds of congressional offices, and he told himself that this was his time. He was well known in Idaho as a legislator, an Indian spokesman, a war veteran, and a frequent speaker to service and civic clubs. He was featured on radio and television, often honored for patriotic and community service, and pictured in newspapers. Joe Garry was surely the most prominent Indian name in Idaho.

He could cast his candidacy as altruistic: A Native American in Congress to speak with a strong voice for his Indian people. Garry did not doubt that he was as capable as many of the members of Congress he dealt with. He understood the system, he had political experience, and he had earned his reputation for integrity.

Quite a few Indians saw Garry's candidacy in this light, as one explained to Helen Peterson: "With this one man, we would have a wedge in the seat of Gov't., we all know that Mr. Garry would work hard to better the Indian situation if it was in his Power."[21]

Garry thought his presidency of the NCAI would be an asset in his senatorial candidacy, but Peterson and Rainer feared his campaign would jeopardize the carefully wrought nonpartisan image of the NCAI. Garry eventually came around to their view. Two weeks before the NCAI convention, he wrote Clarence Wesley a warm letter: "Six years ago in Phoenix, you nominated me for the presidency of the National Congress of American Indians. I have honored this trust; I have given my best. . . . We are back in Phoenix again this year, and I would like the privilege of nominating you for the highest office of the National Congress of American Indians."[22]

Wesley was pleased, of course. While he was independent and outspoken, he believed in Garry's program. With Wesley in office, Garry could be sure that his work of six years would not be dismantled—six years, 1953–59, during which the tide of Indian legislation had turned away from termination. If the battle against termination was truly the last Indian war, Garry had led the Indians to victory.

Garry's convention call to delegates reminded them that "1960 is an election year. Our strongest weapon is our vote. We must work more earnestly to see that every eligible Indian is registered and votes in 1960." The conclave theme was to be: "Register—Inform Yourself—Vote—Participate in the Political Party of Your Choice."

The 1959 convention at the sleekly redone Westward Ho Hotel was perhaps the most memorable in the NCAI's first fifteen years. While there were plenty of mishaps and controversies, the western correspondent for the *Christian Science Monitor* judged that "few could improve on this NCAI six-day meeting for parliamentary procedure, for sifting resolutions, for outspoken debate, for careful analysis of the financial report, or for fun."[23]

Approximately 200 delegates from seventy tribes came "in variegated garb ranging from colorful squaw dresses to expensive business suits," reported the *New York Times*. Its correspondent detected an upbeat spirit "inconceivable in terms of the Indian outlook of even a decade ago," and "a recent awakening in Federal legislation and executive quarters to Indian problems."[24] Newspaper attention was more than welcome to the NCAI, for conventioneers spent one full day discussing how to improve public relations.

The Crows of Montana promised two buffalo for a barbecue picnic at the Phoenix Indian school on the night before the convention opened. But in December the Crows were snowed in, and the Department of the Interior found other animals for the feast. One, a large male penned at a rodeo grounds, broke loose, thundering across the desert, ripping out fences and trailing a full clothesline. Finally, it had to be shot. The other, a small cow, was supposed to be chased by a pony-riding Indian with bow and arrow, in order to demonstrate aboriginal hunting techniques, but the cow was too quick and had to be dispatched by riflemen. At least both beasts were eventually ready for the Indian cooks.[25]

Then someone told Garry the wrong time for the arrival of Marie Racine—the Blackfeet Miss Indian America of 1959—and Joe missed her at the airport. Accompanied by her grandmother, she took a limousine to the convention. Walter Wetzel, Blackfeet chairman, intended that Miss Indian America add a touch of glamour to his candidacy for president, and he loudly protested that she had been intentionally ignored. Mutterings continued for months, until Helen, weary of the talk, declared: "I myself re-checked no less than five or six times with the Blackfeet delegates. . . . In no way could it be charged that she was not given the best and top spot on our biggest, opening session."[26]

Nearly everyone at the meeting had heard that Garry would not run again, and Wesley and Wetzel had emerged as the leading candidates to succeed him. The corridors buzzed with platforms and promises. Peterson, who did not like Wetzel, scoffed after the voting that he "campaigned desperately. . . . He lost, but he never quit; he gave press statements all the way back to Montana."[27]

Wetzel's campaign manager at Phoenix, Meade Swingley, and Edward "Posey" Whiteman, a Montana Crow, arranged for Sen. Mike Mansfield of Montana to send a supportive telegram to Phoenix newspapers. It read, in part: "Have just learned that my former student at Montana State University and long-time friend, Walter Wetzel, has received one of the nominations for the presidency of the National Congress of American Indians. The Montana [congressional] delegation are happy indeed that this honor has been bestowed on one of our own people and we know . . . he will represent the First Americans ably and well."[28]

The wire backfired, because no copy went to the convention managers or to the NCAI, and several delegates complained that Wetzel had tried to influence them through the press. (The indignation of NCAI officers was more feigned than real.) As keynote speaker, Wesley got in the first campaign lick, and he carried Garry's endorsement. Wetzel lost by fourteen votes. His manager challenged the result on the plea that fifteen votes were unconstitutional proxies from Oklahoma Osages, but the credentials committee turned Wetzel down.

At age forty-six, Wesley had been a member of the San Carlos Apache tribal council since 1940, and its chairman since 1954. He was, by calling, a farmer and stockman. Paschal Sherman called Wesley "the direct one." In the NCAI he, Rainer, and Garry were comrades who usually saw eye to eye. "They'd get together and sing Indian songs," Helen Peterson recalled. "We'd joke among ourselves that Joe never learned to sing Apache songs. It was a thrill to sit with those three and hear them sing."[29]

The convention delegates split over raising dues, but otherwise the meeting ran harmoniously. They applauded Garry loudly for his six years at their head. In his last presidential address Joe recalled the battles against forced termination: "All of us working together in NCAI were able to stem the tide on those [termination] bills largely through our organized efforts starting with the emergency conference in early 1954."

He told the gathering, "You have supported me faithfully. . . . Personally, I appreciate this more than words can express, and organizationally, I say that this represents real growth in the organization because it means we know no tribal boundaries in our efforts to fight for common causes."[30]

Garry promoted an amendment to the constitution extending the president's term to two years. Wesley would be in office until at least the convention of 1961, and if all went as Garry hoped, he would then be seated in the U.S. Senate.

The delegates adopted forty-one resolutions, most of them restatements from earlier meetings. The first urged the Department of the Interior to leave determinations of tribal membership to tribes; another called for speeding up the work of the Indian Claims Commission; three called atten-

Clarence Wesley (standing) delivering his keynote address. Seated, left to right: Joe Garry; Paul Pitts (Osage); and NCAI's first president Justice N. B. Johnson. (From NCAI's *Pictorial Highlights*)

tion to Indian hospital and school closures; one asked that Congress grant economic assistance to tribes; another supported Senate Concurrent Resolution 12 "only as an improvement on HCR 108" (while the executive council had voted Garry down on this qualifying phrase, he managed to have it included in the resolution); and a final resolve affirmed the NCAI statement of policy adopted in 1956.

The *New York Times* summed up the five days at Phoenix as demonstrating that the Indians "were inseparable in their self-identification as Indians, in their desire to maintain this identity in the face of an almost overwhelming white civilization, to defend their property against white manipulation and encroachment and to improve their circumstances." The *Christian Science Monitor*'s assessment: "If any one thing dominated this convention . . . it was deep concern for the achievement of unity for reservation Indians everywhere."[31]

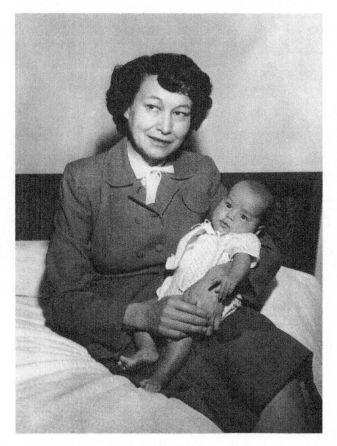

Leona Garry with Ursala, nicknamed "Cubby." (Family)

Soon after the convention, Clarence Wesley wrote a conciliatory letter to NCAI officers, intended to soothe any bruised feelings from
Phoenix. He invited them to correspond with one another between meetings, to "renew our fighting spirit, and cooperate to get the job done."
He closed: "We need one another in these crucial years on Indian affairs,
and may we assume our responsibilities in the spirit of unity and through
divine guidance." [32]

When Leona Garry typed a friendly letter to Mrs. Wesley, to "wish you
well in your work as 'NCAI president's wife,'" she reminded the new leader's

wife that the presidency had kept Joe away from home for long periods. "The more I attended NCAI meetings with him," she wrote, the more "I learned how valuable such work is to all of us Indians, and I found myself working for NCAI almost as hard as Joe." Leona had indeed thrown herself into Joe's work for the NCAI and the Coeur d'Alenes, so much so that some in the tribe considered her overbearing.[33]

Despite his departure from the presidency, some NCAI members worried that Garry's Senate campaign would inevitably cast their organization in a partisan light. "I would very much hate to see this organization [NCAI] used for any political or 'personal gain' behind the disguise of its American Indian membership," warned Allen Slickpoo, secretary of the Idaho State Intertribal Council, in a letter to Peterson. The NCAI, he believed "should remain unbiased and not support any specific candidates, irregardless of any personal acquaintance or friendship."[34]

Marceline Kevis, an off-reservation Coeur d'Alene who opposed Garry's policies, complained that Peterson had sent out an NCAI letter soliciting support for Garry. She quoted the NCAI constitution to Wesley—article nine, which prohibited the NCAI from partisan political activity—and asserted that Peterson "could jeopardize the effectiveness of the whole organization, and completely destroy the usefulness of our lobby in Washington." Thus Wesley's first months in office were preoccupied with defending the NCAI's nonpartisan image.[35]

Peterson protested that the so-called solicitation had been nothing more than "a personal Christmas card which I sent to Ozzie George, in which I referred to the formation of a National Indian Committee for the campaign of Joe Garry." Her card was "mistakenly understood or maliciously misinterpreted," she added. She fired off copies of her explanation to Slickpoo, Wesley, Kevis, the officers of the NCAI, and the executive council: "I respect our Constitution and seek to abide by it scrupulously." But, she pointed out, in this election year several officers of the NCAI "have spoken to me about taking full advantage of this [opportunity] to get attention to Indian issues."[36]

This might have settled the matter, but Peterson correctly saw Kevis's letter as propaganda to subvert Garry's campaign. Without hinting at this suspicion, Wesley responded tactfully: "Marceline, for years I have encouraged qualified Indian people to seek political office. . . . I must admit that I am very much interested in furthering Joe Garry's nomination and election as U.S. Senator from Idaho. I believe that, if he were elected, his heart and soul would be pledged to better the conditions of the American Indian." [37]

B. J. Youngbird, a regional NCAI vice-president from North Dakota, wrote that NCAI officers "had a meeting day after the N.C.A.I. Convention and decided among ourselves to back Mr. Garry for Senator. . . . For whatever differences we hold amongst our own Indian people, we as Indians should stand together. . . . It is very poor thinking for an Indian fighting to keep an Indian out of office." [38]

But the plot against Garry gathered momentum, feeding on the anticipation of a per-capita distribution of claim monies among the Coeur d'Alene tribe, and merging with Walter Wetzel's resolve to be president of the National Congress of American Indians. The cabal came to a climax at the 1961 annual convention in Lewiston, Idaho, where Wesley had to run to stay in office. Although Wesley had been a dedicated president, Wetzel portrayed him as a "figurehead," called for "new blood" at the helm, and advocated returning the NCAI leadership to the Northwest.

Wesley, in fact, did not have much to show for his two years. The Congress, despite a change in administrations, had moved hardly at all on Indian legislation. Tribal contributions to the NCAI remained parsimonious. The most significant victory had been appointment of a new commissioner of Indian affairs, Philleo Nash. Garry headed the welcoming committee when Nash reached Lewiston by chartered plane.

As Wetzel's strength emerged, Garry and Peterson urged Wesley to step aside voluntarily, and Garry nominated John Rainer. Crushed and bitter, Wesley packed his suitcase and went home before the voting. Wetzel won by a huge margin—a landslide that Rainer acknowledged as a "defeat for the present leaders."

Helen Peterson could not work with Wetzel. She resigned, and the executive committee elected Robert Burnette as executive director. The council encouraged John Cragun, who was ailing, to resign as counsel. The election and new appointments made virtually a clean sweep of the Garry camp. Attorney Robert Dellwo, witnessing the proceedings, gloomily called "the outcome a great tragedy and blow to the Indians." He was perhaps too pessimistic, but the Garry era was at its end for the National Congress of American Indians. [39]

9 Money—and Its Consequences

*A**dversity, that mother of ingenuity* (from the Old French verb meaning "turn"), turned Joe Garry from relative obscurity as a tribal councilman to national eminence in Indian political affairs. Adversity, in the form of the Julia Nicodemus tax case, thrust Garry into prominence among western tribes. The western tribes saw Garry as a leader, and he saw them as a constituency, his springboard to a larger role in Indian affairs.

We have already seen that Garry rode the campaign for tax defense funds to national prominence. This is the story. It begins in 1949. While the tax case tarried in the courts, the Coeur d'Alene tribe sued before the Indian Claims Commission to be paid for lost aboriginal lands. Thus began a Coeur d'Alene decade dominated by taxes and claims, and wrangles over money. Throughout the fifties, Garry was at the nub of controversy both at home, on the Coeur d'Alene reservation, and in the nation's capital.

Born of Coeur d'Alene parents, raised on the Coeur d'Alene reservation, a Coeur d'Alene cattleman by profession, Joe Garry had nonetheless been allotted on the Kalispel reserve. In 1936 the superintendent arbitrarily had transferred him and seven others to the Kalispel rolls.

A tribal council was formed under a constitution framed by Lawrence Nicodemus, the most learned resident of the Coeur d'Alene reservation. (He was a musician, a linguist, and a correspondence-school lawyer.) The Coeur d'Alenes had chosen not to organize under the Indian Reorganization Act of 1934 out of respect for the opinions of elders and old Chief Peter Moctelme, who was soured by his encounters with the federal government, indifferent to political process, clinging to tradition. In August 1934, shortly after the balloting, Moctelme died.[1]

Nicodemus's constitution established a seven-member council elected from residents on the reservation. The council was empowered to deal with "outside agencies," borrow money for the tribe, pass and enforce ordinances, set up a tribal court, employ legal counsel, and administer tribal real estate. Chaired by Paschal George, they called themselves a "temporary tribal council," partly study club and partly advisory to the tribe.

The Coeur d'Alenes owned little tribal property—a maximum of 13,000 acres, mostly hilltops—and their thin budget, which they could spend only with Bureau of Indian Affairs approval, rarely exceeded $12,000. Most of the money went for attorneys' fees, a welfare program, law enforcement, prizes for fairs, and a few tribal business trips.

Nicodemus and younger members of the tribe realized that the tribe needed a council to deal with its business during changing times, and Nicodemus ardently wished to make life better for his people. With a little experience now behind him, he wrote a second constitution. Its preamble spoke of building "an independent and honorable life" and providing for the common welfare.[2]

The new constitution of 1947 sucked away whatever authority remained for chiefs. Joseph Seltice, hereditary chief, took part in the council until his death in 1949. His successor, Ignace Garry, the last of these patriarchs without patrimony, was a realist: He worked as tribal policeman before moving to Montana to get out of the way of the new order.

And then abruptly the council faced a crisis. Agents of the Internal Revenue Service brazenly descended on the reservation, claiming that income from crops on alloted lands was subject to income tax. They handed out deficiency notices, imposed penalties, demanded more money than the Indians could pay, and seized harvests. Many Indians did not comprehend their predicament; they knew only that the government had taken their crops and savings, and that they were now destitute, hungry, and powerless.[3]

One of nineteen Coeur d'Alenes beset by federal revenue men was Lawrence Nicodemus's mother, the widow Julia Nicodemus, who possessed not only her own 135-acre allotment but 400 acres inherited from her parents, Louis and Susan Antelope. Another of the nineteen was Joe Garry, and his landholdings included a one-ninth interest in his grandmother's allotment, one-sixth of another, one-fourth of a third, all of a fourth, and one-third of his mother's tract. He had paid tax on grain sold, but the Feds alleged he was $195.60 short.

The tribal council pushed Garry forward to resist the tax raids. He and Father Cornelius E. Byrne, a Jesuit stationed at DeSmet, and son of a noted Spokane pioneer family, gathered documents from the accused Indians and took them to N. D. Wernette, a Spokane attorney who had practiced in Idaho for years. In the lawyer's opinion the Indians were, in fact, subject to income tax.[4]

The Reverend Cornelius Byrne, S.J., chats with Will Rogers, Jr., at a National Congress of American Indians convention. (Dellwo collection)

When the Indians decided they could not accept Wernette's view, Garry turned to an untested alliance with the Affiliated Tribes of Northwest Indians. He had attended its organizing session as a Coeur d'Alene delegate. When two of the session's conveners—Frank George (Colville) and Alex Saluskin (Yakima)—deferred to him, Garry was elected president. Now he resolved to make the tax raids a war cry—a call to action for the Affiliated Tribes—and he formed a delegation to Washington, D.C., to appeal for "a uniform exemption from taxes" through legislation.

The assistant commissioner of Indian affairs, William Zimmerman, Jr., advised Garry to write a letter rather than spend money for travel. But Garry believed that live Indians would attract more notice from the public and Congress, and he wanted his people to feel the streets of Washington under their feet and the exhilaration of directly confronting their congressional representatives. He wanted to strip away any reluctance among his people to bait the national beast.[5]

Idaho representative Compton I. White and a Montana attorney with a string of Indian clients, Kenneth R. L. Simmons, arranged meetings with members of Congress from the Northwest. But Garry's pleas failed to move the lawmakers. The North Idaho superintendent, Archie Phinney, tried to intervene, but was brought up short by the commissioner's unyielding view that "the Supreme Court . . . has held that Indians are subject to federal income tax laws unless specifically exempted by law or treaty." This was the inflexible view, as well, of the Internal Revenue Service and the Department of Justice.[6]

Simmons, however, took on Julia Nicodemus as a client. Although she was portrayed for the tax case as a poor widow, Julia was a bright—and, until the tax raid, prosperous—woman who had interpreted for anthropological reporter James Teit and had served as an informant for the language studies of Gladys Reichard. A decision in her case might become a precedent for all of the Coeur d'Alene tax suits, and Simmons was handling a somewhat parallel case in his defense of Horton Capoeman, Quinault vice-chairman, who had been assessed for his income from the sale of timber logged on his ninety-three-acre allotment. Simmons filed suit in district court seeking recovery of the taxes collected from Julia Nicodemus.[7]

Garry engaged the Wilkinson firm to handle his case. Simmons, therefore, became one prong in a three-pronged legal team: He represented Julia Nicodemus; Wilkinson handled whatever needed to be done in Washington D.C. (including negotiations with federal offices); and the Spokane attorney who succeeded Wernette as Coeur d'Alene tribal counsel, Robert D. Dellwo, dealt with Indians on the Coeur d'Alene reservation. This turned out to be an effective team, working together, respecting one another's views, and keeping Julia Nicodemus before the courts.

The outcome of Julia's case "will fundamentally affect every Indian holder of allotted land and every Indian tribe in the United States," warned the Affiliated Tribes. "It is the problem of all of us." Nicodemus would loom as an ominous backdrop over players on the stage of Indian affairs for six years.[8]

A federal District Court decided, in Capoeman's appeal, that the timber he sold was part of the land, and that its sale was really a sale of an interest in the land. It was therefore exempt from taxation as income. The IRS then took this decision to the Ninth Circuit Court of Appeals, asking for a reversal. By this time, Judge Chase Clark of the Idaho District

Court had heard and judged arguments in the Julia Nicodemus case, and had written his memorandum decision, ruling against Julia.

With the case for Julia going badly, Simmons unexpectedly died, and continuing the Nicodemus suit in Idaho courts fell to Dellwo. Meanwhile, the Affiliated Tribes began to collect funds from Northwest tribes to pay for Nicodemus's defense, because "participation by all Northwest Tribes would have far greater impact than by one single tribe," Garry wrote to tribal chairmen throughout the Northwest. When the Umatillas offered $1,000, and the Blackfeet $3,000, for the defense fund, the Affiliated Tribes realized they had no system for bookkeeping. "Operating in the past with practically no funds whatever," Garry explained, "our Northwest organization has had no need for a bonded treasurer" or for accounting for contributions.[9]

In order to handle defense monies, the Coeur d'Alene council employed Garry as "public relations officer" for three months at a salary of $400 per month, to manage an emergency fund and solicit contributions.[10]

In retrospect, this assignment to canvass for money was pivotal in Joe Garry's career. It launched him on a regional mission that spread across the West. Joe traveled beyond the Northwest to solicit, and western tribal leaders were impressed by this handsome, well-spoken, intelligent, lively man from the Coeur d'Alenes. Joe grasped the moment. Declaring that Nicodemus "stood for every Indian in the United States," he turned his crusade into a national cause.[11]

While Joe solicited funds, Lawrence Nicodemus, finding collections slow, grew impatient, and perhaps a little envious of Garry's emerging eminence. He wrote to the lawyers: "Our very existence as Indians is at stake. Liquidation of our assets would result in disunity among us, and disunity will wipe us out of existence from this earth."[12]

For the moment, the best Dellwo could manage was to delay an adverse decision from the Idaho District Court, persuading Judge Clark to put off a formal ruling against Julia Nicodemus and wait for the Ninth Circuit Court to issue its decision. That decision turned out to be a simple statement upholding Capoeman: His profit from timber was not taxable as income.

Dellwo now wrote to Judge Clark, urging that he withdraw his memorandum ruling against Julia Nicodemus. Dellwo argued that the federal government had been a contracting party in dealing with Indians and could not now honorably or legally step away from this relationship.

"I still believe that the greatest single factor in the Julia Nicodemus case, which should persuade you to hold in her favor," Dellwo wrote to Clark, "is the undisputed evidence that the Government, as a contracting party did, during all the life of the income tax, until the Julia Nicodemus case, interpret that contract . . . exactly as the Indians interpreted it. In fact they told the Indians that that was the proper interpretation, issued literature and books on the subject and in general estopped themself [*sic*] as a contracting party to deny their own interpretation. . . . I would, therefore, strongly urge the Court, in considering the Capeoman case . . . to reconsider this factor of estoppel . . . and to finally decide the case in favor of Julia Nicodemus."[13]

Now, Judge Clark agreed, and he issued a final decision holding that income derived by Indians from allotted land was not subject to federal income tax. His order concluded: "This court should not permit an injustice such as this when the income tax statute in question has never been held to apply to Indians for a period of 35 years, and during which time the Indians have been lulled into security that their property held in trust by the government is free from taxation."[14]

The Capeoman case, however, went on to the U.S. Supreme Court. Dellwo submitted an *amicus curiae* (friend of the court) brief arguing that Indian legislation implied exemption from income taxes, and repeating that the government was a contracting party. The court ruled that exemption was implied by the General Allotment Act (1887) and the Indian Reorganization Act (1934). The decision vindicated the Indian position, and Dellwo would come to believe that his brief helped convince the court.[15]

Joe Garry, in the meantime, had lost his own tax case in the U.S. Tax Court in Washington, D.C. When the IRS carried Judge Clark's finding in the Nicodemus case to the Ninth Circuit Court of Appeals, Dellwo took over the Garry case and appealed it as well. By this time, Garry was president of the National Congress of American Indians, and if he did not appeal, observed one of the Wilkinson lawyers, "it might be viewed . . . as an abandonment of the issues involved."[16]

Since Wilkinson's office had handled Garry's case without compensation, it was now more than willing to turn over further litigation to Dellwo. And Dellwo was elated to get notice that the government had moved for dismissal of the Nicodemus case on the ground that it was covered by the Capeoman decision. The long struggle was over. The Indians had *won!*

Wilkinson reported to its clients: "We regard this as a complete victory for the individual Indian taxpayers and feel it should serve materially to clarify the Indian tax situation." Dellwo happily wrote to Helen Peterson: "This is a great victory for the Indians, far more significant than the victory in the. . . . Capoeman case (although that was its foundation) because it extends the exemption to every type of income from trust allotted lands." The Affiliated Tribes gave Dellwo an appreciative plaque.[17]

The income-tax case (which demanded that the tribal attorneys keep in touch) had served the useful purpose of bringing together leaders of western tribes in a common cause, and it also demonstrated that Indians could win in court. While the government action had threatened many, it actually touched few lives.

In contrast, the Coeur d'Alenes' suit seeking compensation for aboriginal lands agitated everyone who was a Coeur d'Alene or wanted to be one.

In 1948 the tribe, acting under its new constitution, adopted Joe Garry by a vote of 60–0, naming him a Coeur d'Alene "for participation in the council only." Garry had been a member of the tribal council only weeks when Archie Phinney drew him and Father Byrne aside to recommend earnestly that the tribe sue through the Indian Claims Commission before its five-year term slipped away. More than 250 suits by other tribes had already been filed.[18]

Some years earlier, before Congress established the Claims Commission, the Coeur d'Alenes had considered petitioning for redress, but attorneys told the chiefs then that they had no hope of success. Their lost lands appeared to be a dead issue, and the chiefs had given up.

But then Phinney selected a lawyer with Indian clients—the hard-driving, florid Simmons—a man who knew the ropes. At Garry's urging, the tribal council contracted with Simmons, who promised to seek per-capita payments of perhaps $1,000 for each member of the tribe, and he assembled a team of witnesses (a historian, an ethnologist, and an anthropologist) to verify the tribe's aboriginal territory. (He signed up the Spokanes and the Kalispels for claims suits, too.) No one then circled the date on his calendar, but this action marked a significant step toward arresting the Coeur d'Alenes' decline since allotment.

Garry was often absent during the early struggles of the tribal council to restore tribal unity and prepare for its role in land litigation. First, he was on the road begging money for the Nicodemus case; then he was recalled to the army to serve in Korea.

Upon his return, Garry found that the fledgling council had sharpened dissents between modern and traditional, between old and young, and between Indians on and off the reservation. Families stuck together against reasonable persuasion. The educated few considered themselves intellectually equipped to make better judgments than the barely literate. Now, with the prospect of a payoff for lost lands, Coeur d'Alenes who had ignored the council pestered it for attention. No one proposed to be left out.

Such contentions should have been no surprise. Western tribes, the Coeur d'Alenes among them, were inexperienced in parliamentary deliberation and conflict resolution. They were unschooled in compromise, and compromise there would be.

The council put Garry to work writing rules for adoption into the tribe, because a roll of those eligible for per-capita payments would be necessary. The last paragraph of the draft was the telling one: "Any person adopted into the Coeur d'Alene Tribe under this ordinance shall participate in any payments or other benefits accruing to the Tribe subsequent to the date of adoption."[19]

Garry finished his draft just as the Indian Claims Commission wound up its hearings on Coeur d'Alene aboriginal territory, seven years after the tribe had filed its suit. The commission accepted traditional boundaries—a domain, defined by occupancy and use, stretching from the Bitterroot Mountains (the border between modern Montana and Idaho) westward almost to the city of Spokane, and from the southern tip of Lake Pend Oreille southward to Steptoe Butte (a landmark of the rich Palouse farming region). In all, the area covered 2,389,924 acres.[20]

Simmons expected to negotiate an award without going through a second hearing (to set a value on ceded lands), but he could neither shame nor bully the Department of Justice into bargaining. After a year of fruitless entreaties and broken promises, he seethed: "The Indians have been shamefully taken advantage of." Glen Wilkinson discovered that the Justice Department had deliberately stalled while covertly proposing amendments to the Claims Commission act that "would have defeated the Coeur d'Alene claim as well as claims of other tribes." He protested that both the Justice Department and the Indian Bureau hindered tribal

attorneys, "making litigation involving Indian tribal claims . . . pro-
tracted, cumbersome, tedious and irregular." Indeed, at that moment, the
Justice Department delayed renewing Dellwo's contract as tribal counsel, and another Spokane attorney, Lyle Keith, learned that the department was asking the Senate Subcommittee on Indian Affairs to remove
from jurisdiction of the Indian Claims Commission those "claims based
upon or arising out of original Indian title." He urged Sen. Henry Jackson
to block any such action.[21]

During one of the Coeur d'Alene tribe's discussions of an award, Garry
had mentioned (perhaps dissembling) that since he was not an enrolled
Coeur d'Alene, he would not share in it. Oswald George, a councilman,
interposed, "Mr. Garry has done as much as anybody. . . . I think it is altogether fitting and proper that each of us who share in the per capita give
Mr. Garry something," to which Paschal George responded, "We have had
this matter in mind."[22]

Waiting and arguing, the Coeur d'Alenes perceived their council as weak.
Often it could not act for lack of a quorum. Disheartened, Paschal George
resigned as chair. Felix Aripa took over and soon quit. Lawrence Nicodemus
stepped forward, declaring that the Coeur d'Alenes' contentiousness and
apathy demonstrated their "lack of a system of tribal government." He
would create a system, and "in order that my words will not be twisted
any more, it is my purpose to put in writing the statements I will make at
each meeting."[23]

In "this hour of dire need," Nicodemus appointed a three-member committee to compare the U.S. Constitution with the Coeur d'Alenes' 1887
contract with the government. The contract, he maintained, "is our only
safeguard against the encroachment of those who are plotting to get our
last land holdings out of Indian hands."[24]

Nicodemus and Garry agreed wholeheartedly that Indians must hold
onto their lands. Now in 1955, Joe Garry, as president of the National
Congress of American Indians, pleaded with tribes to keep their remaining lands as an economic base to preserve tribal identity. When a bureau
employee resigned, Garry and Nicodemus traveled together to Portland
to petition the area director to divert the man's salary into the purchase
of fractionated acreages put up for sale on the reservation, in order "to
conserve the land base of the Coeur d'Alene Tribe." Most sales were by

off-reservation Indians, and the two leaders had learned that, in the view of the bureau, the tribe did not have enough money to support a land-purchase program.[25]

As friends and professional colleagues working together, Garry and Nicodemus presented contrasting leadership styles. Nicodemus composed thoughtful letters to his tribe. Garry crisscrossed the West, appearing at tribal meetings, at conclaves of Indian advocates, before chambers of commerce and civic clubs, at church services—taking his cause in person to any who would listen.

Nicodemus was more comfortable with written words. A trim, didactic man of medium height (he had been a schoolboy baseball pitcher), he was confronted from the outset of his chairmanship by obstacles, among them empty files. Tribal documents, bylaws, constitution, fiscal accounts, copies of resolutions, and so on were held in agency files at Lapwai. He wrote to Lapwai requesting them, with an admonition for the superintendent: "I might say in passing that you as superintendent have the responsibility of familiarizing yourself with all our activities. But you cannot do this by altogether staying away from our meetings. To depend entirely on a reading of our minutes and other reports would be inadequate."[26]

In six anguished months as chairman, Nicodemus was unable to stir the tribe or to quiet bickering over prospective award money. Sorrowfully, he resigned. "I have done all I could, said all I could, on behalf of the tribe," he wrote to his people. As the "only full-blooded Coeur d'Alene" on the council, "I have been too often made not to feel at home . . . [and] have taken a lot of abuses."[27]

The rising generation of tribal activists rallied to the magnetic Joe Garry. They elected him chairman, and he fashioned a council of Coeur d'Alene men and women aligned with him. For this, his detractors would call him a dictator.

Late in 1957 the Indian Claims Commission, after hearings, published its opinion that the forfeited Coeur d'Alene lands were worth $4,659,663, based on the fair-market value of agricultural and timber lands and mining-claim surfaces in 1889, the year the Coeur d'Alenes ceded roughly half of the reservation.

Ralph Wiggenhorn, a partner of the late Kenneth Simmons, wrote to Garry: "While we are all disappointed in the amount . . . and expected and deserved a larger award," an appeal for reconsideration might consume several more years and result in a lesser amount. "It would seem that it probably would be wise to accept the present award. . . . It is at least a very substantial one and amounts to nearly $10,000.00 for every individual in the tribe."[28] The Coeur d'Alenes accepted the award. And to make sure an appropriation bill did not specify per-capita distribution of the whole amount, Wilkinson arranged an award in the name of the tribe.

Garry had already persuaded the council and general tribe to approve a resolution to compile a new roll of tribal members who would share in the award. Even Indians with a quantum of Coeur d'Alene blood would have to be named on the roll to share. The resolution produced an unintended effect: Some feared they would be squeezed out, and they renewed a clamor to be recognized as tribal members.[29]

The meeting at which Garry explained the award was the largest general council ever held on the reservation. One-hundred twenty-five enrolled adults attended, crowding into the fathers' gymnasium at DeSmet on an airless June day—some in chairs, some seated on the floor, and others lining the walls. Entire families came. Sounds of children at play outside echoed through open windows. The tribe fed 300 or more at noon.

Garry gave them a detailed history of the Claims Commission and the Coeur d'Alenes' award. A supplemental appropriation by Congress had been signed by the president on August 27, 1958, nine years after the tribe initially filed its claim. (Garry intended, in telling the whole story, to demonstrate his mastery of the moment.) He discreetly praised the tribal council for its role, and calculated that after deductions for government services, litigation, and other costs, the net award would total $3,887,507.03. The funds were on deposit in the U.S. Treasury, at 4 percent interest, to the credit of the tribe, and the tribe now needed to come up with a plan to spend the money.[30]

In order to plan, bustle back and forth between DeSmet and Washington, D.C., pay a secretary to compile a tribal roll, and so on, the tribe needed money up front. Garry set out to arrange a loan for "operating expenses," to be repaid from the judgment funds.

"For the past week he [Joe] has been in my office for several hours a day . . . in what may be a fruitless effort to borrow money either from a local bank or from the government to give the Tribe operating capital for the coming year," Dellwo confided to Don Gormley of the Wilkinson office. "What Joe really has in mind is the need for his services in possible trips, tribal roll work, etc., and that he may not be able to do any of this work

Coeur d'Alene agency housing near Plummer, Idaho. Joe Garry and his family occupied one of these houses (at thirty dollars per month) for several years while he served as tribal council chairman. (Author's collection)

unless he has some kind of a salary. And you may know the Tribe is completely broke and cant [*sic*] pay anything."[31]

Garry's plan for reviving the tribe was only beginning to take shape in his mind, but he knew that he would concentrate on the reservation. His concern was for the 150 or so families remaining on the reservation who existed largely on small incomes from leasing their lands or from part-time farm and mill jobs. He would spend money to improve their living conditions, health, and education, and to establish a business to employ tribal members. Of that, he was sure. He would buy Indian land put up for sale to consolidate the tribe's holdings, for without a homeland, the Coeur d'Alenes would cease to be a tribe.

For Garry, preserving the reservation community was essential. The government tended to recognize persons of one-quarter or more Indian blood as Indians wherever they lived. Garry, and many Indian leaders on other reservations, insisted that *real* Indians were bound, both by choice and ancestry, to their lands. But not all Coeur d'Alenes cherished the reservation. The tribe in Garry's time was, in fact, an amalgam of several tribes or bands—the Spokanes, for example—dumped on the reservation by the government to get them out of the way of white settlement, with the unforeseen result that their allotment conferred upon them membership in the Coeur d'Alene tribe. Of a voting population of perhaps 375, approximately two-thirds lived off the reservation. For them, Garry foresaw little more than a per-capita distribution.

Garry did not want his planning slowed by endless deliberations or old rivalries. Once the money was awarded, he wanted to move crisply forward. To do so, he concluded that he would have to be in control, from compiling a roll of tribal members, to writing plans and budgets, to blocking the meddling of the Bureau of Indian Affairs. He would need a tribal council that supported him. He would need to be resolute, convincing, and stubborn.

Unyielding leadership is seldom honored in its own time. Only later do the accomplishments of such a leader emerge as heroic or wise or discerning. In Garry's mind, the Coeur d'Alenes needed a dogged leader. He intended to be that leader, and for his resolve he would be upbraided as greedy and ambitious.

Determined to move forward, Garry sent Sen. Frank Church a draft bill to authorize release of some judgment funds for "purposes determined by the tribal council." It was never considered in Congress. He steered the council to extending his contract and salary as program director, as well as those of Lena Louie, the secretary.

"His reaching for money at this time not only has a bad effect on the tribe," Dellwo (as the man on the scene) fretted to the Wilkinson office, "but has an extremely bad effect on the Indian Bureau. . . . Joe seems to get unanimous approval on things, but on the other hand there is quite a bit of foment within the tribe that doesn't come to the surface and much of this business is done at tribal council meetings with very few if any members of the tribe present." [32]

Garry, truly, had run afoul of the Indian Bureau. He had earlier conspired with Rep. Compton I. White to abolish the Portland area office—a plan that fell through —and now he chafed at loggerheads with a new superintendent at Lapwai, William E. Ensor, Jr., transferred from a Michigan post to the North Idaho Agency late in 1957. Ensor, a paternalistic veteran of the Indian Service marking time to retirement, wanted his agency run by the book and his tenure at Lapwai to be placid. He scorned Joe as an uppity, devious Indian flouting bureau procedures. Garry wrote directly to the secretary of the interior more than once, demanding Ensor's removal.

Ensor could only hope Garry would go too far. "If Joe depletes what few funds there are on his salary," Dellwo feared, "the reaction against him within the tribe will reach a boiling point and they may vote him out. This . . . I believe, is what the Indian Bureau is looking for. Without Joe the tribal council would be relatively leaderless."[33]

Leona Garry, hearing rumors, obtained an affidavit from a Coeur d'Alene who portrayed the area director, Don C. Foster, as angrily voicing "his dissatisfaction over the handling of the Indian affairs by the [Coeur d'Alene] Council and particularly . . . the activities of Joseph Garry. . . . Mr. Foster accused Mr. Garry of domination over the Tribal Council and further felt that and stated that Mr. Garry did not represent the best interests of the Coeur d'Alene Tribe in his handling and management and program concerning tribal lands and monies." Foster, the informant swore, urged him to talk to other members of the tribe "for the purpose of creating dissatisfaction" with Garry, and to circulate petitions to oust Joe from the council. (Dellwo believed that Foster dragged his feet on reservation development because he believed termination inevitable.)[34]

A number of Coeur d'Alenes—especially those off the reservation—were uneasy about the emerging judgment-fund plans. Several began attending council sessions, and one, Marceline Kevis, was nominated for a seat. She was a candidate of unusual merit—former council member, politically active in Spokane (where she owned nursing homes), educated, and informed. And she was, above all, a Seltice, daughter of the late chief Joseph Seltice. In the minds of many Coeur d'Alenes, her heritage entitled her to a place, but at a special meeting the council disqualified her because she did not live on the reservation. They reelected Lawrence Nicodemus instead.[35]

Nicodemus missed the election because he was giving a music lesson. When he heard about it, he fired off a stern letter to Garry, demanding a review. He acknowledged that the constitution (which he had written) required residence on the reservation, but it also required membership in the tribe. If the council followed the rules, "You, Joseph R. Garry, will jeopardize your own legal placement on the council since you are not even a member of the Coeur d'Alene tribe." He asked for another meeting, "with sufficient notice so this meeting can be termed a legal one," and declared, "Marceline Kevis has always worked for the betterment of the Tribe and we should always bear in mind that her ancestral heritage gives her priority rights." Kevis did own land on the reservation and maintained a part-time residence there.[36]

Although no meeting took place to reconsider the voting, Kevis was not easily put off, and the council had provoked Nicodemus. In the meantime, Ensor questioned council resolutions employing Garry as program director and Lena Louie as secretary. Just what did these people do? he asked. And then he pounced on Garry's enrollment as a Kalispel. If Joe were not a Coeur d'Alene, Ensor ruled (and the commissioner concurred), he could not be a member of the tribal council. Consequently, Oswald George took over, as vice-chairman, and Garry continued to participate as program director.

Garry took the occasion of his address at Memorial Day ceremonies in the pine-shaded DeSmet cemetery to appeal for tribal harmony to more than 200 Coeur d'Alenes present. "If we expect to maintain our existence and improve ourselves," he declared, "we must stick together as a Tribe. We must think and act for the welfare of the whole Tribe and not merely strive for our personal interests." Then he led a procession to place wreaths at the graves of war veterans and at the headstones of Joseph Seltice, Paschal George, and Hilary Falcon, the late chief and council members.[37]

Faced with Ensor's challenge, Garry applied to the council to adopt him and his daughter, Ursula. The council immediately convened a special session. "Whereas, there has been an overwhelming demand by members of the Coeur d'Alene Tribe that Joseph R. Garry remain active as a member of their council," their adoption resolution read in part, "the Coeur d'Alene Tribal Council . . . hereby declares that said Joseph R. Garry be adopted . . . and that his name be entered as a duly enrolled member of said Tribe entitled to all the rights and benefits of membership." The bureau approved the action six months later.[38]

Garry's adoption coincided with good news from Washington, D.C.;

The judgment-fund bill had been signed into law by the president (without a requirement to terminate), and the Department of Justice had at last approved a Wilkinson attorney contract. "I would like you to know," Gormley advised Garry, "that a good deal of the credit for successfully pursuing these two items . . . should go to Helen [Peterson]. . . . I am becoming more and more convinced that her usual level headed and quiet way of trying to get things done is becoming more and more effective at Interior and has gained wide respect for her."[39]

While the tribe had been waiting, quite impatiently, for the signing of their judgment bill, committees had been busy on programs to use the money. For the imperative per-capita payment, the council decreed that Coeur d'Alenes of any age, enrolled or entitled to be enrolled as of midnight July 17, 1959, would share. July 17 was six months past, and the council also provided that any person who had been adopted into the tribe by January 1, 1960, might also share. A majority of the tribe whose names appeared on the most recent census roll (1940) had moved off the reservation. Some of them had been vocal about allocating the judgment funds, but a good many others presumably did not even know an award had been made. Lena Louie busily traced them. Letters signed by Garry, Dellwo, or Louie went to the most recent addresses of those unaccounted for.[40]

The lost were generally happy to be found. Alton Rinker, the pianist who migrated from Spokane to Hollywood with Bing Crosby, wrote, "I have been aware of this [claims] suit for years, but I did not know it had been settled." (His mother had been a member of the tribe.) He added a postscript: "Thanks for the trouble you took in looking up my address." That was the sentiment of most.[41]

The council tentatively budgeted $800,000 for per-capita distribution— $1,000 each to 800 persons expected to qualify for tribal membership. The largest budget item, however, was $1.1 million to buy allotted lands up for sale on the reservation. An additional $75,000 would be used to consolidate lands into "adequate economic units" and to drain, clear, and level tillable acres.[42]

The council had talked with area farmers and the bureau about prospects for a seed-treating and -cleaning plant to employ members of the tribe. It set aside $350,000 for that project, expecting to use some of the amount for surveys of mineral, oil, water, agricultural, and other resources that might be developed. Other items that appeared in the budget included: housing, sanitation, a health clinic for preventive examinations, and a fund to buy eyeglasses, dentures, hearing aids, and so on for ailing Coeur d'Alenes; a tribal police force and courts; and scholarships for promising students. One budget item calculated stipends for council members unpaid since January 1958.

An outline with little detail had been sketched when Garry, on the campaign trail for the U.S. Senate, folded the preliminary budget for mailing to Dellwo, adding a hastily penned note: "After several days of trying to get the enclosed . . . in more presentable form, I more or less gave it up for the time and am sending it on to you for presentation or transmittal to Lapwai, Portland, and the Washington office. . . . Sorry to be so late with this. . . . I am campaigning to beat thunder down here [in southern Idaho]."[43]

Even the brightest dream can lose some of its glitter when it is reduced to a typewritten list. And yet, if the Coeur d'Alenes could realize what was essentially Joe Garry's dream for them, if they could establish a business, hold their land, build modern homes, install water and sewer systems, and educate their children, they would free themselves, at last, from the suffocating embrace of a well-meaning government. Even with money and a plan, making this dream real was going to take hard work. For a century the Coeur d'Alenes had endured overregulation, paternalism, and underfunding. Now it was time to shake off the conventional, time to do the undone.

10 "I Enjoyed Working with the People"

*J*oe Garry's plan to spend judgment funds to rehabilitate the Coeur d'Alenes, to make the award his derrick to hoist them out of poverty and lethargy, was slow getting under way. And Garry's gordian personal agenda did not help: He was, at once, program director acting as chairman of the tribe, president of the Affiliated Tribes of Northwest Indians, and candidate for the U.S. Senate. He was also thinking seriously of making another run for the presidency of the National Congress of American Indians.

In the middle of 1960, Garry concentrated on his campaign for the Senate. While Joe stumped, Dellwo grumbled that "the entire [award] program . . . is ground to a standstill. There isn't a single thing being done. . . . [And] Garry, carrying on a cause celebre fight with the Indian Bureau and the Superintendent, doesn't help any."[1]

But Garry had been encouraged by Sen. Frank Church and Cong. Gracie Pfost of Idaho, and had spent an hour or two with Sen. Henry C. Dworshak, a member of Congress almost continuously since 1941 and the likely Republican candidate for the Senate in the coming election. Newspapers, speculating that Garry might become the first full-blood American Indian in the Senate, printed his campaign biography: born in a tepee, spoke no English until he was ten years old, great-grandson of Spokane Garry, hardworking rancher who rose to lead the one all-Indian political organization, and so on. An Idaho political columnist wrote that "Garry made no enemies in his two terms in the Legislature . . . is personable and a good speaker," and he predicted Joe might carry northern Idaho.[2]

Garry's friends in the NCAI organized a drive to raise $30,000 for his campaign. Paul Pitts, an Oklahoma Osage, chaired the group, and John Rainer, a Taos Pueblo, served as treasurer. They solicited by mail. "It is reported that Garry will have plenty of money at his disposal," observed the *Daily Idahonian* (Moscow), opining that oil-rich Indians "around

Oklahoma and northern Texas" could "buy new automobiles every Monday morning if they wish," and might spend freely to boost an Indian into the Senate.[3]

Marceline Kevis carried her faction's quarrel with Garry to the NCAI, insisting that its constitution barred partisan political activism. She won few cohorts. B. J. Youngbird, in a typical rejoinder, wrote: "We as Indians should stand together and fight for our rights. We need a man like Mr. Garry in the Senate."[4]

Garry opened campaign offices in Coeur d'Alene and Rexburg, mailed broadsides throughout the state, and set out on an exhausting tour of speech making. In one week, for example, he visited Salmon, Challis, Mackay, and Arco in one day; Shoshone, Hager, Buhl, Filer, and Twin Falls the next; then Kimberly, Jerome, Wendell, and Gooding the third day; Pocatello for a whole day; and American Falls, Burley, and Rupert on the fifth. He gave set talks: At Buhl he stated his opposition to imports that competed with Idaho's mines; at Pocatello he called for more federal aid to education; and everywhere he warned against Russian communism.

At a rally for Frank Church in Rexburg, Garry won a straw ballot, and the *Daily Idahonian* reported: "Garry, with a fine bearing, handsome face, and fluent tongue . . . might do better at the polls than any other Northern Idaho candidate has in many years." An Idaho farm weekly remarked: "Garry . . . might emerge with enough strength to win the nomination without a runoff."[5]

Yet for all its energy, Garry's campaign was a one-man band. "He has been doing nothing more than a personal contact job, traveling, talking, and not much else," noted an editor. His tan stationery bore the slogan, "All American for All America." Most mailings appealed for money. The fund drive by Indians fizzled, and one week before election day Garry volunteers issued a desperate appeal: "We are now out of funds. . . . Unless we receive additional money . . . this gallant effort could falter and even fail." Their cry echoed in an empty cash box.[6]

In all, Garry spent roughly $5,000 on a campaign that needed five times as much, and he finished fifth among five primary candidates. "He had to depend on volunteer workers and press releases and these were cut [by editors] to paragraphs when large ads failed to materialize," a Rexburg editor summed up. "It is a real compliment to Joe Garry that he was able to amass 11,000 votes."[7]

In his diary Joe wrote simply: "Car repair finished but too late to continue campaign. Lost nomination for U.S. Senate." And to Gracie Pfost: "I wanted to win so badly, but I guess the 'Great White Chief' above had other plans for me."[8]

Despite the demands of Garry's campaign, the tribal plan for its judgment funds took shape, and Lena Louie drew a tentative payroll of Coeur d'Alenes, on and off the reservation, eligible for per-capita distribution. To Joe's dismay, however, the tribe broke into factions: A large group followed Garry; but a small, noisy ring challenged him as despotic, and it fused with off-reservation Coeur d'Alenes demanding representation on the council and with the rising choler of bureau men in Portland and Lapwai.

Dellwo wrote to Don Gormley of the Wilkinson office to warn of "the almost psychopathic antagonism Ensor has for Joe . . . because Joe has sent a series of . . . telegrams, phone calls, etc., to [Assistant] Secretary [of the Interior] Ernst demanding Ensor's removal." Ensor's jaundice sifted upward to the bureau in Washington, which continued to challenge Garry's return to the tribal council, even after Helen Peterson personally intervened with the commissioner's office.[9]

Lawrence Nicodemus, meanwhile, wrote to Sister Providencia asking her to recall the dates of Joe's work in Washington for her father, Cong. John Tolan, hoping to show that Garry had not complied with residency rules for council members. "This is just between ourselves, you understand," Nicodemus cautioned the nun. "If you tell Joe our purposes will be defeated. . . . More and more he has been dictating to the Tribe what they must do." Providencia passed the letter to an Indian friend, who sent it to Dellwo, with the notation, "You should know what needs doing."[10]

And Marceline Kevis complained to the secretary of the interior of "the incompetent management of . . . tribal officers." Her concern was off-reservation Indians. "These people have been disenfranchised and attempts have been made to deny them a vote." She urged the secretary to "call for a referendum" among the Coeur d'Alenes on the use of judgment funds.[11]

Garry had offered an outline plan for judgment funds to the tribe at a general meeting on February 6, 1960. It called for a per-capita payment of $1,000 to members enrolled as of midnight July 17, 1959, and to members adopted by January 1, 1960. The skeleton budget totaled $2,762,900 and included land purchase, land consolidation, health, education, welfare, law enforcement, industrial development, a loan fund, better housing, and a domestic water system. There were also line items for "special donations" to the mission and to the NCAI, and for back pay to council members. The largest single expenditure was $1.1 million for the purchase of allotted lands, designed to keep Indian acres in Indian hands.[12]

The program—other than the per-capita payments—aimed to benefit Coeur d'Alenes on the reservation, and the more than $1 million to buy land was especially vexing to off-reservation Indians, who itched to have that money distributed individually. Designating themselves an "advisory committee," the off-reservation people petitioned the commissioner of Indian affairs to order a referendum on Garry's proposals, as the bureau had in disputes over assets of terminating tribes.

For its part, the bureau ruled that the tribal council did not have constitutional authority either to develop a tribal roll or to buy land. These were nit-picking technicalities. Nearly a year would pass in revising the constitution and per-capita payroll, and in defeating the call for a referendum, before the first per-capita payments of $1,000 were made in October 1960.[13]

Garry, more impatient each month with the bureau's delays, appealed to Idaho's congressional delegation and to the National Congress of American Indians to push for action. But there was no discernible movement. When the Lapwai office circulated a newsletter critical of the Coeur d'Alene tribal council, Joe exploded in a seven-page letter to Superintendent Ensor, with copies to members of the tribe, to the commissioner, and to the Interior Department: "Since your arrival . . . [at Lapwai] in 1957 the Coeur d'Alene Tribal Council has had to do at least three times more work to get anything accomplished for the tribe as they have been required to do in the past. . . . By confusion and delay, you have attempted to suppress every honest effort . . . to help the tribe. . . . You seem to prefer to work with individuals who are constantly trying to arouse a minority element of the tribe to subvert the program of the Council." In sum, Joe accused Ensor of "trying to manufacture" trouble within the tribe.[14]

Joe's harsh indictment of Ensor might have blown over, but Dellwo, who usually took the role of peacemaker, in this case shared Joe's anger. He wrote to his friend Philleo Nash, the new commissioner of Indian affairs: "I am certain that this whole matter [challenges to the judgment program] resulted from a concerted program by Bureau officials to hamstring and discredit Joe Garry. We went through that era when everything we tried . . . was bottled up with endless obstacles and splitting of hairs. . . . At the same time there was copious propaganda released to Coeur d'Alene members trying to give the impression of incompetence, callousness and greed on the part of the Council members and of Joe Garry in particular." Dellwo urged a change of heart in the Indian office, pointing out that "the various policies and principles of Joe during the past ten years are now the official policy of the Bureau of Indian Affairs."[15]

Garry was given a personal opportunity to impress Nash as the new commissioner's official escort at the 1961 NCAI convention in Lewiston, Idaho. (Garry had met Nash earlier in the year when Joe attended a meeting of an Interior Department task force studying the Indian Bureau. Nash, a former lieutenant governor of Wisconsin, was a task-force member.) In Lewiston, Joe delivered the keynote address, hoping to recapture the presidency, but he found Walter Wetzel's coterie entrenched—Marceline Kevis, among them, as Portland-area vice-president.

Shortly after the convention, Nicodemus addressed Fern Fisher, an Oklahoma Otoe, who was the newly elected secretary of the NCAI, telling her that he was busy gathering signatures on a petition to the commissioner "to oust our present council. . . . We are trying to get Joe Garry and his clique out of tribal affairs, just as we have had to do in NCAI. Joe has become a dictator."[16]

Fisher expressed surprise, observing that Garry had referred to Nicodemus, in recent conversation, as a lifetime good friend: "The example of dignity and kindness to others I have seen him exhibit and the ideals that he has encouraged have certainly impressed me. . . . Can anyone with the background Mr. Garry has had, all of the achievements that he has won, all of the good that he has accomplished not only for your tribe but for all of the Indian tribes . . . change to the complete opposite? Your tribe is famous among the Indians nationally due to his efforts and example of leadership. . . . We have come too far on a national basis to lose that which is important to all of us—regard and loyalty to one another." Fisher's reaction was not what Nicodemus had hoped for. The lifetime good friend continued to scheme to sink Joe Garry.[17]

Garry had lost two of his faithful friends on the council: David Garrick died in 1960 and Lena Louie in 1961. Lena's place as tribal secretary went to a clever, motherly woman, Evangeline Abraham. She too admired Garry,

A Public Health Service survey in the fifties found Indian homes consisting of three rooms and no water supply or sanitary facilities. (Dellwo collection)

but did not much care for Leona Garry's sharp tongue. One story has it that gentle Evangeline, during a noisy council meeting, took Leona by an arm, led her to the door, and shoved her out.

The council's judgment-award program slowly took shape. They also renewed Garry's contract. "Whereas," the council resolution for Garry read, "the Coeur d'Alene Tribe lacks skilled, educated members who are available to work for the tribe and is reliant on a handful of members and primarily on Joseph R. Garry," his title, program director, was changed to chairman.[18]

A professional team surveyed reservation sanitary facilities, counting sixty-five Indian homes—frame structures, usually with three rooms—for a population of 254. Nearly half of the Indian dwellings had no water supply, and of those with water, two-thirds were polluted. Ninety percent had "unsatisfactory refuse disposal facilities." The survey would result in a cooperative project between the tribe and the Public Health Service to build an adequate system, whereby they agreed to split the costs and to rely on homeowners to dig their own ditches and install their own fixtures.[19]

The council invested $126,000 in the Benewah County Development

Corporation, organized by local citizens to meet the requirements for loans from the federal Area Redevelopment Administration. The money was divided between a lumber (planing) mill at Plummer and a plywood manufacturer at St. Maries. Both promised dividends and jobs for Indians. The council bought 320 acres of trust farmland and finished preliminary planning for a Land Purchase Program, proposing to spend $1.25 million over time to acquire trust lands for farming or development. (The bureau approved the land program on September 28, 1965.) From returns on these ventures, council members hoped to realize enough income for annual per-capita distributions. By early 1963 they had progressed far enough in a law-and-order program to order office furniture for judges and police officers. And they considered putting money into a mutual fund for scholarships.[20]

Of the varied potential uses of judgment funds, industrial development was doubtless the most hazardous. With few exceptions Indian tribes could not attract industries, because of poor locations and transportation routes. What else could be expected after a century of awarding to Indians the least valued lands? The John F. Kennedy Administration, promising new vigor and fresh ideas, formed yet another task force to study Indian administration. After meetings with Indians in seven key cities, the task-force report recommended that the bureau shift emphasis from termination to economic development but offered no original or useful ideas for doing so.[21]

Consequently, in putting their funds into local businesses, the Coeur d'Alenes were little different from many other tribes struggling to build an economic base. The Confederated Salish tried tourism on Flathead Lake. The Kalispels put their money into a local aluminum-fabricating plant. In the sixties, industries looking for locations in the inland Northwest were those exploiting raw materials or cheap electrical energy. Indian reservations rarely offered either.

A flux of dissent rocked the council's efforts. Off-reservation members, egged on by bureau personnel, urged the commissioner to cut off judgment funds for the council and order a referendum on a new constitution that would create a general council of enrolled adults. A fluctuating minority listened to Lawrence Nicodemus and Marceline Kevis spread rumors of boodle and tyranny. The St. Joe River, rippling its way through Lake Coeur d'Alene, creating a collision of currents, offered a metaphor of the Coeur d'Alene tribe.

As whispers aimed at Garry unfurled within the NCAI, Joe received a sharp letter from Executive Director Robert Burnette: "I am very concerned about the rumors that have been reaching me. . . . I believe that I can prove that you used NCAI for your own gain and I will if you continue to try to destroy NCAI." Jack Deno, a Spokane advertising man fronting for off-reservation Coeur d'Alenes (of an uncertain number), circulated petitions to dissolve the tribal council. In rebuttal the council sent out a tribal newsletter asserting that Deno's people intended "to take over the reservation, replace the council, and finally divide up all the cash assets of the tribe. Once they succeed . . . they will be glad to hand a crippled, broken reservation back to the council to rebuild."

In the ensuing months the council adamantly rejected both a referendum and a new constitution. Father Byrne held a prayer meeting to sermonize against a new constitution, and Lawrence Aripa drew compelling campaign posters. Garry talked individually to Deno's dissenters, eventually winning over enough to quiet their demands.[22]

When Marceline Kevis, as regional vice-president of the NCAI, asked the council to pay her travel expenses to an executive council meeting, they turned her down, observing that the Coeur d'Alenes "have a capable representative, who is a [tribal] council member and resident of the Reservation." A few weeks later the council reelected Garry and Evangeline Abraham to three-year terms.[23]

Conflict on his home reservation notwithstanding, Joe Garry remained a man of distinction in the larger community. He was frequently invited to participate in symposia on Indian affairs, and regarded as a headliner. He participated (as did Nicodemus) in a well-publicized University of Chicago conference convened to write a new declaration of Indian purpose. (The Montana Intertribal Policy Board and Sister Providencia, among others, withdrew from the American Indian Chicago Conference, and criticized the NCAI for its part in helping to organize and staff the meeting. Put off by "inflexibility" of its planners, including D'Arcy McNickle, the dissenters felt that tribal leaders who attended had been coopted by elitist insiders.)[24]

At All-American Indian Days in Sheridan, Wyoming, in 1961 Joe was named the nation's outstanding Indian. He remained a director of Arrow, Inc. Garry regularly attended Idaho State Indian Conference meetings and in 1964 would be elected chairman. He also took part in the American

When off-reservation Coeur d'Alenes circulated petitions for a new tribal constitution, Lawrence Aripa, a Garry supporter, drew this poster opposing them. (Cheney Cowles Museum/Eastern Washington State Historical Society, Spokane.)

On a visit to Washington, Garry laid a wreath at the grave of the slain president, John F. Kennedy. (Arlene Owen family collection)

Indian Capital Conference at the national cathedral in Washington, D.C. The La Grande, Oregon, Festival of Indian Arts named him president. Senator Church arranged for Garry to place a wreath at President Kennedy's grave, with military escort, cannon salute, and a bugler sounding taps.

The inaugural committee for President Lyndon B. Johnson invited Garry to ride as one of thirty Indian horsemen in the parade. He and Walter Wetzel, with Miss Indian America between them, led the Indian marchers. At the reviewing stand, Garry noted, "President Johnson raised his hand in a military salute and held it as the Indian units of over one hundred" passed. "Despite the four hour mount, spent mostly waiting, the thrill and excitement of having ridden horseback down Pennsylvania Avenue . . . distracted all attention from aches and pains, as well as the chill of the late winter afternoon." Garry rented a dinner jacket and borrowed a black topcoat from Father Michael Shannon, now Jesuit superior at DeSmet, to attend the "gala" inaugural events.[25]

With the new federal administration came changes in Portland and Lapwai: a new area director in Portland and a new superintendent, Thomas H. St. Clair, in Lapwai. Soon St. Clair addressed the Coeur d'Alenes in an open letter: "Ever since I have been your superintendent, there has been a steady circulation of anonymous letters on your Reservation, which, to say the least, is disgraceful and despicable. . . . I earnestly hope that we will have no more of this un-American, cowardly attempt to destroy the members of your Tribe. . . . I urge all Coeur d'Alenes to make every effort to work together and solve differences in a democratic fashion."[26]

For its part, the tribal council addressed a resolution to the NCAI: "Whereas at the annual convention . . . no members of our authorized delegation . . . were delegated to serve on any committee, or participate in the program in any manner, although two members of the Coeur d'Alene Tribe, namely Lawrence Nicodemus and Marceline Kevis, who are constantly working in opposition to the authorized governing body of the tribe . . . were given committee assignments and allowed to participate in the program, now therefore, the Coeur d'Alene Tribal Council hereby makes known its objections to the present policy of the President and Executive Director . . . in recognizing individuals who are not authorized tribal delegates." Shortly after, the council voted to withhold dues from the NCAI in protest.[27]

The council, dissent aside, continued to push forward with its judgment program. It adopted a code for housing construction and remodeling, and formed a citizens' advisory committee for housing; it gathered information about housing needs, as part of its application for financial and technical assistance to the Public Housing Administration; and, to quiet new rumors, it issued a disclaimer: "Do not be concerned that the tribe is 'spending all of our money' on this housing project. The funds for this project are from the federal housing authority. Coeur d'Alene tribal funds will not be used." Better housing stands today as a visible legacy of Joe Garry.[28]

A 1990s view of Indian housing at Sacred Heart Mission, DeSmet, Idaho. The mission cemetery lies in the clump of high pines visible in the background. (Author's collection)

For two days the council conducted a "tribal affairs institute" for enrolled members—a "little convention . . . tailored to the needs of the Coeur d'Alene Reservation." The purpose, of course, was to discuss council policies and procedures, hear from informed guests, and familiarize Coeur d'Alenes with tribal business.

To carry out its scholarship plan, the council invested $150,000 in a mutual stock-and-bond fund with a Spokane broker, Murphey Favre, Inc. The investment, intended to create income for scholarships, was said to be the first in stocks and bonds by an Indian tribe. It had taken eight years, with paperwork bouncing back and forth from tribe to attorney to Washington, to satisfy the U.S. solicitor's legal concerns. The scholarships

Joseph R. Garry, a portrait taken during
his campaign for the Idaho State Senate.
(Arlene Owen family collection)

would be available to enrolled Coeur d'Alenes, on or off the reservation,
for vocational, high school, or college studies.[29]

The land program progressed: The tribe bought 487 acres that had been
a Civilian Conservation Corps camp in the thirties, and it acquired the allotments of six members who wanted to sell. The council hired an independent appraiser because bureau appraisals ran consistently high.

As the day approached for tribal elections, Garry circulated an appeal
for votes. "Our main objective now," he said, "is to build up tribal assets
in order that dividend payments can be assured each year. We want to
increase our land base, develop the land now owned by the tribe, and promote full use of tribally owned timber in order to gain more income for
the tribe." He was reelected.[30]

Garry, in the meantime, had run for and won a seat in the Idaho state senate, representing the new Third District, formed by reapportionment. He set off for the thirty-ninth legislative session, opening January 2, 1967 — back to the familiar sandstone capitol, the crowded chambers with shabby desks, the shared offices, and Idaho's tight budgets. The elation of a decade earlier, when he arrived as a representative, had evaporated. Garry was tired and ailing. He missed opening day, to be sworn in later alone as legislators gathered for the governor's message.

A small-business owner from Sandpoint, an ultraconservative Republican who surprised even his own party by winning the governor's chair, Don W. Samuelson had been senator from Bonner County during Garry's second term in the house. Amid bickering among Republicans, Samuelson took an unyielding position on finance. This 1967 session would seem rudderless, and it was one of the longest, at eighty-nine days. Garry was absent twenty-seven of them.[31]

As an experienced legislator, Garry was assigned to active committees much involved with the state budget: agriculture and livestock, education, local government, and public health and welfare. While there was no more horseplay with war bonnet and tomahawk, when the legislators considered restrictions on gambling that seemed to threaten Indian stick games, Garry organized a stick game, with drumming and feathered regalia, on the floor of the capitol rotunda, as a demonstration of this ancient native pastime.

Garry, for the most part, worked quietly. He introduced two bills to exempt veterans from certain property taxes and from nonbusiness sales taxes. He offered two bills for veterans' pensions. None passed. He steered Senate Joint Memorial 6, urging the Indian Bureau to keep the Northern Idaho Indian agency at Lapwai or move it to Coeur d'Alene if the Colvilles accepted termination.

Samuelson, stubbornly resisting the legislature's budget, delayed adjournment. Garry joined a knot of Democrats who voted against all fiscal measures in protest, and they killed a proposal to designate Boise College as a state institution. The education committee, one of Garry's assignments, leveraged increased funding for the state university against the governor's recommendation, and it endorsed enrolling school employees in Idaho's retirement system for the first time.

When the governor vetoed a bill to raise legislators' pay (one of thirty-nine vetoed), Garry and five others tried unsuccessfully to gather enough

votes to override. A Garry committee pushed through funding for community mental health and retardation centers; another voted to end a tax
on merchants' inventories. As the session wheezed toward adjournment,
Garry slipped out to join delegates from Idaho tribes gathering in Boise
for the annual state Indian conference. The legislature, exhausted, left a
dozen pressing issues unresolved.

Except for brief visits, Garry had been gone from the reservation for
three months. He came home in agony from recurring headaches, to find
that Ozzie George, as vice-chairman, had kept the tribal council's judgment plan on Garry's track. But Garry was too ill to resume command:
He resorted to alcohol for relief, and when able to attend meetings, sat
dumbly. In July, as Joe lay in St. Luke's hospital in Spokane awaiting
exploratory brain surgery, the council elevated George to acting chairman.
"Whereas, our chairman Joseph Garry is quite ill . . . we do not want him
to feel pressed to resume his duties too early," its resolution read, "and
will like nothing better than to have him back . . . managing tribal affairs
with the skill and dedication that he has demonstrated." The council would
rely on George to "keep the tribal business in a current condition." [32]

Leona was another matter. Protective of Joe, she waxed more outspoken, became bossier, and sometimes combative. Joe was back in the chair
temporarily in October when the council resolved to fire Leona as a tribal
employee "in the interest of efficiency and harmony in the tribal office
and for the good of the Tribe as a whole." As the council's intent became
apparent, Joe left his seat and went home. In the next few days he told
friends that he and Leona might move to Denver, and then he talked opti-
mistically of attending a special session of the legislature in late January.
Garry was passed over for a place on the board of the Museum of Native
American Cultures, then taking shape at Gonzaga University, because he
"was so greatly influenced" by Leona. [33]

But he went back to the hospital, rather than to the legislative special
session, and he was pictured by a newspaper in hospital bathrobe signing
a contract for the tribe to buy the grain elevator at Tilma, a railroad sid-
ing near Tekoa, as an investment. He issued a chairmanly statement: "This
fits in with our land purchase program to purchase a million dollars [worth]
of productive wheat properties. . . . Now the tribe will have a marketing
facility."

A few weeks later, Garry was again deathly ill. He underwent a second

The Coeur d'Alene Tribal Council at work. Second from right, reaching for papers, is Marceline Kevis. (Dellwo collection)

brain operation and, after fluid buildup, a third. He appeared to be dying. He lay in the hospital in January when the tribal council voted him an "award of merit for lifelong service," in absentia. Joe's sister, Celina, who spent hours by his bedside cheering him with Indian stories in Salish, accepted the award for Garry at a general meeting of the tribe.[34]

To Ozzie George fell the task of writing a memorandum about the Coeur d'Alenes' immediate concerns for Sen. Frank Church, who would confer with tribal representatives at St. Maries. (Church had not shown much interest in Indians, but he was conscientious, and he wanted to hear reactions to his heirship bill before Congress.)

Joe Garry in front of the Coeur d'Alene tribal
administration building at its dedication to him
in 1975. (Arlene Owen family collection)

Since neither George nor Garry would be available to meet with
Church, George summarized the Garry program in a memorandum that
did not name Joe. He expressed the tribe's opposition to the "type of termination" contained in the Colville bill —still floating in congressional
air—and pointed out that mixed families of Colvilles and Coeur d'Alenes
owned allotments on both reservations that would pass out of Indian title.
"This would mean that the entire Coeur d'Alene Reservation would find
itself speckled with fractional terminated interests," George wrote.[35]

The Coeur d'Alenes, he explained, evolving "toward an ever more self-
sufficient unit," owned a grain elevator and had invested in mutual funds
and mills. "Our tribe is interested in developing its resources and establishing a firm economic base . . . in enterprises which maintain employ-

ment for our members and in land to secure our future economic strength."
George added that industries balked at the short leases imposed by the
bureau, and he urged Church to assist the Coeur d'Alenes in convincing
Congress to enact the tribe's land-consolidation bill.

In regard to the tribe's investment in the St. Maries plywood plant,
George complained that the owners, Potlatch Forests and Atlas Tie
Company, had expanded the mill but kept their accounts in such a way
that they showed neither profit nor earned surplus, and had thus avoided
paying the tribe either interest or installments on the principal. By the Coeur
d'Alenes' reckoning, the plant was $30,000 in arrears.[36]

An informed reader, perusing George's memo, would see that the Coeur
d'Alenes' program resonated with Joe Garry's preachments as president
of the National Congress of American Indians; with his pleas for Indians
to cherish their land and their culture, to preserve tribal unity, to educate
their children, to build a tribal economic base; with echoes of the days
when he gave Indians their national voice as Indians, and rallied them to
resist forced assimilation.

And the reader might then consider the transformation in federal attitude, if not action, in three decades. To be sure, with House Joint
Resolution 108 still on the books, Indians sniffed for any odor of termination in new legislation, although now presidents and Congresses
espoused termination only with tribal consent.

Garry made of his home reservation a real-life field trial of his gospel.
He encountered the frustrations of dealing with a heavy-handed, regula-
tion-wary bureau. He knew firsthand the perils of a tribal leader at the end
of the bureaucratic line where legislation and edict fell heaviest. He risked
reputation and status to contend for the tribe's right to manage its own
business. And he honored his commitment to improve the material lives
of his people.

With Garry's goading, the tribe's proud spirit revived. Families returned
to the reservation, believing there might, after all, be a future for them there.
By 1970 the Coeur d' Alene's enrollment rose to 941. More than 400 lived
on the reservation. But full-time jobs on or near the reserve were still scarce.
In fact, creating payrolls was a major concern of the council when it
wrapped its various businesses into a Coeur d'Alene Development Enterprise to manage its farm (yielding lentils and grains), timber, swine herd,
and service station.[37]

Oswald George, who as vice-chairman had held Garry's council together with good humor, died in 1970. Father Byrne appealed to Garry to come back. "How much Oswald was credited with doing cannot replace the foundation you laid in the magnificent years of your leadership," the priest wrote to Joe. "Perhaps, Joe, the passing of Oswald is a call—a call to you to step back into the breach. I think it is." [38]

But with Garry's health failing, taking hold again was beyond him. The old days were gone. New faces appeared at the council table, and new members saw Garry as outworn when he struggled for coherence during their deliberations. At the election on May 8, 1972, Joe Garry was defeated as a candidate for the council for the first time since 1948. He rose from his chair, remarked that he had been the council's oldest member, and had enjoyed "working with the people." Then he went to the door, turned to scan the room, and with a jaunty salute, stepped out into gathering darkness.

Epilogue

In December 1971 the Alaska Native Claims Settlement Act granted Alaskan natives title to more than 40 million acres and compensation of nearly $1 billion.

In December 1973 the Menominee Restoration Act restored the tribe to federal trust status.

The Indian Self-Determination Act of 1975 expressed a federal policy of effective and meaningful participation by Indians in federal programs, and laid a foundation for eventually turning over many programs to the management of tribes. It empowered tribes to create their own resource policies and regulatory agencies.

Joe Garry died on December 31, 1975, after a long illness. He lies beside Leona and Cubby in the shady cemetery at DeSmet.

Notes

While the notes demonstrate my heavy reliance on Joe Garry's papers, I searched a number of archives. These are identified, in abbreviated form, as follows:

AP   Archie Phinney Papers, Pacific Alaska Region, National Archives
EW   Eastern Washington State Historical Society, Spokane
HP   Helen Peterson Papers, National Anthropological Archives, Smithsonian Institution
HJ   Henry M. Jackson Papers, University of Washington Libraries
MU   Museum of Native American Cultures, archives in the care of the Eastern Washington State Historical Society
NA   National Archives
NCAI National Congress of American Indians Papers, National Anthropological Archives, Smithsonian Institution
OPA   Oregon Province Archives, Society of Jesus, Gonzaga University, Spokane
RD   Robert D. Dellwo Papers
SI   Smithsonian Institution
SP   Sister Providencia Papers, Eastern Washington State Historical Society

Books, articles, government documents, dissertations, and theses are cited fully when they first appear in the notes; thereafter, by shortened references.

Letters, documents, minutes, transcripts, and other sources for which no location is provided in the notes are among the Garry papers. In this regard, be advised that a number of individuals sent Garry letters and documents they felt he should know about, although he is neither addressee nor signer.

1. Emergency!

1. Joe Garry, "justification," carbon copy of trip expenses, (n.d.) Helen Peterson, interview (June 2, 1989), no. 0993 (Idaho Oral History Center, Boise), 11.

2. Peterson, ibid., 11–12.

3. Garry, "justification."

4. Call to emergency conference (Feb. 9, 1954). Those who handled arrangements for the conference included Vincent McMullen and Winifred

Pomeroy (both volunteers in the NCAI office), Jim Hayes, Ruth Muskrat Bronson, Elizabeth Roe Cloud, and Helen Peterson. D'Arcy McNickle advised Peterson, Bronson and Roe Cloud raised money. The Indians met at the Raleigh Hotel—one of those lining Pennsylvania Avenue, facing federal office buildings—where conferees were offered single rooms at six dollars or doubles at ten.

    5. Felix S. Cohen, "The Erosion of Indian Rights, 1950–1953," *Yale Law Journal* 68 (Feb. 1953):348–90 passim.

    6. *Congressional Record,* 84th Cong., 2d sess. (June 26, 1956), A5037, 106. According to the Washington *Evening Star* (Mar. 1, 1954), Wesley gave this talk at the emergency conference called by Garry.

    7. *New York Times* (Mar. 20 and July 16, 1953).

    8. Helen Peterson, interview with author (Sept. 11, 1993); "Resume of the Emergency Conference" (n.d.).

    9. McNickle's testimony was quoted in *New York Times* (Feb. 27, 1954). The description of Watkins is based on William W. White, "Portrait of a 'Proper Washingtonian,'" *New York Times* magazine (Aug. 5, 1954). Under the Legislative Reorganization Act of 1946, the committees on Indian affairs were abolished in both houses of Congress, and a Subcommittee on Indian Affairs was created, with five members, under the Senate Committee on Public Lands.

    10. "Resume of Emergency Conference."

    11. Adopted Feb. 28, 1954. See *Congressional Record,* 83rd Cong. 2d sess. (Mar. 11, 1954), NCAI reprint.

    12. Typescript (n.d.).

2. *"The Chance of Our Indian Lifetimes"*

    1. Call to the NCAI organizing convention (Oct. 2, 1944), AP. Garry had risen to the rank of sergeant, in charge of men of various patrimonies whom the army had thrust into his rifle platoon. He had won his place as a leader, not as an Indian.

    2. McNickle to Mrs. John Rogers, Jr. (Apr. 28, 1944), AP. The letter was written in search of funds for the convention.

    3. Phinney to McNickle (Dec. 15, 1943), AP.

    4. Phinney typescript, "The Indian Intelligencia [*sic*]" (n.d.), AP, box 2; the Society of American Indians is recalled in a letter from Arthur C. Parker, a cofounder, to Phinney (Sept. 1, 1942), AP, box 10. Parker identifies Thomas L. Sloan as the man with the political ambition.

    5. AP, box 10, f.

    6. Phinney to Dwight (Sept. 30, 1938), AP, box 10.

    7. Dorothy R. Parker, *Singing an Indian Song: A Biography of D'Arcy McNickle* (Lincoln: University of Nebraska Press, 1992), 93.

8. McNickle to Phinney (June 11, 1943), AP, box 10.

9. Transcript of Phinney's talk to a Chicago group (Feb. 9, 1944), AP, box 10.

10. Parker, *Singing an Indian Song,* 106; Phinney, "History and Scope of National Indian Unity," manuscript (n.d.), AP, box 2. Phinney was then closing out his roving assignment. He was named superintendent of the Fort Totten agency, North Dakota, in January 1944 and was promoted to his home reservation, the Nez Perce, as superintendent of the Northern Idaho agency in November of that year.

11. Phinney to McNickle (Nov. 15, 1943), AP, box 10.

12. "Summary of Proceedings" (May 25, 26, and 27, 1944), AP, box 10; Kent FitzGerald, temporary chairman, to McNickle (n.d.), AP, box 10.

13. Heacock to Phinney (Sept. 1, 1942); Phinney to McNickle (Dec. 15, 1943), AP, box 10.

14. *Morning Star,* Coeur d'Alene tribal newspaper (Sept. 23, 1945). The account of Basil Two Bears' war whoop is based on McNickle's recollection in Parker, *Singing an Indian Song,* 107.

15. Transcript, resolution 4, NCAI, SI. Johnson, a Cherokee, graduated in law from Cumberland University in Tennessee. He had been a city and county attorney, a member of the board of the Oklahoma Historical Society and the Governors' Interstate Indian Council, and president of the Intertribal Council of the Five Civilized Tribes. His recollections appear in his article, "The National Congress of American Indians," *Chronicles of Oklahoma* 30 (1952):140–48.

16. A brief account of the convention appears in Denver *Rocky Mountain News* (Nov. 18, 1944).

17. Johnson to Phinney (Aug. 24, 1946), AP. For discussions of the Indian Claims Commission, see Glen A. Wilkinson, "Indian Tribal Claims before the Court of Claims," *Georgetown Law Journal* 55 (Dec. 1966): 511–28; and Nancy O. Lurie, "The Indian Claims Commission Act," *Annals of the American Academy of Political and Social Science* 311 (May 1957):56–70.

18. McNickle to Collier (Nov. 20, 1944); Larry J. Hasse, "Termination and Assimilation, Federal Indian Policy 1943–61" (Ph.D. diss., Washington State University, Pullman, 1974), 51.

19. Ickes's statement appeared in *New York Times* (Dec. 24, 1944). The extension of the Wheeler-Howard act to Alaska in 1936 (49 *Stats* 1250) gave the secretary of the interior the authority to fix boundaries on Indian villages, but no reservations were designated until 1943. See Claus-M. Naske, "Ernest Gruening and Alaska Native Claims," *Pacific Northwest Quarterly* 62, 4 (Oct. 1991):140–48.

20. Bronson to Phinney (Apr. 25, 1947), AP, box 10.

21. John Rainer's analysis of NCAI finances was appended to the 1958 summary of activities.

22. Bronson to Garry (July 9, 1949). This account of Garry's initial inter-

est in the NCAI is based on the author's interview with Helen Peterson (Sept. 28, 1993).

23. William Zimmerman, Jr., "Role of the Bureau of Indian Affairs since 1933," *Annals of the American Academy of Political and Social Science* 311 (May 1957):36; Arthur V. Watkins, "Termination of Federal Supervision: The Removal of Restrictions over Indian Property and Person," ibid., 49.

24. Johnson, "National Congress of American Indians," 147.

25. Appendix, "Table of Financing," attached to a proposal from NCAI to Robert Marshall Civil Liberties Trust (Nov. 26, 1958).

26. Peterson, interview (Sept. 28, 1993). Peterson was born on the Pine Ridge reservation, an enrolled Oglala Sioux. She earned a bachelor of science degree in business education from Chadron State College. She was employed by the federal Resettlement Administration, and then directed the Rocky Mountain Council on Inter-American Affairs, establishing a field program later adopted by the extension division of the University of Colorado. She was working as the first director of the Denver Community Relations Commission in 1948 when she learned of the NCAI.

27. William J. Van den Heuvel, "Arrow Inc. and NCAI: An Appraisal of Their Relationship," typescript (n.d.), HP, box 11, SI. NCAI *Bulletin,* convention issue (1949). According to Peterson, Yeffe Kimball, in the role of administrator, ran Arrow, Inc., into debt, and Will Rogers, Jr., agreed to pay it off if the NCAI took control of the corporation. See Peterson, interview (Sept. 28, 1993).

28. An undated telegram to members of Congress from Washington, Idaho, Oregon, and Montana asked that they amend the current appropriations bill to ban funding for area offices; it was signed by the Kalispel, Coeur d'Alene, Nez Perce, Warm Springs, Flathead, Yakima, and Umatilla tribes. Carbon copies of the NCAI statement opposing area offices and White's amendment to H.R. 7786. According to a staff memo to Congressman White, Henry Jackson of Washington counseled against the White amendment, saying "if the amendment is offered and defeated, it will be impossible to get the Department [of the Interior] to do anything about it thereafter, as Congress will have voted against the measure."

29. Hasse, "Termination and Assimilation," 127–28.

30. Cohen, "Erosion of Indian Rights," 381 n. 129.

31. James E. Curry, "Report to the Seventh Annual [NCAI] Convention," 7.

32. *New York Times* (Oct. 16 and Nov. 18, 1950).

33. *New York Times* (Nov. 9, 1951; Dec. 2, 1950; and Oct. 15, 1951).

34. *New York Times* (Nov. 3, 1951).

35. D'Ary McNickle, "A Ten-Point Program for American Indians," typescript (June 24–27, 1951).

36. Proposal to Marshall Trust (Nov. 26, 1958), 6

37. Frank George, a full-blooded Nez Perce, graduated from the Chemawa

Indian School and the Haskell Institute. In 1956 he would be the Colville Business Council's nominee as "Outstanding American Indian." George resigned his post as Colville tribal-relations officer to take the NCAI position. He was a founder and secretary-treasurer of the Affiliated Tribes of Northwest Indians, and a charter member of the Governors' Interstate Council (organized June 18–22, 1950, "to work toward the solution of Indian problems").

38. Minutes (paraphrased), Affiliated Tribes of Northwest Indians annual meeting (Sept. 17–19, 1953), 3.

39. George to Ramon Robideaux, Fort Pierre, South Dakota, a member of the NCAI executive council (Nov. 16, 1953); Peterson, interview (June 2, 1989). The *New York Times* of July 16, 1953, reported Emmons's appointment.

40. George, ibid.; Peterson, ibid.

41. Garry, call to Affiliated Tribes meeting (Nov. 28, 1953); Peterson, ibid.

42. Peterson, ibid.

3. *The Crucial Year*

1. 83d Cong., 1st sess. (1953), P.L. 277 (liquor), P.L. 280 (state jurisdiction), and P.L. 281 (firearms).

2. H.R. 2680, 83d Cong., 2d sess. (Sept. 20, 1954), v, 6–12.

3. Peterson to Short (May 7, 1954).

4. Peterson, interview (Sept. 28, 1993).

5. Peterson to Rev. B. A. Cullen, Marquette League (July 24, 1954).

6. Peterson, interview (Sept. 28, 1993); Van den Heuvel, "Arrow Inc. and NCAI," 3. The opening of Arrow's New York office was reported in the *New York Times* (June 25, 1953). For that occasion Susan B. Hyde gave $25,000 for a mobile health center at Crown Point, New Mexico, in memory of her archaeologist husband, Frederick E. Hyde.

7. Garry to McNickle (Mar. 27, 1954). While Joe was in New York, Corinna Smith arranged a party, at which Joe received a fine Stetson hat and met potential NCAI donors.

8. Kalispel resolution (July 22, 1954); Peterson to executive council (June 4, 1954); "Table of Finances," appended to 1958 proposal to Marshall Trust; audit (Aug. 25, 1955), by Leopold & Linowes, certified public accountants.

9. NCAI press release, "Indians came out better than expected in 83d Congress" (n.d., ca. Jan. 1955).

10. Robert D. Dellwo, interview (May 2, 1994).

11. Seminole Indian Association of Florida to NCAI (Jan. 19, 1954), with an enclosed statement to the area director at Muskogee, dated Oct. 16, 1953.

12. H.R. 2680, v, 15.

13. Hearings on "Termination . . . Part 7, Flathead Indians" (Feb. 25–27, 1954), Gov. John Aronson, 870; Sen. James Murray, 802; Dellwo interview (May 2, 1994). Robert Dellwo was present at the hearings.

14. "Termination . . . Part 7, Flathead Indians," Richard Shipman, vice-president of the Montana Farmers Union, 786.

15. Ibid., 909; *New York Times* (Feb. 26 and 27, 1954).

16. Peterson to Walter McDonald, Flathead council (June 19, 1954).

17. "Summary Statement of the 'Indian Viewpoint' on 1954 Legislative Proposals," NCAI press release (n.d.), SP; H.R. 4985, 83d Cong., 1st sess. Cohen is quoted in a transcript of his testimony (July 7, 1953), SP.

18. Affiliated Tribes *Bulletin* (Jan. 1954):5–6 (attacking H.R. 4985 and a companion bill, S. 335); author's sampling of Peterson letters in Garry files; Garry to Cullen (June 24, 1954).

19. Transcript of Cohen testimony (July 7, 1953), SP.

20. Cohen, supplementary memo (July 8, 1953), SP; Vigil (June 1, 1954), copy to NCAI.

21. Peterson to Garry (July 22, 1954).

22. Peterson to Garry (July 22, 1954). Garry's statement expressing tribal consensus was made at a meeting on Mar. 1, 1957.

23. Telegram, George to Peterson (June 1, 1954); Peterson to George (June 6, 1954); Peterson to Garry (July 22, 1954).

24. Three years after the transfer, Garry would commend the surgeon general for the increase "in quality and quantity" of services to Indians. But he passed along complaints as well: A regulation requiring Indians to live on trust lands to be eligible for health services barred many. "Disease is not located by the status of the title to the land," Garry wrote. "It is inconsistent to terminate trusteeship on land on the one hand, but to grant service only to those who live on trust land." Indians, he went on, object to the degree blood is used as a criterion for service, to "an intensive drive to require patients to pay," to "non-professional people—even clerks—deciding whether, a person shall be admitted," and to a lack of understanding of Indian ways and values. Garry to surgeon general (June 20, 1958), HP, box 7, SI.

25. *New York Times* (July 18, 1954); Peterson to Garry (July 23, 1954); NCAI summary of 83d Cong. (1953–54).

26. NCAI legislative bulletin on bills before the 83d Congress (n.d.). Although the Bureau of Indian Affairs claimed that no California tribes opposed Public Law 280, Garry's files suggest the opposite. See Erin Forrest to Garry (Apr. 27, 1954).

27. California Senate Interim Committee, "Progress Report on Indian Affairs" (Jan. 1955).

28. Peterson to Garry (July 22, 1954).

29. Ibid. Emphasis is Peterson's.

30. Typescript, Wilkinson statement (July 8, 1954).

31. Peterson to NCAI council and tribal chairmen, Information Letter No. 1 (1956).

32. Report 357, Part 2, 84th Cong., 1st sess., "Minority Views."

33. H.R. 2680, summarized in *New York Times* (Oct. 4, 1954).
34. NCAI legislative bulletin summarizing Indian legislation in 83d Cong. (n.d.).
35. *New York Times* (July 18, 1954).

4. Turning Points

1. Transcript, introduction by Paschal Sherman, of the NCAI financial report for 1954, reviewed Aug. 29, 1955. Sherman held five university degrees, including one in law. Modest, slender, balding, he did not impress physically, but in the Indian community he was considered an intellectual and held in high regard. It was said that when Sherman entered a meeting, a respectful hush fell over those present.
   On the issue of consent, Secretary of the Interior Douglas McKay wrote to Oliver La Farge, on Nov. 30, 1955, that consent meant "giving Indians, over and above normal rights of citizenship, a special veto power over legislation which might affect them."
2. NCAI press release, "Indians Come Out Better Than Expected" (n.d.). Emphasis in original. For her efforts during that year, Helen Peterson was named "Outstanding Indian Citizen of 1955" at the annual Anadarko Indian Exposition.
3. Dorothy Bohn, Great Falls, to McNickle and NCAI (Oct. 1, 1954).
4. See Joan Bishop, "From Hill 57 to Capitol Hill: 'Making the Sparks Fly,'" *Montana: The Magazine of Western History* 43, 3 (summer 1993):16–29; Bohn to tribal chairmen (Oct. 11, 1954). Sister Providencia was stationed at Sacred Heart Mission from 1937 to 1941. In 1955, the NCAI would vote her its National Merit Award.
5. Peterson to Garry (Nov. 6, 1954).
6. Omaha *Sunday World Herald* (Nov. 21, 1954); *New York Times* (Nov. 22, 1954).
7. McNickle, "Statement of the Eleventh Annual Convention, NCAI, Concerning Report Number 2680," transcript packaged with convention resolutions.
8. Peterson, interview (Sept. 28, 1993).
9. Quoted by Rev. Cornelius Byrne, S. J., in "Termination . . . Part 7, Flathead Indians," 911.
10. Peterson to Garry (Nov. 6, 1954). The estimate is taken from a statement of the commissioner of Indian affairs, in a transcript of hearings on Indian heirship land problems (Apr. 2 and 3, 1962), 206–11.
11. John Cragun, memo to attorneys (Feb. 1, 1955).
12. Ibid., with notation by Peterson.
13. H.R. 7190, 84th Cong., 2d sess., enacted as P.L. 772 on July 24, 1956; acting commissioner to Portland area director (June 13, 1951).
14. Peterson to James D. White (Jan. 24, 1955).

15. George to McNickle (Jan. 14, 1955); transcript of Horan conference (Aug. 30, 1954), MU, EW; White to commissioner of Indian affairs (Apr. 8, 1955), MU, EW. For discussions of Colville conflicts, see John Alan Ross, "Political Conflict on the Colville Reservation," *Northwest Anthropological Research Notes* 2, 1 (1968):29–91; Kathleen A. Dahl, "Battle over Termination on the Colville Indian Reservation," *American Indian Culture and Research Journal* 18, 1 (1994):29–53; and Kathleen A. Dahl, "Sovereignty, Environmental Use and Ethnic Identity on the Colville Indian Reservation" (Ph.D. diss., Washington State University, Pullman, 1990).

16. Transcript, hearings on H.R. 6154 and H.R. 7190 (1955), 94.

17. "Statement of Coeur d'Alene Tribe" (Oct. 14, 1956), House Committee on Interior and Insular Affairs, Subcommittee on Indian Affairs.

18. Lucy Covington was a granddaughter of the noted chief Kamiakin. She lived on the Colville reservation site of Chief Moses's home. She, Frank George, and others testified and entered statements into the record at the hearings on Colville termination. See H.R. 3051, 90th Cong., 2d sess. (July 12, 1968), 112–21. On June 14, 1969, the Affiliated Tribes of Northwest Indians voted Resolution No. 5, hailing her work against termination and her victory. She "fought an uphill battle against the incumbent terminationists. They had control of the tribal organization with its newspaper and means of communication. She had to work the roads, the streets, and the fields, searching out and talking to tribal members. . . . Her only hope was to build up such a majority of local voters that they would not be outnumbered by the expected avalanche of termination-ist votes from the absentees. . . . She . . . demonstrated to the Indian world and to government and political officials the tragedy and danger of compulsory absentee ballots."

19. Peterson to six tribal chairmen (Jan. 6, 1955).

20. *Christian Century* (Sept. 21, 1955); Parker, *Singing an Indian Song,* 173.

21. Federated Indians of California to Garry (May 19, 1955); Peterson to Garry (June 4, 1955).

22. L. Garry to unknown addressee (n.d.).

23. Minutes, Fort Peck tribal executive council (July 13, 1955).

24. Garry to Saux (Mar. 11, 1955).

25. NCAI *Bulletin* (May 1958).

26. James Murray, *Indian Land Transactions,* 85th Cong., 2d sess., 1.

27. Emmons to Max Gubatayao, Great Falls, Montana (Oct. 8, 1957).

28. Typescript, opening address (Sept. 24, 1956).

29. From Resolution No. 1, 13th convention of NCAI.

30. Ibid. Emphasis in original: For a summary of the convention, see *Christian Century* (Sept. 21, 1955), NCAI reprint.

31. Murray, *Indian Land Transactions,* xviii.

32. NCAI press release (Feb. 23, 1955), SP.

33. *New York Times* (May 14, 1957).

34. McNickle to the Garrys (Jan. 17, 1956).

35. "Request for Moratorium," *Congressional Record* (May 13, 1958):7636–38, NCAI reprint; Sen. James Murray, press release (May 13, 1958).

36. Garry to Murray (May 22, 1958).

37. Robert Burnette, NCAI executive director in 1962, wrote in NCAI *Newsletter,* no. 6 (Dec. 14, 1962): "We are quite vitally concerned with the subtle methods employed in the Grorud 'Indian Associations' because at present five tribal councils are being harassed and intimidated by these organizations. . . . These 'Indian Associations' were organized by Mr. Albert Grorud . . . for the sole purpose of finding ways to ultimately terminate Indian tribes. Unfortunately, there are Indians who are willing to go along . . . without realizing the real intention is to eventually obtain remaining Indian lands. . . . Ways must be found to combat this destructive national movement."

38. Murray, *Indian Land Transactions,* xvii, xix.

39. Typescript, Wesley address to the Arizona Industrial Conference (Mar. 13, 1957). Wesley was, at the time, general manager for the San Carlos Apache tribe's business endeavors.

40. Typescript of testimony (Mar. 26, 1956).

41. Garry to Seaton (Dec. 31, 1956); *Indian Affairs,* Association on American Indian Affairs newsletter, no. 25 (Mar. 1958). A Nebraska newspaper publisher, Seaton had previously served the Eisenhower Administration as assistant secretary of defense and as the president's administrative assistant. He was a short, dapper man, generally soft spoken.

42. Garry to Seaton (Dec. 31, 1956).

43. Paul Jones, chairman, Navajo tribal council, to Garry (Feb. 15, 1956), distributed by NCAI.

44. Transcript, conference of eastern Washington and Idaho tribes with Commissioner Emmons (Sept. 20, 1956), 24, 26.

45. Ibid. (Sept. 21, 1956), 4.

46. *Salt Lake Tribune* (Sept. 25, 1956).

47. Joe Pedro, secretary, Cheyenne and Arapaho, to Garry (July 30 and Aug. 7, 1956).

48. Peterson to Clara Sturges Johnson (Jan. 23, 1955); Sister Providencia to Garry (Sept. 1, 1958).

49. Typescript, itinerary (July 14–Aug. 3, 1956); revised constitution and bylaws, amended Sept. 2, 1955.

50. Bronson memo to Garry and others (Jan. 25, 1956).

51. Garry to executive council (n.d.); Louis Bruce, president of Arrow, to NCAI convention (1956), typescript report and cover letter.

52. Ballot draft (Apr. 24, 1957); minutes, 1957 NCAI convention.

53. "Federal Indian Policy," hearings on S. 809, S.C.R. 3, and S. 331 (85th Cong., 1st sess.), 223. Murray's S.C.R. 3 was identical to his S.C.R. 85, introduced in the Eighty-fourth Congress, on which no hearings were held.

54. Ibid., 225.

55. Ibid., 85–86.

56. Peterson, typescript draft, "Indian Legislation in the First Session of the 85th Congress."

57. "Federal Indian Policy," 263.

58. Peterson, "Indian Legislation."

59. Sherman to Garry (Aug. 14, 1957).

60. Peterson to Sherman, with copies to Garry and others (Sept. 12, 1957).

61. John Rainer, "Report to the Council" (May 9, 1957), with audited financial reports (1947–57); Garry to Sherman (Aug. 17, 1957).

5. Roots: The Coeur d'Alenes

1. There are a number of historical reports on the Coeur d'Alene tribe, but no general history. A partial account, personal and somewhat legendary, is Joseph Seltice's *Saga of the Coeur d'Alene Indians,* ed. by Rev. Edward J. Kowrach and Rev. Thomas E. Connolly, S.J. (Fairfield, WA, Ye Galleon Press, 1990). Some conclusions about population and village siting can be found in Kelly A. Murphey, "Archeological Resources of Southern Lake Coeur d'Alene Northern Idaho" (typescript, Laboratory of Anthropology, University of Idaho, 1994). A witness to early white contact, Rev. Joseph Joset, S.J., left a manuscript, "Short Chronology of the Rocky Mountain Missions," and an undated letter (OPA) to fellow Jesuits, commenting on the origin of the name Coeur d'Alene. Born in the French canton of Berne, Switzerland, in 1810, Joset entered the Jesuit order in 1830 and arrived in the Rocky Mountain mission field in 1846. He died at Sacred Heart Mission in 1900.

2. Rev. Nicholas Point, S.J., *Wilderness Kingdom: Indian Life in the Rocky Mountains, 1840–1847,* ed. and intro. by Rev. Joseph P. Donnelly, S.J. (New York: Holt, Rinehart and Winston, 1967), 8–9.

3. Rev. Gilbert J. Garraghan, S.J., *Jesuits of the Middle United States,* 3 vols. (New York: America Press, 1938), vol. 2, 319. See also Garraghan's essay, "Nicholas Point, Jesuit Missionary in the Montana of the Forties," in *Transmississippi West* (Boulder: University Press of Colorado, 1930).

4. Joset, untitled manuscript, quoted by Robert I. Burns, S.J., "Pere Joset's Account of the Indian War of 1858," *Pacific Northwest Quarterly* 38, 4 (Oct. 1947): 290.

5. I. I. Stevens, *Journal of Operations of Governor Isaac Ingalls Stevens of Washington Territory,* ed. by Rev. Edward J. Kowrach (Fairfield, WA: Ye Galleon Press, 1978), 37.

6. Stevens's message to the legislature can be found in Charles M. Gates, ed., *Messages of the Governors of the Territory of Washington to the Legislative Assembly, 1854–1889* (Seattle: University of Washington Press, 1940), 4.

7. Quoted in Burns, "Pere Joset's Account," 291–92.

8. There are a number of accounts of the Steptoe adventure. The official version appears in *Report of the Secretary of War, and Message of the President,* S. Exec. Doc. 32, 35th Cong., 2d sess. (1859). Scholars have identified the tribes who took part in the skirmish by battlefield artifacts.

9. Quoted in Carl P. Schlicke, *General George Wright: Guardian of the Pacific Coast* (Norman: University of Oklahoma Press, 1988), 154.

10. *Message of the President,* S. Exec. Doc. 2, 35th Cong., 2d sess. (1859), 395.

11. Dispatch from Wright's camp on the Palouse River, ibid. Wright's dispatches commend Joset for "zealous and unwearied exertions" to end the fighting.

12. A. Pleasanton, assistant adjutant general, to DeSmet (Oct. 28, 1858), in *Report of the Secretary of War* (1858), 93.

13. H.R. 1109, 51st Cong., 1st sess. (1890), 23.

14. Gustavus Sohon to Mullan (Mar. 9, 1860), in *Report and Map of Captain John Mullan . . . ,*" S. Exec. Doc. 43, 37th Cong., 3d sess. (1863).

15. *Report of the Secretary of the Interior* (1860), 646.

16. Act of July 1, 1864.

17. This was actually a second petition. The earlier one was filed without action (NA).

18. Ewing to secretary of the interior (Jan. 5, 1873), NA. Seltice is described in *Spokane Falls Review* (July 16, 1885), in an article recalling his peaceful posture during Chief Joseph's war in 1877. Congress voted Seltice the first medal honoring an American Indian.

19. *Report of the Commissioner of Indian Affairs* (1873), 385, 392.

20. Shanks to secretary of the interior (Aug. 1, 1873), enclosing a copy of the Coeur d'Alene compact; Shanks et al. to secretary of the interior (Nov. 17, 1873), NA.

21. Bennett's letter to the editor of the Lewiston *Idaho Signal* (p. 2) was published on Oct. 4, 1873. Emphasis is Bennett's. A letter from Idaho Territorial Governor David Ballard expressed a common view of Indian treaties among Whites. He wrote on Sept. 4, 1866 (NA), that treaties "are designed more for their effect upon the Indians than to compel the government to do justice to them."

22. J. G. Straughn, Idaho surveyor-general, to Commissioner Sparks, General Land Office (Aug. 10, 1887); Sparks to secretary of the interior (Nov. 11, 1887), NA.

23. Right-of-way files, General Land Office, records of "Division F," NA, RG49; see the author's *Inland Empire: D. C. Corbin and Spokane* (Seattle: University of Washington Press, 1965), 35–43. The General Land Office apparently relied on the Executive Order of 1873, establishing boundaries for the Coeur d'Alene tribe.

24. Contract (Mar. 26, 1887), article 5, NA.

25. *Congressional Record* (1888), 6223; 25 Stats 1002; acting commissioner of Indian affairs to secretary of the interior (May 22, 1889), NA.

26. *Message of the President,* S. Exec. Doc. 14, 51st Cong., 1st sess. (1889), includes correspondence, transcripts, and reports of this negotiation; Capt. William A. Thompson to War Department (Aug. 22, 1890), NA, reporting squatters.

27. Commissioner Atkins to Benjamin P. Moore (Mar. 13, 1887), NA.

28. Inspector James Saunders's report (Jan. 17, 1889), NA; untitled manuscript recollections of George, MU, EW. The *Coeur d'Alene Teepee* (Nov. 1939), a tribal newspaper, reprinted an unidentified newspaper clipping dated June 17, 1905, quoting Charles Worley, agent, estimating that two-fifths of the reservation was cultivatable, with three-fifths in timber.

29. There is perhaps no clearer statement than that of Robert F. Kennedy, testifying before the Senate Indian Affairs Subcommittee on March 5, 1968: "The Allotment Act succeeded in the period of the next forty years in diminishing the Indian tribal economic base from 140 million acres to approximately 50 million acres of the least desirable land. Greed for Indian resources and intolerance of Indian cultures combined in one act to drive the American Indian into the depths of a poverty from which he has never recovered." Quoted in *Indian Education: A National Tragedy—A National Challenge,* S. R. 91-501, 91st Cong., 1st sess. (1969), 150.

30. French is quoted in a letter, commissioner of Indian affairs to Colville agent A. M. Anderson (Dec. 5, 1903), NA.

31. Thomas R. Cox, "Tribal Leadership in Transition: Chief Peter Moctelme of the Coeur d'Alenes," *Idaho Yesterdays* 23 (spring):2–9, 25–31. Cox concludes that tribal disintegration commenced with allotment. See *Opening of the Coeur d'Alene Reservation,* Report 3352, 59th Cong. 1st sess. (1906), 3, noting Peter Wildsho [*sic*] and others' protest that allotment was "a violation of faith" and contrary to their contract ratified on March 3, 1891. Commissioner of Indian Affairs Francis E. Leupp's letter to the secretary of the treasury (Apr. 11, 1906) is quoted: "It is believed that all Indian reservations must sooner or later be abolished. . . . The Coeur d'Alene Indians are perhaps in as good condition to receive their lands in severalty as they will be for years to come."

32. Sams quoted in Spokane *Spokesman-Review* (Aug. 16, 1908 and Feb. 3, 1909); Garry and Lena Louie in conversation with the commissioner of Indian affairs (Sept. 21, 1956).

33. Lawrence Nicodemus to R. D. Dellwo (Oct. 16, 1953), RD.

34. Inspector Hugh Scott (Aug. 10, 1922), NA.

6. Boy to Man

1. Rev. Thomas E. Connolly, S.J., to Roselle Chase (Feb. 15, 1984); Hayden enlistment (register, 49, p. 118, line 158, NA) on June 3, 1852, at West Point,

New York; assigned to Troop C, 2d Dragoons; honorable discharge June 3, 1857; Hayden probate, Spokane County, Dec. 17, 1890 (Book of Orders 6:396); Kootenai County deeds C:210, showing a purchase of 209.82 acres from the Northern Pacific Railroad (Aug. 1, 1888); Idaho State Historical Society list of place names, 71.

2. Kalispel allotment 31; allotting agent W. B. Sams, in *Spokesman-Review* (Feb. 2, 1909).

3. Memoir of Celina Garry Goulsby, "My Dad," type-script (n.d.)., unpaged. In possession of heirs.

4. Garry's employment record is listed on his application to the Indian Service (June 10, 1940), U.S. Office of Personnel Management.

5. Joe to Ignace Garry (Oct. 14, 1934).

6. Clipping in Garry files (n.d.).

7. Arlene Owen, interview (Sept. 20, 1994). Weight and height are noted in the 1940 job application.

8. Commissioner of Indian affairs to Paschal George (Sept. 22, 1937).

9. Tolan to commissioner of Indian affairs (Jan. 9, 1939); acting commissioner to Tolan (Feb. 16, 1939). Sister Providencia sent 300 items for display and sale from the Kateri Guild, Coeur d'Alene reservation, which the show manager is said to have called the "largest and finest display from Plateau tribes." See Coeur d'Alene *Council Fires* (Jan. 10, 1990).

10. "My Day," *Spokesman-Review* (Feb. 3, 1941).

11. Sacred Heart Mission house diary (July 17, 1941), OPA; Connolly, interview.

12. Phinney, quoted in Tekoa *Sentinel* (Feb. 23, 1945); Byrne, in house diary (Feb. 28, 1948).

13. Minutes (June 20–22, 1949). Archie Phinney, Frank George, and Garry were named to a committee to write a constitution and bylaws for an organization to be known as the Affiliated Tribes of Northwest Indians.

14. Ballot tally sheet attached to council minutes (May 27, 1948), RD; W. B. Plympton, farm agent, to Northern Idaho agency (May 28, 1948), NA, reporting election.

15. Tekoa *Sentinel* (Aug. 13, 1948).

16. Mimeographed letter, Garry to "All Indians of the Northwest" (Feb. 25, 1950), RD, enclosing questionnaire; Lawrence Nicodemus, in *Spokesman-Review* (Mar. 19, 1950).

17. Associated Press wire story, dateline Washington, published in *Spokesman-Review* (Mar. 30, 1950).

18. Once, on an application for employment, Joe had listed his reading as *Redbook, American,* and *Liberty*. These were popular general-circulation magazines—hardly at the core of American polity—and he did not check, as interests, such categories as civic or community organizations or tribal affairs. Application for employment with Bureau of Indian Affairs (June 8, 1937).

19. From Garry's personal papers.
20. Leonard S. Strahan to William B. Osborne, consulting forester (Oct. 24, 1951), RD.
21. Jeanne Givens, Garry's niece, interview (Nov. 5, 1993).
22. *Idaho Education News* 11, 8 (Apr. 1957): Unless otherwise noted, accounts of Garry's legislative service are based reports in *Idaho Daily Statesman* (Boise) and *Journal of the Idaho State House of Representatives,* 34th sess. (1957).
23. *Idaho Daily Statesman* (Feb. 14 and Mar. 10, 1957).
24. Based on author's review of Garry's 1957 datebook.
25. *St. Maries Gazette-Record* (Oct. 23, 1958).
26. Based on *Idaho Daily Statesman* and *Journal of the Idaho State House of Representatives,* 35th sess. (1959).

7. Toward a Victory of Sorts

1. *Tulsa Tribune* (Oct. 29, 1957); *Claremore Daily Progress* (Oct. 27, 1957).
2. Typescript, Garry's address (Oct. 28, 1957).
3. "Impressions," edited for publication in NCAI *Bulletin* 3, 1 (Oct. 1957):6–10.
4. *Tulsa Tribune* (Oct. 29, 1957).
5. Typescript of Emmons's remarks (Oct. 29, 1957).
6. *Federal Indian Policy and the NCAI,* edited version of Tax's remarks in pamphlet (n.d.), published by NCAI.
7. *NCAI Resolutions: 14th Annual Convention,* mimeographed booklet (1958). John Cragun and Charles Hobbs of the Wilkinson law firm attended, as did Robert Dellwo, who recalls resolutions drafted "to be put in shape by Dellwo."
8. NCAI *Bulletin* 3, 1 (Oct. 1957):7.
9. Donald Janson (Des Moines bureau), *New York Times* (Nov. 3, 1957).
10. *New York Times* (Jan. 4, 1956; Mar. 28, 1958); Garry to All-Pueblo Council (Jan. 16, 1956), reporting Cragun's rumor.
11. *Reader's Digest* (Mar. 1958), condensed from *Freeman; Christian Century* (Apr. 9, 1958); NCAI "Information Letter," No. 2-1958 (May 5, 1958).
12. *Indian Affairs,* no. 26 (May 1958): 1–4.
13. "Proposed Information and Education Program for NCAI," mimeo. (Oct. 1958).
14. Peterson to executive committee, NCAI (Jan. 27, 1958).
15. Ibid.
16. Elizabeth C. Rosenthal, treasurer, Association on American Indian Affairs, to Peterson (Jan. 20, 1958).
17. Peterson to executive committee, NCAI (Jan. 27, 1958).
18. Charles M. Roberts, *Washington Post* (Mar. 3, 1957), E, 1.
19. Ibid.; Herbert Sternau, *Puerto Rico and the Puerto Ricans,* pamphlet pub-

lished by the Council of Spanish American Organizations and the American Jewish Committee (Feb. 1958).

20. *Newsweek* (May 6, 1957).

21. *El Mundo* 1, 8 (Mar. 5, 1957):6–7.

22. Based on Garry's schedules, receipts for purchases, and notes. The account of the Puerto Rican tour is also based, in part, on the minutes of the executive council, NCAI (Mar. 12, 1958), NCAI, SI.

23. "Son of the Sun" is apparently a reporter's misinterpretation of Garry's ancestry. Spokane was said to mean "Children of the Sun." *Island Times* (Mar. 7, 1958).

24. Author's paraphrasing of executive council minutes (Mar. 12, 1958), NCAI, box 54, SI.

25. Ibid.

26. Jackson to Garry (Sept. 18, 1958); Jackson to Garry (Dec. 21, 1958). Jackson had a longtime interest in Indian affairs, stemming from his great aunt, Helen Hunt Jackson, whose report for the Senate Interior Committee, decrying federal Indian policy, was published in 1881 as a book, *A Century of Dishonor.* Helen Jackson also published a novel, *Ramona,* after investigating conditions among the mission Indians of California.

27. Minutes of executive council (Mar. 14, 1958).

28. Form letters (n.d.), attached to Peterson to Garry (May 28, 1958).

29. Garry, Peterson, and John Rainer (as treasurer) to Crow tribal council, copy attached to Peterson to Garry (May 28, 1958).

30. H.R. 8544, 85th Cong., 2d sess., which became P.L. 85-240; NCAI *Bulletin* 4, 2 (May 8, 1958).

31. "Federal Indian Policy," hearings on S. 809, 3, and S. 331 (May 13, 1957), 85. S.C.R.

32. House Committee print No. 38, 85th Cong., 2d sess. (Dec. 31, 1958), *Present Relations of the Federal Government to the American Indian,* 274–75.

33. Garry to Gerard (June 9, 1958).

34. Peterson to Garry (Feb. 12, 1958).

35. Duplicated letter, Sister Providencia to Montana tribal council members (June 24, 1956). On a copy to Garry, she penciled "Good ATNW conference!!!"

36. Typescript, E. Y. Berry, "Indian Problems of Law and Order" (June 16–17, 1958). Berry did not deliver the speech as intended, but his script was appended to the conference proceedings.

37. Sister Providencia to Garry (n.d., "Thursday").

38. Hearings on S. 104, S. 964, S. 1433, and S. 1854, "Area Redevelopment," part 1, 85th Cong., 1st sess. (1957), 780–83. The hearings transcript includes testimony from the previous year. Eisenhower vetoed S. 3683, 85th Cong, 2d sess. on Sept. 6, 1958. Gerald D. Morgan, special counsel, to Garry (Sept. 9, 1958).

39. Sister Providencia to Garry (Sept. 1, 1958).
40. Associated Press report (Sept. 10, 1958).
41. *New York Times* (Sept. 17, 1958).
42. Typescript, Garry address (Sept. 15, 1958).
43. Department of the Interior press release, "Remarks by Secretary of the Interior Fred A. Seaton"; NCAI *Bulletin* 4, 4 (Nov. 1, 1958): 1.
44. NCAI *Bulletin* 4, 4 (Nov. 1, 1958): 1.

8. The Garry Era Ends

1. Peterson to Garry et al. (Aug. 20, 1958).
2. Peterson, interview (Sept. 28, 1993).
3. Minutes of executive council annual meeting (Nov. 1, 1957), NCAI, SI.
4. Peterson, "American Indian Political Participation," *Annals of the American Academy of Political and Social Science* 311 (May 1957):116–25. A survey for the House Committee on Interior and Insular Affairs counted 143,078 Indians of voting age in 1956, of whom 25,582 had voted in recent state or national elections. See *Present Relations of the Federal Government*, 8–9.
5. Minutes of executive council (Feb. 28, 1958), HP, SI.
6. Typescript, Garry address (Mar. 19, 1959), HP, SI; NCAI press release (Mar. 20, 1959), HP, SI.
7. "Federal Indian Policy," 46.
8. Ibid.
9. Minutes of executive council (Feb. 28, 1958), HP, SI.
10. Based on "Legislative Report," Affiliated Tribes of Northwest Indians; NCAI 1959 convention report.
11. Minutes of executive Council (Mar. 16–19, 1959), NCAI, SI, 6–7. As noted previously, hearings on S.C.R. 3 had been combined with hearings on S. 809 and S. 331.
12. Coeur d'Alene resolution 76 (59) (May 2, 1959), NCAI, SI; letters from Garry to members of Congress (June 23, 1959), NCAI, SI.
13. L. Garry to Peterson (July 30, 1959), NCAI, SI.
14. Peterson, interview (Sept. 11, 1993).
15. *Indian Land Transactions,* xvii, xix.
16. *Present Relations of the Federal Government,* 1, 4, 11.
17. Fort Belknap agent to Pat Stump, Box Elder, Montana, (n.d.).
18. "Federal Indian Policy," 8 (Langer), 202 (Goldwater); *Congressional Record* (Jan. 23, 1957), quoted in "Federal Indian Policy," 6–9.
19. Typescript summary of executive council minutes (Mar. 16–20, 1959).
20. Sister Providencia to archbishop of Capetown (who had visited Montana), with copy to Garry (June 28, 1958).
21. Irene Mack, regional NCAI vice-president, to Peterson (Mar. 9, 1960), HP, box 7, SI.

22. Group interview (May 20–21, 1993), 58–59, SI; Garry to Wesley (Nov. 23, 1959), HP, box 4, SI.

23. Kimmis Hendrick, *Christian Science Monitor* (Dec. 16, 1959).

24. Gladwin Hill, *New York Times* (Dec. 13, 1959).

25. *Arizona Republic* (Dec. 5, 1959).

26. Peterson to J. Brooder, Western Airlines (Oct. 28, 1960), HP, box 8, SI. Apparently Western, which had flown in Racine, had been overlooked in the acknowledgment of contributions to the convention.

27. Ibid.

28. Telegram, Mansfield to *Phoenix Gazette* (Dec. 10, 1959); telegram, Mansfield to Wetzel (Dec. 14, 1959).

29. Peterson, interview (Sept. 28, 1993).

30. Transcript, Garry address (Dec. 7, 1959).

31. *New York Times* (Dec. 13, 1959); *Christian Science Monitor* (Dec. 16, 1959).

32. Wesley to officers of NCAI (Jan. 21, 1950), HP, box 4, SI.

33. L. Garry to Mrs. Wesley (Feb. 16, 1960).

34. Slickpoo to Peterson (Feb. 2, 1960).

35. Kevis to Wesley (Jan. 29, 1960).

36. Copy, Peterson to Slickpoo (Feb. 9, 1960).

37. Wesley to Kevis (Feb. 1, 1960).

38. Youngbird to Kevis (Feb. 1, 1960). Copy to Garry.

39. Peterson, interview (Sept. 28, 1993); items in the *Lewiston Tribune,* quoting Peterson and others (Sept. 18–22, 1961): Dellwo to Wilkinson, Cragun and Barker (Oct. 3, 1961), RD.

9. Money—and Its Consequences

1. Cox, "Tribal Leadership," 31, portrays Moctelme as speaking against the Indian Reorganization Act at a Chemawa conference in March 1934.

2. Constitution (June 5, 1947).

3. Robert D. Dellwo, "From Taunah to Anderson: The Bad News of Indian Tax Law," *South Dakota Law Review* 25 (summer 1981): 530; Dellwo to editor, *Spokesman-Review* (Aug. 18, 1955), RD.

4. Dellwo, interview (Aug. 12, 1993). Dellwo recalled that Willard Roe, a young attorney in the Wernette office who eventually became a superior court judge, wrote the memo of opinion for Wernette. Cornelius Byrne was the son of Dr. P. S. Byrne, mayor of Spokane from 1901 to 1903, who was active in politics and real estate. Cornelius entered the Society of Jesus upon graduation from Gonzaga College, studied in Spain and Rome, and was assigned to DeSmet in 1934. He worked to aid the tribe's "middle-aged leaders"—Peter Moctelme, Joseph Seltice, and Paschal George—until he was transferred to St. Ignatius, Montana, in 1950.

5. Zimmerman, quoted in Rep. Compton I. White to Garry (Mar. 22, 1950); Garry to all involved (Mar. 11, 1950).

6. Commissioner to Phinney (Aug. 16, 1949), quoted in Dellwo, "Taunah to Anderson," 531.

7. *Squire* v. *Capoeman,* 351 US 1 (1956); Simmons to Dellwo (Feb. 26, 1953), RD. Dellwo believed that Simmons took on the Nicodemus case as a way to persuade the tribe to contract with him for a claims suit.

8. Resolution No. 1, Affiliated Tribes in convention (Sept 17–19, 1953).

9. Garry to Louise M. Elk, chairwoman, Umatilla tribes (Feb. 15, 1955), RD.

10. Coeur d'Alene council, minutes of special session (Jan. 26, 1955), RD.

11. This language also appears in a supplemental memo in case No. 1898, Idaho Northern District, RD.

12. Nicodemus to Dellwo (Oct. 16, 1955), RD.

13. Dellwo to Clark (Mar. 16, 1955), RD. While the Nicodemus case is discussed here as a single case, the IRS actually filed a number of suits on various reservations and attempted to limit Nicodemus's defense to her original allotment, excluding her inherited or purchased land. There were similar filings in the Pacific Northwest on the Spokane, Flathead, and Colville reservations.

14. 132 Fed. Supp. 608, Northern District of Idaho (1955); *Spokesman-Review* (June 16, 1955), in which Judge Clark is quoted as saying his decision "will affect every Indian allottee in the country."

15. *Squire* v. *Capoeman,* 359 US 1 (1956). The Idaho Northern District Court granted Julia Nicodemus 6 percent interest on her tax payments from Oct. 1, 1949, as well as her costs of litigation. See *Spokesman-Review* (May 9, 1956).

16. Cragun to Dellwo (Aug. 9, 1955), responding to Dellwo inquiry (Aug. 4, 1955), RD.

17. Memo to clients, Wilkinson, Cragun, Barker and Hawkins (July 13, 1956), citing *IR Bulletin,* forthcoming on July 23, 1956; Dellwo to Peterson (July 10, 1956), RD. The plaque is pictured in *Spokesman-Review* (Aug. 30, 1956).

18. Garry, quoted in minutes of a special meeting of the Coeur d'Alene council (May 24, 1952), 3, RD.

19. Draft, "Adoption Ordinance" (Jan. 5, 1952), RD.

20. Indian Claims Commission, "Findings of Fact," paragraph 11, Docket 81, *Coeur d'Alene Tribe* v. *United States* (Aug. 26, 1955).

21. Simmons to Coeur d'Alene council (May 22, 1952), RD; Keith to Jackson (Feb. 24, 1956), HJ.

22. Minutes, general meeting and special council meeting (May 24, 1952), RD. Oswald "Ozzie" George was the son of Paschal George.

23. Nicodemus to members of the Coeur d'Alene tribe (Dec. 5, 1955), RD.

24. Nicodemus to tribe (Dec. 14, 1955).

25. Garry's notes taken at a conference in Portland (Apr. 1, 1955), RD.

26. Nicodemus to Elmo Miller, superintendent of Northern Idaho agency (Nov. 23, 1955), RD.

27. Nicodemus to council (June 5, 1956).

28. Henry J. Murray, "Appraisal," typescript (1956); ICC opinion, Docket 81 (Dec. 6, 1957); Wiggenhorn to Garry (Dec. 6, 1957).
29. Coeur d'Alene resolution 41 (58).
30. Coeur d'Alene general council minutes (June 27, 1959).
31. Dellwo to Gormley (Jan. 13, 1958). Gormley, originally part of Simmons's firm, had moved to the Wilkinson office to handle its Northwest business.
32. Dellwo to Gormley (Apr. 16, 1958), RD.
33. Ibid.
34. Affidavit of Elmer Peone et al. (Apr. 15, 1960), describing an event of April 24, 1959; L. Garry to Dellwo, enclosing a copy of the affidavit (n.d.), RD.
35. Minutes of a special council meeting (May 4, 1959). The meeting, called informally, was declared official after convening.
36. Nicodemus to Garry (May 5, 1959), RD.
37. Coeur d'Alene "News Notes" (July 10, 1959).
38. Adoption resolution 59–60 (July 23, 1959); Ensor to council (Dec. 29, 1959).
39. P.L. 86–95 (July 17, 1959); Gormley to Garry (July 28, 1959).
40. Resolution 31 (60) (Jan. 9, 1960).
41. Rinker to Dellwo (Mar. 14, 1961), RD.
42. Draft outline, Coeur d'Alene resolution 104 (60) (Feb. 6, 1960) council minutes (Feb. 6, 1960).
43. Garry to Dellwo (Apr. 20, 1960), RD.

10. "I Enjoyed Working with the People"

1. Dellwo to Gormley (May 10, 1960), RD.
2. John Corlett, *Lewiston Morning Tribune* (Nov. 6, 1959).
3. *Daily Idahonian* (Nov. 12, 1959).
4. Kevis to Wesley (Jan. 29, 1960); Youngbird to Kevis (Feb. 8, 1960); Wesley to Kevis (Feb. 1, 1960).
5. *Daily Idahonian* (Nov. 12, 1959); *Eastern Idaho Farmer,* Idaho Falls (May 26, 1960).
6. *Eastern Idaho Farmer* (May 26, 1960).
7. Quoted in *Cherokee Times* 5, 41 (July 30, 1960):2.
8. Diary entry (June 8, 1960); Garry to Pfost (Sept. 14, 1960).
9. Dellwo to Gormley (Jan. 8, 1960), RD; Assistant Commissioner Thomas M. Reed to Peterson (Sept. 15, 1959), RD.
10. Nicodemus to Sister Providencia (May 21, 1960), attached to Max Gubatayao to Dellwo (May 23, 1960), RD.
11. Kevis to Secretary Seaton (June 6, 1960), RD.
12. Coeur d'Alene resolution 104 (60), "General Outline of Plan" (Feb. 6, 1960), RD.

13. Recapitulation of events in Commissioner of Indian Affairs John Crow to Garry (Apr. 24, 1961), RD.

14. Garry to Ensor (Sept. 16, 1960), RD. The tribal council designated Garry to answer the agency's "newsletter" by resolution 12 (61) (Sept. 16, 1960).

15. Dellwo to Nash (Nov. 30, 1961), RD.

16. Nicodemus to Fisher (Oct. 16, 1961), RD.

17. Fisher to Nicodemus (Oct. 19, 1961), RD.

18. Resolution 41 (62) (Oct. 5, 1961).

19. William A. Wandersee, "Sanitary Facilities Project, PL 86–121: Summary of Coeur d'Alene Reservation Sanitation Project" (July 1961). Wandersee reported the average reservation family had an annual income of $2,200.

20. Draft resolution on per-capita payments (1963); council minutes (Feb. 14 and Nov. 20, 1963); tribal newsletter (May 8, 1963); a Law and Order Code was adopted July 24, 1962, amended Aug. 30, 1962; *Spokesman-Review* (Apr. 18, 1965).

21. Indian Education, 172–73, quotes Alvin Josephy on task-force report of July 10, 1961; "Federal Indian Policy, 44, lists only six industrial plants that had been persuaded to locate near Indian reservations; Bureau of Indian Affairs press release (Mar. 10, 1961).

22. Burnette to Garry (Dec. 13, 1962); Coeur d'Alene tribal newsletter (Sept. 1, 1961); conversations with Dellwo and Father Connolly.

23. Minutes (Feb. 14 and May 8, 1963).

24. The American Indian Chicago Convention (June 13–20, 1961) was coordinated by Sol Tax. A resolution of the Montana Intertribal Policy Board (May 9, 1961) formally withdrew support for the conference and criticized the NCAI for participating. The NCAI endorsed but did not join in sponsoring the meeting. Sister Providencia to McNickle, cochair of the convention (June 5, 1961), SP.

25. Garry's report to the tribe, "Newsletter" (Jan. 1965).

26. St. Clair, "Open letter to the Coeur d'Alene Tribe" (n.d.).

27. Resolution 51 (64) (Sept. 23, 1963), and cover letter, Evangeline Abraham to members of NCAI (Sept. 27, 1963).

28. The Coeur d'Alene Tribal Housing Authority was organized on May 23, 1963, as a public-housing agency under the Housing Act of 1937. *Spokane Daily Chronicle* (Aug. 20, 1968), describes improved housing.

29. Coeur d'Alene resolution 93 (62) (Dec. 7, 1961); *Spokane Daily Chronicle* (Jan. 23, 1968); deputy assistant commissioner to Dellwo (n.d.); Dellwo to solicitor (Apr. 11, 1966).

30. Garry and Abraham to all members of the Coeur d'Alene tribe (May 1966), OP.

31. Based on senate *Journal* roll calls; for general background, see the sketch of Samuelson in Robert C. Sims and Hope A. Benedict, *Idaho's Governors: Historical Essays on Their Administrations* (Boise, ID: Boise State University, 1992).

32. Resolution (July 29, 1967).

33. Rev. Wilfred P. Schoenberg, S.J., *Indians, Cowboys, and Western Art: A History of MONAC* (Spokane, WA 1981), 18; Dellwo to St. Clair (Oct. 14, 1967); Coeur d'Alene resolution 33 (68) (Oct. 12, 1967).

34. *Spokane Daily Chronicle* (Jan. 6, 1968); conversation with Jeanne Givens.

35. Memo to Senator Church (n.d., ca. Jan. 25, 1968).

36. Dellwo to R. Fuehrer, Portland office, Bureau of Indian Affairs (Jan. 18, 1968), makes a similar observation. He notes in a letter to R. S. Walter, Coeur d'Alene tribal council (Oct. 6, 1982), that interest had been paid under threat of a lawsuit, but the principal was still not retired, RD.

37. Development enterprise, resolution 22 (71) (Aug. 11, 1970); resolution 52 (71) (Sept. 16, 1970); "Overall Economic Development Plan for the Coeur d'Alene Indian Tribe of Idaho" (Mar. 27, 1972), typescript, RD.

38. Byrne to Garry (Oct. 15, 1970), OPA.

Sources

My research on Joseph Garry centered on two private collections: seven boxes of Garry's papers; and more than three dozen boxes of records and historic documents accumulated by Robert D. Dellwo during his service as counsel to the Coeur d'Alene, Spokane, and Kalispel tribes. The Garry papers were loaned by Emogene "Joey" Wienclaw, Leona Garry's daughter, and deposited for safe-keeping in the Cheney Cowles Museum archives, Eastern Washington State Historical Society, Spokane.

I also consulted: the records of the National Congress of American Indians, which are housed in the National Anthropological Archives of the Smithsonian Institution. At this writing, these NCAI records were partially processed, with a series list as guide. The papers of Helen Peterson, forty-one boxes, are also held by the National Anthropological Archives, with a register by Jania R. Garcia.

The U.S. Office of Personnel Management, St. Louis, furnished Garry's military and employment records.

The Eastern Washington State Historical Society holds limited papers of the Coeur d'Alene and Colville tribes, and of Sister Providencia.

The records of the Northern Idaho and Coeur d'Alene agencies, of the Bureau of Indian Affairs, 1875–1952, consist of 160 linear feet in the National Archives—Pacific Alaska Region (Seattle).

The Archie Phinney papers that I drew upon for the early days of the NCAI fill twelve archival boxes in the Pacific Alaska Region collection of the National Archives, with a register by Joyce Justice. Phinney's correspondence related to the NCAI is in boxes 10 and 11.

Correspondence, mission records, and miscellaneous tribal publications may be found in the papers of Father Cornelius Byrne, S.J., in the Oregon Province Archives of the Society of Jesus, Gonzaga University, Spokane.

Henry M. Jackson's papers are held by the University of Washington Libraries, except those relating to his committee work, which are housed in the legislative archives division of the National Archives of the Senate. The Jackson collection was useful as a source of comments on legislation and Indian conditions. A detailed container list is available.

My interpretation of events, and the direction of the narrative, relied largely on interviews, some in person and some by telephone. Several lasted nearly a full day. In alphabetical order by last name, they were:

Rev. Thomas E. Connolly, S.J., November 6, 1993 (phone); jointly with Joey Wienclaw, Arlene Owen, and Jeanne Givens, September 20, 1994.

Robert D. Dellwo, August 12, 1993; January 4, March 8, and May 12, 1994.
Forrest Gerard, October 6, 1993 (phone).
Jeanne Givens, November 5, 1993 (phone).
Marceline Kevis, February 8, 1995 (phone).
Judge Owen Panner, September 27, 1993 (phone).
Helen Peterson, September 11 and 28, 1993 (phone); September 6, 1994.
John A. Ross, September 9, 1995.
In addition, I made use of a partial transcript of an NCAI oral history meet-
ing, May 20–21, 1993, moderated by Thomas W. Cowger and sponsored by
the National Anthropological Archives. The participants included Mary
Elizabeth Ruwell, John C. Rainer, Helen Peterson, Arthur T. Manning, Rose
W. Robinson, Erma H. Walz, and Robert L. Bennett.
I also consulted transcripts of interviews conducted by Idaho Public
Television with Peterson, Givens, and Dellwo for a 1990 telecast on Idaho
history.

Books

Arrington, Leonard J. *History of Idaho*. 2 vols. Moscow: University of Idaho
Press, 1994.
Ashby, LeRoy, and Rod Gramer. *Fighting the Odds: The Life of Senator Frank
Church*. Pullman: Washington State University Press, 1994.
Bernstein, Alison R. *American Indians and World War II: Toward a New Era
in Indian Affairs*. Norman: University of Oklahoma Press, 1991.
Berry, William A., and James Alexander. *Justice for Sale: The Shocking Scandal
of the Oklahoma Supreme Court*. Macedon, 1996. Allegations of bribery involv-
ing Justice N. B. Johnson.
Bordewich, Fergus M. *Killing the White Man's Indian: Reinventing Native
Americans at the End of the Twentieth Century*. New York: Doubleday, 1996.
Brophy, William A., and Sophie D. Aberle, comps. *The Indian: America's
Unfinished Business*. Norman: University of Oklahoma Press, 1966. Report
of the Commission on Rights, Liberties, and Responsibilities of the
American Indian, established by the Fund for the Republic.
Burt, Larry W. *Tribalism in Crisis*. Albuquerque: University of New Mexico
Press, 1982.
Fey, Harold, and D'Arcy McNickle. *Indians and Other Americans*. New York:
Harper & Brothers, 1959.
Fixico, Donald L. *Termination and Relocation: Federal Indian Policy, 1945–1960*.
Albuquerque: University of New Mexico Press, 1990.
Garraghan, Gilbert J., S.J. *Jesuits of the Middle United States*. 3 vols. New York:
America Press, 1938.
Hertzberg, Hazel W. *The Search for American Indian Identity: Modern Pan-
Indian Movements*. Syracuse, NY: Syracuse University Press, 1971.

Indian Tribes As Sovereign Governments: A Sourcebook of Federal-Tribal History, Law and Policy. Oakland, CA: American Indian Lawyer Training Program, Inc., 1988.

Kelly, Lawrence C. *Assault on Assimilation: John Collier and the Origins of Indian Policy Reform.* Albuquerque: University of New Mexico Press, 1983.

Kelly, William H., ed. *Indian Affairs and the Indian Reorganization Act: The Twenty Year Record.* Tucson: University of Arizona, 1954. Publication of papers read at a symposium on December 30, 1953. Some of the papers are cited separately as articles, following.

Kvasnicka, Robert K., and Herman J. Viola, eds. *The Commissioners of Indian Affairs, 1824–1977.* Lincoln: University of Nebraska Press, 1979.

National Lawyers Guild Committee on Native American Struggles, ed. and comp. *Rethinking Indian Law.* New Haven, CT: Advocate Press, 1981.

O'Brien, Sharon. *American Indian Tribal Governments.* Norman: University of Oklahoma Press, 1989.

Parker, Dorothy R. *Singing an Indian Song: A Biography of D'Arcy McNickle.* Lincoln: University of Nebraska Press, 1992.

Prucha, Francis Paul, S. J. *American Indian Policy in the Formative Years.* (Cambridge, MA: Harvard University Press, 1962.

———. *The Great Father: The U.S. Government and the American Indians.* 2 vols. Lincoln: University of Nebraska Press, 1984.

———. *Indians in American Society.* Berkeley: University of California Press, 1985.

Reichard, Gladys A. *Analysis of Coeur d'Alene Indian Myths.* Philadelphia: American Folklore Society, 1947.

Schlicke, Carl P. *General George Wright: Guardian of the Pacific Coast.* Norman: University of Oklahoma Press, 1988.

Schoenberg, Wilfred P., S. J. *Indians, Cowboys and Western Art: A History of MONAC.* Spokane, WA: privately printed, 1981. MONAC stands for Museum of Native American Cultures. Its collections merged with those of the Eastern Washington State Historical Society, Spokane.

Shames, Deborah, ed. *Freedom with Reservation: The Menominee Struggle.* Madison, WI: National Committee To Save the Menominee People and Forests, 1972.

Sims, Robert C., and Hope A. Benedict, eds. *Idaho's Governors: Historical Essays on Their Administrations.* Boise, ID: Boise State University, 1992.

White, Robert H. *Tribal Assets: The Rehabilitation of Native America.* New York: Henry Holt & Co., 1990.

Articles

Barney, Ralph A. "Legal Problems Peculiar to Indian Claims." *Ethnohistory* 2 (Fall 1955): 255–62.

Barris, Allan. "Washington's Public Law 280 Jurisdiction on Indian Reservations." *Washington Law Review* 53, 4 (October 1978): 701–27.

Barsh, Russel L. "Issues in Federal, State and Tribal Taxation." *Washington Law Review* 54, 3 (June 1979): 531–86.

Bishop, Joan. "From Hill 57 to Capitol Hill: Making the Sparks Fly." *Montana Magazine of Western History* 43, 3 (Summer 1993): 16–29. An article about Sister Providencia's concerns.

Black, Charles L., Jr. "Counsel of Their Own Choosing." *American Indian* (Fall 1951): 3–17.

Cohen, Felix S. "Erosion of Indian Rights, 1950–53." *Yale Law Journal* 62 (February 1953): 348–90.

———. "Original Land Title." *Minnesota Law Review* 32, 1 (December 1947): 28–59.

Collier, John. "The Genesis and Philosophy of the Indian Reorganization Policies." In Kelly, ed., *Indian Affairs*, 2–8.

Connolly, Thomas E., S. J., "American Indians in Council." *America* 94, 4 (October 22, 1955): 100.

———. "New Last Frontier." *America* 105, 11 (June 10, 1961): 417

Cotroneo, Ross R., and Jack Dozier, "A Time of Disintegration: The Coeur d'Alenes and the Dawes Act." *Western Historical Quarterly* 5 (1974): 405–19.

Cox, Thomas R. "Tribal Leadership in Transition: Chief Peter Moctelme of the Coeur d'Alenes." *Idaho Yesterdays* 23 (Spring 1979): 2–9, 25–31.

Dahl, Kathleen A. "The Battle over Termination on the Colville Indian Reservation." *American Indian Culture and Research Journal* 18, 1 (1994): 29–53.

Dellwo, Robert D. "From Taunah to Anderson: The Bad News of Indian Tax Law." *South Dakota Law Review* 26 (Summer 1981): 529–46.

Dozier, Jack. "Coeur d'Alene Country: The Creation of the Coeur d'Alene Indian Reservation in North Idaho." *Idaho Yesterdays* 6, 3 (Fall 1962): 2–7.

Fenwick, Robert W. "America's Lost People." Series of twelve articles published in the *Denver Post,* January 3–15, 1960; reprinted in the *Congressional Record,* January 22, 1960: 947–58.

Garraghan, Gilbert J., S.J. "Nicholas Point, Jesuit Missionary in the Montana of the Forties." Collected essays, in *Transmississippi West.* Boulder, CO: 1930.

Garry, Joseph. "The Indian Reorganization Act and the Withdrawal Program." In Kelly, ed., *Indian Affairs*, 35–37.

Haas, Theodore. "The Indian Reorganization Act in Historical Perspective." In Kelly, ed., *Indian Affairs*, 9–25.

Johnson, Napoleon B. "The National Congress of American Indians." *Chronicles of Oklahoma* 30 (Summer 1952): 140–48.

Kane, Albert E. "Jurisdiction over Indians and Indian Reservations." *Arizona Law Review* 6 (1965): 243–55.

LeDuc, Thomas. "The Work of the Indian Claims Commission under the Act of 1946." *Pacific Historical Review* 26 (February 1957): 1–16.

Leverino, Anthony. Three articles on federal-Indian relations in the *New York Times,* November 1, 2, and 3, 1951. Titles and page locations vary.

Lurie, Nancy O. "The Voice of the American Indian: The Chicago Conference." *Current Anthropology* 2, 5 (December 1961): 478–500.

Mirrielees, Edith R. "Cloud of Mistrust." *Atlantic* 190, 2 (February 1957): 55–59. On the relocation program.

Nader, Ralph. "American Indians: People without a Future," *Harvard Law Record* 22, 10 (May 10, 1956): 3–5.

Naske, Claus-M. "Ernest Gruening and Alaska Native Claims," *Pacific Northwest Quarterly* 62, 4 (October 1991): 140–48.

Ourada, Patricia K. "Dillon Seymour Myer, 1950–53." In Kvasnicka and Viola, eds., *Commissioners of Indian Affairs,* 293–99.

Peterson, Helen L. "American Indian Political Participation." *Annals of the American Academy of Political and Social Science,* no. 311 (May 1957): 116–25.

Reichard, Gladys A. "Coeur d'Alene." In *Handbook of American Indian Languages.* New York: J. J. Augustine, 1938.

Ross, John Alan. "Political Conflict on the Colville Reservation," *Northwest Research Notes* 2, 1 (1968): 29–91.

Teit, James A. "Salishan Tribes of the Western Plateaus." In Franz Boas, ed., *45th Annual Report of the Bureau of American Ethnology (1927–28).* 70th Cong., 2d sess., 1930. H. Doc. 380.

Watkins, Arthur V. "Termination of Federal Supervision: The Removal of Restrictions over Indian Property and Person." *Annals of the American Academy of Political and Social Science,* no. 311 (May 1957): 47–55.

Wesley, Clarence. "Tribal Self-Government under the Indian Reorganization Act," in Kelly, ed., *Indian Affairs,* 26–28.

Wilkinson, Glen A. "Indian Tribal Claims before the Court of Claims." *Georgetown Law Journal* 55 (December 1966): 511–28.

Zimmerman, William, Jr. "The Role of the Bureau of Indian Affairs since 1933," *Annals of the American Academy of Political and Social Science,* no. 311 (May 1957): 31–46.

Unpublished and Miscellany

"Archie Phinney and the Formation of the National Congress of American Indians." Documents selected from the archives of the National Archives — Pacific Alaska Region, 1994.

Boyd, Robert F. "Introduction of Infectious Diseases among Indians of the Pacific Northwest, 1774–1874." Ph. D. diss., University of Washington, 1985.

Bennett, Robert L. (commissioner of Indian affairs). "First Commissioner's Report to Indian Peoples." Typescript of address to NCAI, September 30, 1968.

Coeur d'Alene Teepee. Vols. 1–3 (1937–40). Collection of fifty tribal newsletters, edited by Su Harms. Mimeographed at Plummer, Idaho, July 1980.

Curry, James E. "Report to the Seventh Annual Convention of the NCAI." August 30, 1950. Mimeographed, 12 pages.

"Emergency Conference of American Indians on Legislation." February 25–28, 1954. Mimeographed summary distributed by the NCAI.

Federal Indian Legislation and Policies. Booklet for 1956 workshop on American Indian Affairs, University of Chicago.

Garry, Joseph. "State Control and Administration of Indian Affairs." Typescript of panel presentation at the 1949 NCAI convention.

Goulsby, Celina Garry. "Memoirs." Personal recollection of the Ignace Garry family, undated. In possession of the family.

Hasse, Larry. "Termination and Assimilation: Federal Indian Policy, 1943–61." Ph.D. diss., Washington State University, 1974.

Hayes, Susanna A. "Resistance to Education for Assimilation by the Colville Indians, 1872–1972." Ph.D. diss., University of Michigan, 1973.

Josephy, Alvin M., Jr. "The American Indian and the Bureau of Indian Affairs." Typescript, February 24, 1969. Delivered to James Keogh, of the Nixon Administration, at the White House.

Murphey, Kelly A. "Archeological Resources of Southern Lake Coeur d'Alene, Northern Idaho." Typescript, Laboratory of Anthropology, University of Idaho, 1994.

Murray, Henry T. "Appraisal of Aboriginal Lands of the Coeur d'Alene Indian Tribe." Typescript, May 5, 1956. (For tribe's claim, Indian Claims Commission, docket 81.)

"NCAI Oral History Meeting," log of conversations, Albuquerque, New Mexico, May 20–21, 1993. Typescript in the National Anthropological Archives.

Orfield, Gary. "Study of the Termination Policy." Paper prepared for the NCAI convention, Denver, 1966.

Palmer, Garry B. "Indian Pioneers: Coeur d'Alene Farming from 1842 to 1876." Typescript of journal article, 1981.

Pomeroy, Kenneth B. "Terminating Federal Supervision over Indian Forests." Address of November 12, 1957, before the annual meeting of the Society of American Foresters. Mimeograph.

Potter, Andrew Ray. "Climbing into the Ring: Indian Employees in the Office of Indian Affairs, 1934–1946." Master's thesis, Western Washington University, 1992.

Rassier, Phillip J (assistant attorney general, Idaho). "Indian Water Rights: A Study of Historical and Legal Factors Affecting Water Rights of Indians of the State of Idaho." Idaho Department of Water Resources. Typescript, June 1978.

"Report to the Secretary of the Interior by the Task Force on Indian Affairs." Typescript, July 10, 1961.

Sternau, Herbert, comp. "Puerto Rico and the Puerto Ricans." February 1958.

Pamphlet distributed by the Council of Spanish American Organizations and the American Jewish Committee.

"Summary of Public Housing and Urban Removal Programs in Puerto Rico." Public relations office of the Puerto Rico Housing Authority. Mimeographed, October 1957.

Tax, Sol. "Federal Indian Policy and the National Congress of American Indians." Edited version of an impromptu speech delivered at the NCAI convention, 1957. Distributed by the NCAI.

Trulove, W. Thomas. "The Economics of Paternalism: Federal Policy and the Klamath Indians." Ph.D. diss., University of Oregon, 1973.

Van den Heuvel, William J. "Arrow Inc. and NCAI: An Appraisal of Their Relationship." Undated typescript in Helen Peterson papers, box 11.

Wandersee, William A. "Summary of Sanitary Facilities Project P.L. 86–121." July 1961. Sanitary project on the Coeur d'Alene reservation.

Index

Mullan Road: as railroad route, 76

Murray, Sen. James E.: offers Senate Concurrent Resolution 3, 62; mentioned, 46, 55–56, 140

Myer, Dillon S. (Commissioner of Indian Affairs): as commissioner, 5, 23–26; resigns, 6; attorney rules, 25; mentioned, 35

Nash, Philleo, 171, 172

National Congress of American Indians: emergency meeting, 4–9; organizing of, 10–16; naming of, 16; first days, 15–20; and NCAI Fund, 22, 61; and 83rd Congress proposals, 34, 44; campaign against competency, 38–39; advances an Indian program, 45, 119, 136, 137, 140; finances, 61, 65, 128; Point nine program, 55–56; revise constitution, 60; public relations, 123; Puerto Rico tour, 123–26. *See also* Conventions, NCAI

Navajo Tribe, 58

Nez Perce war, 81

Nicodemus, Julia: tax suit, 151, 154–57, 205*n.13*

Nicodemus, Lawrence: writes Coeur d'Alene constitution, 151–52; on tax suit, 155; as tribal chairman, 159–60; opposes Garry, 170, 172, 174; mentioned, 105, 164–65, 175, 178

"North American Indian Today" (seminar in Toronto), 11

Northern Pacific Railroad, 76, 77, 80, 83

Northwest Indian Commission, 85

Old Mission. *See* Sacred Heart Mission

Orozco, Charlotte, 13

Panner, Owen, 62–63

Peterson, Helen, 6, 21; shapes NCAI strategy, 4, 52–53, 65; opinion of Garry, 30, 60; on NCAI advances, 45, 116, 140; on Indian aims, 64; on Indian voting, 136; mentioned, 3, 34, 52, 61, 62, 115, 128, 191*n.26*

Pfost, Rep. Gracie, 39, 170

Phinney, Archie: urges Indian organizing, 10, 11, 12; mentioned 13, 14, 103, 154, 157

Pierce, President Franklin, 71

Point, Rev. Nicholas, 67–68

Point Nine Program, 55

Poverty, 58

Powlas, Peter, 13

Providencia, Sister: chides "Butter-fly" Garry, 60, 133; on health services, 143; mentioned, 46–47, 130, 170

Public Health Service, 40

Public Law 280: debate on extending, 41; California questions, 41–42; mentioned, 29

Pyramid Lake, 24, 25

Rainer, John, 24, 60

Ravalli, Anthony, 68, 71

Robert Marshall Civil Liberties Trust, 65, 118, 127

Rogers, Ed, 13

Rogers, Will Jr., 15, 23

Sacred Heart Mission: relocated, 81; mentioned, 68–70, 71

St. Clair, Thomas H., 178

Seaton, Fred (Secretary of the Interior): and termination policy, 134; mentioned, 58

Seltice, Andrew, 79, 89; in Nez Perce war, 81; on Union Pacific railroad, 85–86; mentioned, 78, 198*n.18*

Seminole Tribes, 35

Semple, W. F.: and Inter-Tribal Indian Council, 11

Settlers, 80–81, 86–87

Shanks, Rep. John P. C., 79

Sherman, Paschal, 49, 60, 64–65, 116–18, 194*n.1*

Simpson, Alva A., 28

Short, William W.: as second NCAI president, 28–29; mentioned, 15, 61, 121

Simmons, Kenneth R. L., 154, 155, 157, 158

Slickpoo, Allen, 149

CPSIA information can be obtained at www.ICGtesting.com
Printed in the USA
BVOW08s0007210815

414366BV00002B/23/P